Paul Krugman is the recipient of the 2008 Nobel Prize in Economics. The author of a twice-weekly column for the op-ed page of the *New York Times* and a daily blog, 'The Conscience of a Liberal', derived from his book of the same name, Krugman has been named Columnist of the Year by *Editor and Publisher* magazine. He is a professor of economics and international affairs at Princeton University, and is the author or editor of twenty books and more than two hundred professional journal articles. For more information, visit Krugmanonline.com.

Paul Krugman

THE RETURN OF DEPRESSION ECONOMICS AND THE CRISIS OF 2008

PENGUIN BOOKS

PENGUIN BOOKS

Published by the Penguin Group
Penguin Books Ltd, 80 Strand, London WC2R 0RL, England
Penguin Group (USA) Inc., 375 Hudson Street, New York, New York 10014, USA
Penguin Group (Canada), 90 Eglinton Avenue East, Suite 700, Toronto, Ontario, Canada M4P 2P3
(a division of Pearson Penguin Canada Inc.)
Penguin Ireland, 25 St Stephen's Green, Dublin 2, Ireland (a division of Penguin Books Ltd)
Penguin Group (Australia), 250 Camberwell Road, Camberwell, Victoria 3124, Australia
(a division of Pearson Australia Group Pty Ltd)
Penguin Books India Pvt Ltd, 11 Community Centre, Panchsheel Park, New Delhi – 110 017, India
Penguin Group (NZ), 67 Apollo Drive, Rosedale, North Shore 0632, New Zealand
(a division of Pearson New Zealand Ltd)
Penguin Books (South Africa) (Pty) Ltd, 24 Sturdee Avenue, Rosebank, Johannesburg 2196, South Africa

Penguin Books Ltd, Registered Offices: 80 Strand, London WC2R 0RL, England

www.penguin.com

First published in the United States of America by W. W. Norton & Company 1999
First published in Great Britain by Allen Lane 1999
This edition with new material first published in Great Britain by Penguin Books 2008
13

Copyright © Paul Krugman, 1999, 2008
All rights reserved

The moral right of the author has been asserted

Printed in England by Clays Ltd, St Ives plc

ISBN: 978-1-846-14239-0

www.greenpenguin.co.uk

Penguin Books is committed to a sustainable
future for our business, our readers and our
planet. This book is made from paper certified
by the Forest Stewardship Council.

Contents

THE RETURN OF
DEPRESSION ECONOMICS
AND THE CRISIS OF 2008

INTRODUCTION

Most economists, to the extent that they think about the subject at all, regard the Great Depression of the 1930s as a gratuitous, unnecessary tragedy. If only Herbert Hoover hadn't tried to balance the budget in the face of an economic slump; if only the Federal Reserve hadn't defended the gold standard at the expense of the domestic economy; if only officials had rushed cash to threatened banks, and thus calmed the bank panic that developed in 1930–31; then the stock market crash of 1929 would have led only to a garden-variety recession, soon forgotten. And since economists and policymakers have learned their lesson—no modern treasury secretary would echo Andrew Mellon's famous advice to "liquidate labor, liquidate stocks, liquidate the farmers, liquidate real estate . . . purge the rottenness out of the system"—nothing like the Great Depression can ever happen again.

Or can it? In the late 1990s a group of Asian economies—economies that produced about a quarter of the world's output and were home to two-thirds of a billion people—experienced an economic slump that bore an eerie resemblance to the Great Depression. Like the Depression, the crisis struck out of a clear blue sky, with most pundits predicting a continuing boom even as the slump gathered momentum; as in the 1930s the conventional economic medicine proved ineffective, perhaps even counterproductive. The fact that something like this could happen in the modern world should have sent chills up the spine of anyone with a sense of history.

It certainly sent chills up my spine. The first edition of this book was written in response to the Asian crisis of the 1990s. Where some saw the crisis as a specifically Asian phenomenon, I saw it as a troubling omen for all of us, a warning that the problems of depression economics have not disappeared in the modern world. Sad to say, I was right to be worried: as this new edition goes to press, much of the world, very much including the United States, is grappling with a financial and economic crisis that bears even more resemblance to the Great Depression than the Asian troubles of the 1990s.

The kind of economic trouble that Asia experienced a decade ago, and that we're all experiencing now, is precisely the sort of thing we thought we had learned to prevent. In the bad old days big, advanced economies with stable governments—like Britain in the 1920s—might have had no answer to prolonged periods of stagnation and deflation; but between John Maynard Keynes and Milton Friedman, we thought we knew enough to keep that from happening again. Smaller countries—like Austria in 1931—may once have been at the mercy of financial tides, unable to control their economic destiny; but nowadays sophisticated bankers and government officials (not to mention the International Monetary

Fund) are supposed to quickly orchestrate rescue packages that contain such crises before they spread. Governments—like that of the United States in 1930–31—may once have stood by helplessly as national banking systems collapsed; but in the modern world, deposit insurance and the readiness of the Federal Reserve to rush cash to threatened institutions are supposed to prevent such scenes. No sensible person thought that the age of economic anxiety was past; but whatever problems we might have in the future, we were sure that they would bear little resemblance to those of the 1920s and 1930s.

But we should have realized a decade ago that our confidence was misplaced. Japan spent most of the 1990s in an economic trap that Keynes and his contemporaries found completely familiar. The smaller economies of Asia, by contrast, went from boom to calamity virtually overnight—and the story of their calamity reads as if it were taken straight out of a financial history of the 1930s.

At the time, I thought of it this way: it was as if bacteria that used to cause deadly plagues, but had long been considered conquered by modern medicine, had reemerged in a form resistant to all the standard antibiotics. Here's what I wrote in the introduction to the first edition: "So far only a limited number of people have actually fallen prey to the newly incurable strains; but even those of us who have so far been lucky would be foolish not to seek new cures, new prophylactic regimens, whatever it takes, lest we turn out to be the next victims."

Well, we were foolish. And now the plague is upon us.

Much of this new edition is devoted to the Asian crisis of the 1990s, which turns out to have been a sort of rehearsal for the global crisis now in progress. But I've added a lot of new material as well, in an effort to explain how the United States found itself looking like Japan a decade earlier, how Iceland found itself looking like Thailand, and how the original crisis countries of the 1990s have, to their horror, found themselves once again at the edge of the abyss.

About This Book

Let me admit at the outset that this book is, at bottom, an analytical tract. It is not so much about *what* happened as *why* it happened; the important things to understand, I believe, are how this catastrophe can have happened, how the victims can recover, and how we can prevent it from happening again. This means that the ultimate objective is, as they say in business schools, to develop the theory of the case—to figure out how to think about this stuff.

But I have tried to avoid making this a dry theoretical exposition. There are no equations, no inscrutable diagrams, and (I hope) no impenetrable jargon. As an economist in good standing, I am quite capable of writing things nobody can read. Indeed, unreadable writing—my own and others'—played a key role in helping me arrive at the views presented here. But what the world needs now is informed action; and to get that kind of action, ideas must be presented in a way that is accessible to concerned people at large, not just those with economics Ph.D.'s. Anyway, the equations and diagrams of formal economics are, more often than not, no more than a scaffolding used to help construct an intellectual edifice. Once that edifice has been built to a certain point, the scaffolding can be stripped away, leaving only plain English behind.

It also turns out that although the ultimate goal here is analytical, much of the writing involves narrative. Partly this is because the story line—the sequence in which events happened—is often an important clue to what theory of the case makes sense. (For example, any "fundamentalist" view of economic crisis—that is, a view that economies only get the punishment they deserve—must come to grips with the peculiar coincidence that so many seemingly disparate economies hit the wall in the space of a few months.) But I am also aware that the story line provides a necessary context for any attempts at explanation and that most people have not spent the last eighteen months obsessively following the unfolding drama. Not everyone recalls what Prime Minister Mahathir said in Kuala Lumpur in August 1997 and relates it to what Donald Tsang ended up doing in Hong Kong a year later; well, this book will refresh your memory.

A note about intellectual style: one temptation that often afflicts writers on economics, especially when the subject is so grave, is the tendency to become excessively dignified. Not that the events we are concerned with aren't important, in some cases matters of life and death. Too often, though, pundits imagine that because the subject is serious, it must be approached solemnly: that because these are big issues, they must be addressed with big words; no informality or levity allowed. As it turns out, however, to make sense of new and strange phenomena, one must be prepared to play with ideas. And I use the word "play" advisedly: dignified people, without a whimsical streak, almost never offer fresh insights, in economics or anywhere else. Suppose I tell you that "Japan is suffering from fundamental maladjustment, because its state-mediated growth model leads to structural rigidity." Well, guess what: I haven't said anything at all; at best I have conveyed a sense that the problems are very difficult, and there are no easy answers—a sense that may well be completely wrong. Suppose, on the other hand, that I illustrate Japan's problems with the entertaining tale of the ups and downs of a baby-sitting co-op (which will, in fact, make several appearances in this book). Maybe it sounds silly, maybe the levity will even offend your sensibilities, but the whimsicality has a purpose: it jolts the mind into a different channel, suggesting in this case that there may indeed be a surprisingly easy way out of at least part of Japan's problem. So don't expect a solemn, dignified book: the objectives here are as serious as can be, but the writing will be as silly as the subject demands.

And with that, let's begin our journey, starting with the world as it seemed to be, just a few years ago.

1

"THE CENTRAL PROBLEM
HAS BEEN SOLVED"

In 2003 Robert Lucas, a professor at the University of Chicago and winner of the 1995 Nobel Memorial Prize in Economics, gave the presidential address at the annual meetings of the American Economic Association. After explaining that macroeconomics began as a response to the Great Depression, he declared that it was time for the field to move on: the "central problem of depression-prevention," he declared, "has been solved, for all practical purposes."

Lucas didn't claim that the business cycle, the irregular alternation of recessions and expansions that has been with us for at least a century and a half, was over. But he did claim that the cycle had been tamed, to the point that the benefits of any further taming were trivial: smoothing out the wiggles in the economy's growth, he argued, would produce only trivial gains in public welfare. So it was time to switch focus to things like long-term economic growth.

Lucas wasn't alone in claiming that depression-prevention was a solved problem. A year later Ben Bernanke, a former Princeton professor who had gone to serve on the board of the Federal Reserve—and would soon be appointed as the Fed's chairman—gave a remarkably upbeat speech titled "The Great Moderation," in which he argued, much as Lucas had, that modern macroeconomic policy had solved the problem of the business cycle—or, more precisely, reduced the problem to the point that it was more of a nuisance than a front-rank issue.

Looking back from only a few years later, with much of the world in the throes of a financial and economic crisis all too reminiscent of the 1930s, these optimistic pronouncements sound almost incredibly smug. What was especially strange about this optimism was the fact that during the 1990s, economic problems reminiscent of the Great Depression *had*, in fact, popped up in a number of countries—including Japan, the world's second-largest economy.

But in the early years of this decade, depression-type problems had not yet hit the United States, while inflation—the scourge of the 1970s—seemed, finally, to be well under control. And the relatively soothing economic news was embedded in a political context that encouraged optimism: the world seemed more favorable to market economies than it had for almost ninety years.

Capitalism Triumphant

This is a book about economics; but economics inevitably takes place in a political context, and one cannot understand the world as it appeared a few years ago without considering the fundamental political fact of the 1990s: the collapse of socialism, not merely as a ruling ideology, but as an idea with the power to move men's minds.

That collapse began, rather oddly, in China. It is still mind-boggling to realize that Deng Xiaoping launched his nation on what turned out to be the road to capitalism in 1978, only three years after the Communist victory in Vietnam, only two years after the internal defeat of radical Maoists who wanted to resume the Cultural Revolution. Probably Deng did not fully realize how far that road would lead; certainly it took the rest of the world a long time to grasp that a billion people had quietly abandoned Marxism. In fact, as late as the early 1990s China's transformation had failed fully to register with the chattering classes; in the best-sellers of the time, the world economy was an arena for "head to head" struggle between Europe, America, and Japan—China was thought of, if at all, as a subsidiary player, perhaps part of an emerging yen bloc.

Nonetheless, everyone realized that something had changed, and that "something" was the collapse of the Soviet Union.

Nobody really understands what happened to the Soviet regime. With the benefit of hindsight we now think of the whole structure as a sort of ramshackle affair, doomed to eventual failure. Yet this was a regime that had maintained its grip through civil war and famine, that had been able against terrible odds to defeat the Nazis, that was able to mobilize the scientific and industrial resources to contest America's nuclear superiority. How it could have ended so suddenly, not with a bang but with a whimper, should be regarded as one of the great puzzles of political economy. Maybe it was simply a matter of time—it seems that revolutionary fervor, above all the willingness to murder your opponents in the name of the greater good, cannot last more than a couple of generations. Or maybe the regime was gradually undermined by the stubborn refusal of capitalism to display the proper degree of decadence: I have a private theory, based on no evidence whatsoever, that the rise of Asia's capitalist economies subtly but deeply demoralized the Soviet regime, by making its claim to have history on its side ever less plausible. A debilitating, unwinnable war in Afghanistan certainly helped the process along, as did the evident inability of Soviet industry to match Ronald Reagan's arms buildup. Whatever the reasons, in 1989 the Soviet empire in Eastern Europe suddenly unraveled, and in 1991 so did the Soviet Union itself.

The effects of that unraveling were felt around the world, in ways obvious and subtle. And all of the effects were favorable to the political and ideological dominance of capitalism.

First of all, of course, several hundred million people who had lived under Marxist regimes suddenly became citizens of states prepared to give markets a chance. Somewhat surprisingly, however, this has in some ways turned out to be the least important consequence of the Soviet collapse. Contrary to what most people expected, the "transition economies" of Eastern Europe did not quickly become a major force in the world market, or a favored destination for foreign investment. On the contrary, for the most part they had a very hard time making the transition: East Germany, for example, has become Germany's equivalent of Italy's Mezzogiorno, a permanently depressed region that is a continual source of social and fiscal concern. Only now, almost two decades after the fall of Communism, are a few countries—Poland, Estonia, the Czech Republic—starting to look like success stories. And Russia itself has become a surprisingly powerful source of financial and political instability for the rest of the world. But let's reserve that story for Chapter 6.

Another direct effect of the collapse of the Soviet regime was that other governments that had relied on its largesse were now on their own. Since some of these states had been idealized and idolized by opponents of capitalism, their sudden poverty—and the corresponding revelation of their previous dependency—helped to undermine the legitimacy of all such movements. When Cuba seemed a heroic nation, standing alone with clenched fist confronting the United States, it was an attractive symbol for revolutionaries across Latin America—far more attractive, of course, than the gray bureaucrats of Moscow. The shabbiness of post-Soviet Cuba is not only disillusioning in itself; it makes painfully clear that the heroic stance of the past was possible only because of huge subsidies from those very bureaucrats. Similarly, until the 1990s North Korea's government, for all its ghastliness, held a certain mystique for radicals, particularly among South Korean students. With its population literally starving because it no longer receives Soviet aid, the thrill is gone.

Yet another more or less direct effect of Soviet collapse was the disappearance of the many radical movements that, whatever their claims to represent a purer revolutionary spirit, were in fact able to operate only because Moscow provided the weapons, the training camps, and the money. Europeans like to point out that the radical terrorists of the seventies and eighties—Baader-Meinhof in Germany, the Red Army Brigades in Italy—all claimed to be true Marxists, unconnected with the corrupt old Communists in Russia. Yet we now know that they were deeply dependent on Soviet-bloc aid, and as soon as that aid vanished, so did the movements.

Most of all, the humiliating failure of the Soviet Union destroyed the socialist dream. For a century and a half the idea of socialism—from each according to his abilities, to each according to his needs—served as an intellectual focal point for those who disliked the hand the market dealt them. Nationalist leaders invoked socialist ideals as they blocked foreign investment or repudiated foreign debts; labor unions used the rhetoric of socialism as they demanded higher wages; even businessmen appealed to vaguely socialist principles when demanding tariffs or subsidies. And those governments that nonetheless embraced more or less free markets did so cautiously, a bit shamefacedly, because they always feared that too total a commitment to letting markets have their way would be seen as a brutal, inhumane, anti-*social* policy.

But who can now use the words of socialism with a straight face? As a member of the baby boomer generation, I can remember when the idea of revolution, of brave men pushing history forward, had a certain glamour. Now it is a sick joke: after all the purges and gulags, Russia was as backward and corrupt as ever; after all the Great Leaps and Cultural Revolutions, China decided that making money is the highest good. There are still radical leftists out there, who stubbornly claim that true socialism has not yet been tried; and there are still moderate leftists, who claim with more justification that one can reject Marxist-Leninism without necessarily becoming a disciple of Milton Friedman. But the truth is that the heart has gone out of the opposition to capitalism.

For the first time since 1917, then, we live in a world in which property rights and free markets are viewed as fundamental principles, not grudging expedients; where the unpleasant aspects of a market system—inequality, unemployment, injustice—are accepted as facts of life. As in the Victorian era, capitalism is secure not only because of its successes—which, as we will see in a moment, have been very real—but because nobody has a plausible alternative.

This situation will not last forever. Surely there will be other ideologies, other dreams; and they will emerge sooner rather than later if the current economic crisis persists and deepens. But for now capitalism rules the world unchallenged.

The Taming of the Business Cycle

The great enemies of capitalist stability have always been war and depression. War, needless to say, is still with us. But the wars that almost brought capitalism to an end in the middle years of the twentieth century were giant conflicts among great powers—and it's hard to see how that kind of war could erupt in the foreseeable future.

What about depression? The Great Depression came close to destroying both capitalism and democracy, and led more or less directly to war. It was followed, however, by a generation of sustained economic growth in the industrial world, during which recessions were short and mild, recoveries strong and sustained. By the late 1960s the United States had gone so long without a recession that economists were holding conferences with titles like "Is the Business Cycle Obsolete?"

The question was premature: the 1970s was the decade of "stagflation," economic slump and inflation combined. The two energy crises of 1973 and 1979 were followed by the worst recessions since the 1930s. But by the 1990s the question was being asked again; and as we just saw, both Robert Lucas and Ben Bernanke went on record a few years ago with the claim that while the economy would continue to suffer from occasional setbacks, the days of really severe recessions, let alone worldwide depressions, were behind us.

How would you make up your mind about such a claim, other than by noticing that the economy has not had a major recession lately? To answer that question we need to make a digression into theory and ask ourselves what the business cycle is all about. In particular, why do market economies experience recessions?

Whatever you do, don't say that the answer is obvious—that recessions occur because of X, where X is the prejudice of your choice. The truth is that if you think about it—especially if you understand and generally believe in the idea that markets usually manage to match supply and demand—a recession is a very peculiar thing indeed. For during an economic slump, especially a severe one, supply seems to be everywhere and demand nowhere. There are willing workers but not enough jobs, perfectly good factories but not enough orders, open shops but not enough customers. It's easy enough to see how there can be a shortfall of demand for *some* goods: if manufacturers produce a lot of Barbie dolls, but it turns out that consumers want Bratz instead, some of those Barbies may go unsold. But how can there be too little demand for goods in general? Don't people have to spend their money on *something*?

Part of the problem people have in talking sensibly about recessions is that it is hard to picture what is going on during a slump, to reduce it to a human scale. But I have a favorite story that I like to use, both to explain what recessions are all about and as an "intuition pump" for my own thought. (Readers of my earlier books have heard this one before.) It is a true story, although in Chapter 3 I will use an imaginary elaboration to try to make sense of Japan's malaise.

The story is told in an article by Joan and Richard Sweeney, published in 1978 under the title "Monetary Theory and the Great Capitol Hill Baby-sitting Co-op Crisis." Don't recoil at the title: this is serious.

During the 1970s the Sweeneys were members of, surprise, a baby-sitting cooperative: an association of young couples, in this case mainly people with congressional jobs, who were willing to baby-sit each other's children. This particular co-op was unusually large, about 150 couples, which meant not only that there were plenty of potential baby-sitters but also that managing the organization—especially making sure that each couple did its fair share—was not a trivial matter.

Like many such institutions (and other barter schemes), the Capitol Hill co-op dealt with the problem by issuing scrip: coupons entitling the bearer to one hour of baby-sitting. When babies were sat, the baby-sitters would receive the appropriate number of coupons from the baby-sittees. This system was, by construction, shirkproof: it automatically ensured that over time each couple would provide exactly as many hours of baby-sitting as it received.

But it was not quite that simple. It turns out that such a system requires a fair amount of scrip in circulation. Couples with several free evenings in a row, and no immediate plans to go out, would try to accumulate reserves for the future; this accumulation would be matched by the running down of other couples' reserves, but over time each couple would on the average probably want to hold enough coupons to go out several times between bouts of baby-sitting. The issuance of coupons in the Capitol Hill co-op was a complicated affair: couples received coupons on joining, were supposed to repay them on leaving, but also paid dues in baby-sitting coupons that were used to pay officers, and so on. The details aren't important; the point is that there came a time when relatively few coupons were in circulation—too few, in fact, to meet the co-op's needs.

The result was peculiar. Couples who felt their reserves of coupons to be insufficient were anxious to baby-sit and reluctant to go out. But one couple's decision to go out was another's opportunity to baby-sit; so opportunities to baby-sit became hard to find, making couples even more reluctant to use their reserves except on special occasions, which made baby-sitting opportunities even scarcer . . .

In short, the co-op went into a recession.

Okay, time out. How do you react to being told this story?

If you are baffled—wasn't this supposed to be a book about the world economic crisis, not about child care?—you have missed the point. The only way to make sense of any complex system, be it global weather or the global economy, is to work with models—simplified representations of that system which you hope help you understand how it works. Sometimes models consist of systems of equations, sometimes of computer programs (like the simulations that give you your daily weather forecast); but sometimes they are like the model airplanes that designers test in wind tunnels, small-scale versions of the real thing that are more accessible to observation and experiment. The Capitol Hill Baby-sitting Co-op was a miniature economy; it was indeed just about the smallest economy capable of having a recession. But what it experienced *was* a real recession, just as the lift generated by a model airplane's wings is real lift; and just as the behavior of that model can give designers valuable insights into how a jumbo jet will perform, the ups and downs of the co-op can give us crucial insights into why full-scale economies succeed or fail.

If you are not so much puzzled as offended—we're supposed to be discussing important issues here, and instead you are being told cute little parables about Washington yuppies—shame on you. Remember what I said in the introduction: whimsicality, a willingness to play with ideas, is not merely entertaining but essential in times like these. Never trust an aircraft designer who refuses to play with model airplanes, and never trust an economic pundit who refuses to play with model economies.

As it happens, the tale of the baby-sitting co-op will turn out to be a powerful tool for understanding the not-at-all-whimsical problems of real-world economies. The theoretical models economists use, mainly mathematical constructs, often sound far more complicated than this; but usually their lessons can be translated into simple parables like that of the Capitol Hill co-op (and if they can't, often this is a sign that something is wrong with the model). I will end up returning to the baby-sitting story several times in this book, in a variety of contexts. For now, however, let's consider two crucial implications of the story: one about how recessions can happen, the other about how to deal with them.

First, why did the baby-sitting co-op get into a recession? It was *not* because the members of the co-op were doing a bad job of baby-sitting: maybe they were, maybe they weren't, but anyway that is a separate issue. It wasn't because the co-op suffered from "Capitol Hill values," or engaged in "crony baby-sittingism," or had failed to adjust to changing baby-sitting technology as well as its competitors. The problem was not with the co-op's ability to produce, but simply a lack of "effective demand": too little spending on real goods (baby-sitting time) because people were trying to accumulate cash (baby-sitting coupons) instead. The lesson for the real world is that your vulnerability to the business cycle may have little or nothing to do with your more fundamental economic strengths and weaknesses: bad things can happen to good economies.

Second, in that case, what was the solution? The Sweeneys report that in the case of the Capitol Hill co-op it was quite difficult to convince the governing board, which consisted mainly of lawyers, that the problem was essentially technical, with an easy fix. The co-op's officers at first treated it as what an economist would call a "structural" problem, requiring direct action: a rule was passed *requiring* each couple to go out at least twice a month. Eventually, however, the economists prevailed, and the supply of coupons was increased. The results were magical: with larger reserves of coupons couples became more willing to go out, making opportunities to baby-sit more plentiful, making couples even more willing to go out, and so on. The co-op's GBP—gross baby-sitting product, measured in units of babies sat—soared. Again, this was not because the couples had become better baby-sitters, or that the co-op had gone through any sort of fundamental reform process; it was simply because the monetary screwup had been rectified. Recessions, in other words, can be fought simply by printing money—and can sometimes (usually) be cured with surprising ease.

And with that let us return to the business cycle in the full-scale world.

The economy of even a small nation is, of course, far more complex than that of a baby-sitting co-op. Among other things, people in the larger world spend money not only for their current pleasure but also to invest for the future (imagine hiring co-op members not to watch your babies but to build a new playpen). And in the big world there is also a capital market in which those with spare cash can lend it at interest to those who need it now. But the fundamentals are the same: a recession is normally a matter of the public as a whole trying to accumulate cash (or, what is the same thing, trying to save more than it invests) and can normally be cured simply by issuing more coupons.

The coupon issuers of the modern world are known as central banks: the Federal Reserve, the European Central Bank, the Bank of Japan, and so on. And it is their job to keep the economy on an even keel by adding or subtracting cash as needed.

But if it's that easy, why do we ever experience economic slumps? Why don't the central banks always print enough money to keep us at full employment?

Before World War II, policymakers, quite simply, had no idea what they were supposed to be doing. Nowadays practically the whole spectrum of economists, from Milton Friedman leftward, agrees that the Great Depression was brought on by a collapse of effective demand and that the Federal Reserve should have fought the slump with large injections of money. But at the time this was by no means the conventional wisdom. Indeed, many prominent economists subscribed to a sort of moralistic fatalism, which viewed the Depression as an inevitable consequence of the economy's earlier excesses, and indeed as a healthy process: recovery, declared Joseph Schumpeter, "is sound only if it [comes] of itself. For any revival which is merely due to artificial stimulus leaves part of the work of depressions undone and adds, to an undigested remnant of maladjustment, new maladjustment of its own which has to be liquidated in turn, thus threatening business with another [worse] crisis ahead."

Such fatalism vanished after the war, and for a generation most countries did try actively to control the business cycle, with considerable success; recessions were mild, and jobs were usually plentiful. By the late 1960s many started to believe that the business cycle was no longer a major problem; even Richard Nixon promised to "fine-tune" the economy.

This was hubris, and the tragic flaw of full-employment policies became apparent in the 1970s. If the central bank is overoptimistic about how many jobs can be created, if it puts too much money into circulation, the result is inflation. And once that inflation has become deeply embedded in the public's expectations, it can be wrung out of the system only through a period of high unemployment. Add in some external shock that suddenly increases prices— such as a doubling of the price of oil—and you have a recipe for nasty, if not Depression-sized, economic slumps.

But by the middle of the 1980s inflation had fallen back to tolerable levels, oil was in abundant supply, and central bankers finally seemed to be getting the hang of economic management. Indeed,

the shocks the economy experienced seemed, if anything, to rein-
force the sense that we had finally figured this thing out. In 1987,
for example, the U.S. stock market crashed—with a one-day fall
that was as bad as the first day's fall of the 1929 crash. But the
Federal Reserve pumped cash into the system, the real economy
didn't even slow down, and the Dow soon recovered. At the end of
the 1980s central bankers, worried about a small rise in inflation,
missed the signs of a developing recession and got behind the curve
in fighting it; but while that recession cost George H. W. Bush his
job, eventually it responded to the usual medicine, and the United
States entered into another period of sustained expansion. By the
late 1990s it seemed safe to say that the business cycle, if it had not
been eliminated, had at least been decisively tamed.

Much of the credit for that taming went to the money managers:
never in history has a central banker enjoyed the mystique of Alan
Greenspan. But there was also a sense that the underlying structure of the economy had changed in ways that made continuing
prosperity more likely.

Technology as Savior

In a strict technological sense you could say that the modern information age began when Intel introduced the microprocessor—the
guts of a computer on a single chip—back in 1971. By the early
1980s products that put this technology to highly visible use—fax
machines, video games, and personal computers—were becoming
widespread. But at the time it didn't feel like a revolution. Most
people assumed that the information industries would continue to
be dominated by big, bureaucratic companies like IBM—or that
all of the new technologies would eventually go the way of the fax
machine, the VCR, and the video game: invented by innovative

Americans but converted into a paying product only by faceless Japanese manufacturers.

By the nineties, however, it was clear that the information industries would dramatically change the look and feel of our economy.

It is still possible to be skeptical about how large the ultimate economic benefits of information technology will be. What cannot be denied is that the new technologies have had a more *visible* impact on how we work than anything in the previous twenty or thirty years. The typical modern American worker, after all, now sits in an office; and from 1900 until the 1980s the basic appearance of and working of a business office—typewriters and file cabinets, memos and meetings—was pretty much static. (Yes, the Xerox machine did do away with carbon paper.) Then, over a fairly short time, the whole thing changed: networked PCs on every desk, e-mail and the Internet, videoconferencing and telecommuting. This was qualitative, unmistakable change, which created a sense of major progress in a way that mere quantitative improvements could not. And that sense of progress helped bring with it a new sense of optimism about capitalism.

Moreover, the new industries brought back what we might call the romance of capitalism: the idea of the heroic entrepreneur who builds a better mousetrap, and in so doing becomes deservedly wealthy. Ever since the days of Henry Ford, that heroic figure had come to seem ever more mythical, as the economy became increasingly dominated by giant corporations, run not by romantic innovators but by bureaucrats who might just as well have been government officials. In 1968 John Kenneth Galbraith wrote, "With the rise of the modern corporation, the emergence of the organization required by modern technology and planning and the divorce of the owner of capital from control of the enterprise, the entrepreneur no longer exists as an individual person in the mature industrial enterprise." And who could be enthusiastic about capitalism that seemed more or less like socialism without the justice?

The information industries, however, shook up the industrial order. As in the nineteenth century, the economic story became one of remarkable individuals: of men (and, at least occasionally, women) who had a better idea, developed it in their garage or on their kitchen table, and struck it rich. Business magazines actually became interesting to read; and business success came to seem admirable, in a way that it hadn't for more than a century.

And this provided fertile ground for free-market ideas. Forty years ago, defenders of the free market, of the virtues of untrammeled entrepreneurship, had an image problem: when they said "private enterprise," most people thought of General Motors; when they said "businessman," most people thought of the man in the gray flannel suit. In the 1990s the old idea that wealth is the product of virtue, or at least of creativity, made a comeback.

But what really fed economic optimism was the remarkable spread of prosperity—not merely to the advanced nations (where, indeed, the benefits were not as widely spread as one might have wished) but to many countries that not long ago had been written off as economically hopeless.

The Fruits of Globalization

The term "Third World" was originally intended as a badge of pride: Jawaharlal Nehru coined it to refer to those countries that maintained their independence, allying themselves neither with the West nor with the Soviet Union. But soon enough the political intention was overwhelmed by the economic reality: "Third World" came to mean backward, poor, less developed. And the term came to carry a connotation not of righteous demand but of hopelessness.

What changed all of that was globalization: the transfer of technology and capital from high-wage to low-wage countries, and the resulting growth of labor-intensive Third World exports.

It is a bit hard to remember what the world looked like before globalization; so let's try to turn the clock back for a moment, to the Third World as it was a generation ago (and still is, in many countries). In those days, although the rapid economic growth of a handful of small East Asian nations had started to attract attention, developing countries like the Philippines, or Indonesia, or Bangladesh were still mainly what they had always been: exporters of raw materials, importers of manufactures. Small, inefficient manufacturing sectors served their domestic markets, sheltered behind import quotas, but these sectors generated few jobs. Meanwhile, population pressure pushed desperate peasants into cultivating ever more marginal land, or into seeking a livelihood in any way possible, such as homesteading on the mountains of garbage found near many Third World cities.

Given this lack of other opportunities, you could hire workers in Djakarta or Manila for a pittance. But in the mid-1970s cheap labor was not enough to allow a developing country to compete in world markets for manufactured goods. The entrenched advantages of advanced nations—their infrastructure and technical know-how, the vastly larger size of their markets and their proximity to suppliers of key components, their political stability and the subtle but crucial social adaptations that are necessary to operate an efficient economy—seemed to outweigh even a ten- or twentyfold disparity in wage rates. Even radicals seemed to despair of reversing those entrenched advantages: in the 1970s demands for a New International Economic Order were centered on attempts to increase the price of raw materials, rather than to bring Third World countries into the modern industrial world.

And then something changed. Some combination of factors that we still don't fully understand—lower tariff barriers, improved tele-communications, the advent of cheap air transport—reduced the disadvantages of producing in developing countries. Other things being the same, it is still better to produce in the First World—stories of firms that moved production to Mexico or East Asia, then decided to move back after experiencing the disadvantages of the Third World environment at first hand are actually quite common—but there were now a substantial number of industries in which low wages gave developing countries enough of a com-petitive advantage to break into world markets. And so countries that previously made a living selling jute or coffee started produc-ing shirts and sneakers instead.

Workers in those shirt and sneaker factories are, inevitably, paid very little and expected to endure terrible working conditions. I say "inevitably" because their employers are not in business for their (or their workers') health; they will of course try to pay as little as possible, and that minimum is determined by the other opportunities available to workers. And in many cases these are still extremely poor countries.

Yet in those countries where the new export industries took root, there has been unmistakable improvement in the lives of ordi-nary people. Partly this is because a growing industry must offer its workers a somewhat higher wage than they could get elsewhere just in order to get them to move. More important, however, the growth of manufacturing, and of the penumbra of other jobs that the new export sector created, had a ripple effect throughout the economy. The pressure on the land became less intense, so rural wages rose; the pool of unemployed urban dwellers always anxious for work shrank, so factories started to compete with one another for workers, and urban wages also began to rise. In countries where the process has gone on long enough—say, in South Korea or Taiwan—wages have reached advanced-country levels. (In 1975 the average hourly wage in South Korea was only 5 percent of that in the United States; by 2006 it had risen to 62 percent.)

The benefits of export-led economic growth to the mass of people in the newly industrializing economies were not a matter of conjecture. A place like Indonesia is still so poor that progress can be measured in terms of how much the average person gets to eat; between 1968 and 1990 per capita intake rose from 2,000 to 2,700 calories a day, and life expectancy rose from forty-six years to sixty-three. Similar improvements could be seen throughout the Pacific Rim, and even in places like Bangladesh. These improvements did not take place because well-meaning people in the West did anything to help—foreign aid, never large, shrank in the 1990s to virtually nothing. Nor was it the result of the benign policies of national governments, which, as we were soon to be forcefully reminded, were as callous and corrupt as ever. It was the indirect and unintended result of the actions of soulless multinational corporations and rapacious local entrepreneurs, whose only concern was to take advantage of the profit opportunities offered by cheap labor. It was not an edifying spectacle; but no matter how base the motives of those involved, the result was to move hundreds of millions of people from abject poverty to something that was in some cases still awful but nonetheless significantly better.

And once again, capitalism could with considerable justification claim the credit. Socialists had long promised development; there was a time when the Third World looked to Stalin's five-year plans as the very image of how a backward nation should push itself into the twentieth century. And even after the Soviet Union had lost its aura of progressiveness, many intellectuals believed that only by cutting themselves off from competition with more advanced economies could poor nations hope to break out of their trap. By the 1990s, however, there were role models showing that rapid development was possible after all—and it had been accomplished not through proud socialist isolation but precisely by becoming as integrated as possible with global capitalism.

Skeptics and Critics

Not everyone was happy with the state of the world economy after the fall of Communism. While the United States was experiencing remarkable prosperity, other advanced economies were more troubled. Japan had never recovered from the bursting of its "bubble economy" at the beginning of the 1990s, and Europe still suffered from "Eurosclerosis," the persistence of high unemployment rates, especially among the young, even during economic recoveries.

Nor did everyone in the United States share in the general prosperity. The benefits of growth were unequally shared: inequality of both wealth and income had increased to levels not seen since the Great Gatsby days, and by official measures real wages had actually declined for many workers. Even if the numbers were taken with a grain of salt, it was pretty clear that the American economy's progress had left at least 20 or 30 million people at the bottom of the distribution slipping backward.

Some people found other things to be outraged about. The low wages and poor working conditions in those Third World export industries were a frequent source of moralizing—after all, by First World standards those workers were certainly miserable, and these critics had little patience with the argument that bad jobs at bad wages are better than no jobs at all. More justifiably, humanitarians pointed out that large parts of the world were completely untouched by the benefits of globalization: Africa, in particular, was still a continent of ever-deepening poverty, spreading disease, and brutal conflict.

And as always, there were doomsayers. But ever since the 1930s there have been people predicting a new depression any day now; sensible observers have learned not to take such warnings seriously. And that's why ominous developments in Latin America during the first half of the 1990s—developments that did, we now know, signal the possibility of a return to depression economics—were generally ignored.

2

WARNING IGNORED:
LATIN AMERICA'S CRISES

I magine playing word association—in which one person says a word or phrase, and the other is supposed to reply with the first thing that pops into his mind—with an experienced international banker, finance official, or economist. Until very recently, and perhaps even now, if you said, "Financial crisis," he would surely reply, "Latin America."

For generations, Latin American countries were almost uniquely subject to currency crises, banking failures, bouts of hyperinflation, and all the other monetary ills known to modern man. Weak elected governments alternated with military strongmen, both trying to buy popular support with populist programs they could not afford. In the effort to finance these programs, governments resorted either to borrowing from careless foreign bankers, with the end result being balance-of-payments crisis and default, or to the printing press, with the end result being hyperinflation. To this day, when economists tell parables about the dangers of "macroeconomic populism," about the many ways in which money can go bad, the hypothetical currency is by convention named the "peso."

But by the late 1980s it seemed that Latin America had finally learned its lesson. Few Latins admired the brutality of Augusto Pinochet; but the economic reforms he launched in Chile proved highly successful and were preserved intact when Chile finally returned to democracy in 1989. Chile's return to the Victorian virtues—to sound money and free markets—began to look increasingly attractive as the country's growth rate accelerated. Moreover, the old policies seemed finally to have reached the end of the road: the Latin American debt crisis that began in 1982 dragged on for most of the decade, and it became increasingly clear that only some radical change in policy would get the region moving again.

And so Latin America reformed. State-owned companies were privatized, restrictions on imports lifted, budget deficits trimmed. Controlling inflation became a priority; as we will see, some countries adopted drastic measures to restore confidence in their currencies. And these efforts were quickly rewarded not only with greater efficiency but also in the renewed confidence of foreign investors. Countries that had spent the 1980s as financial pariahs—as late as 1990, creditors who wanted out of Latin debt and sold their claims to less risk-averse investors received, on average, only thirty cents on the dollar—became darlings of the international markets, receiving inflows of money that dwarfed the bank loans that got them into the original debt crisis. International media began to talk about the "new" Latin America, in particular about the "Mexican miracle." In September 1994 the annual World Competitiveness Report, prepared by the people who run the famous Davos conferences, featured a special message from the hero of the hour, the Mexican president, Carlos Salinas.

Three months later, Mexico plunged into its worst financial crisis yet. The so-called tequila crisis caused one of the worst recessions to hit an individual country since the 1930s. The repercussions of that crisis spread across Latin America, coming perilously close to bringing down Argentina's banking system. In retrospect, the tequila crisis should have been seen as an omen, a warning that the good opinion of the markets can be fickle, that today's good press does not insulate you from tomorrow's crisis of confidence.

But the warning was ignored. To understand why, we need to look at the strangely ignored story of Latin America's great crisis.

Mexico: Up from the 1980s

Nobody could describe Mexico's government as unsophisticated. The president's inner circle, the so-called Científicos, were well-educated young men who wanted Mexico to become a modern nation and believed that this required close integration with the world economy. Foreign investors were welcomed, their property rights assured. And, impressed with the progressive leadership, such investors came in large numbers, playing a crucial role in the country's modernization.

Okay, I've just played a trick on you. I'm not describing a recent Mexican government. I'm describing the regime of Porfirio Díaz, who ruled Mexico from 1876 until his regime was overthrown by a popular uprising in 1911. The stable government that emerged after the ensuing decade of civil war was populist, nationalist, suspicious of foreign investors in general and the United States in particular. Members of the new regime, the wonderfully named Institutional Revolutionary Party, or PRI, wanted to modernize Mexico, but they wanted to do it their way: industries were developed by domestic companies to serve the domestic market, sheltered from more efficient foreigners by tariffs and import restrictions. Foreign money was acceptable, as long as it did not bring foreign control; the Mexican government was happy to let its companies borrow from U.S. banks, as long as the voting shares remained in local hands.

This inward-looking economic policy may have been inefficient; aside from the *maquiladoras*, export-oriented factories that were allowed to operate only in a narrow zone near the U.S. border, Mexico failed to take advantage of the rising tide of globalization. But once established, Mexico's development policy became deeply entrenched in the country's political and social system, defended by an iron triangle of industrial oligarchs (who received preferential access to credit and import licenses), politicians (who received largesse from the oligarchs), and labor unions (which represented a "labor aristocracy" of relatively well-paid workers in the sheltered industries). Until the 1970s, it must also be said, Mexico was careful not to overreach financially; growth was disappointing, but there were no crises.

In the late 1970s, however, that traditional caution was thrown to the winds. The Mexican economy entered a feverish boom, fed by new oil discoveries, high prices for that oil, and large loans from foreign banks. As the economy heated up and money came rolling in, few people saw the warning signs. There were scattered press stories suggesting some emerging financial problems, but the general view was that Mexico (and Latin America in general) posed few financial risks. This complacency can be quantified: as late as July 1982 the yield on Mexican bonds was slightly *less* than that on those of presumably safe borrowers like the World Bank, indicating that investors regarded the risk that Mexico would fail to pay on time as negligible.

In the middle of the next month, however, a delegation of Mexican officials flew to Washington to inform the U.S. treasury secretary that they were out of money and that Mexico could no longer honor its debts. Within a few months the crisis had spread through most of Latin America and beyond, as banks stopped lending and began demanding repayment. Through frantic efforts—emergency loans from the U.S. government and international agencies like the Bank for International Settlements, "rescheduling" of loan repayments, and what was politely known as "concerted lending" (in which banks were more or less coerced into lending countries the money they needed to pay interest on outstanding loans)— most countries managed to avoid an outright default. The price of this narrow avoidance of financial catastrophe, however, was a severe recession, followed by a slow and often sputtering recovery. By 1986 Mexican real income per capita was 10 percent lower than it had been in 1981, and real wages, eroded by an average inflation rate of more than 70 percent over the preceding four years, were 30 percent below their pre-crisis level.

Enter the new generation of reformers. Over the course of the 1970s a "new class" had become increasingly influential within Mexico's ruling party and government. Well educated, often with graduate degrees from Harvard or MIT, fluent in English and internationalist in outlook, they were Mexican enough to navigate the PRI's boss-and-patronage political waters, but Americanized enough to believe that things should be different. The economic crisis left the old guard, the "dinosaurs," at a loss for answers; the "technopols," who could explain how free-market reforms had worked in Chile, how export-oriented growth had worked in Korea, how inflation stabilization had been achieved in Israel, found themselves the men of the hour. They were not alone: by the mid-1980s many Latin American economists had abandoned the statist views of the fifties and sixties in favor of what came to be called the

Washington Consensus: growth could best be achieved via sound budgets, low inflation, deregulated markets, and free trade.

In 1985 President Miguel de la Madrid began to put this doctrine into effect, most dramatically through a radical freeing up of Mexico's trade: tariffs were slashed, and the range of imports requiring government licenses drastically reduced. The government began selling off some of the enterprises it owned, and loosened the strict rules governing foreign ownership. Perhaps most remarkable of all, de la Madrid designated as his successor not one of the usual PRI bosses but a champion of the new reformers: Planning and Budget Secretary Carlos Salinas de Gortari, himself possessed of a degree from Harvard's Kennedy School of Government, and surrounded by a staff of highly regarded economists trained mainly at MIT.

I use the phrase "designated as his successor" advisedly. Mexico's political system from 1920 to 1990 was truly unique. On paper it was a representative democracy; in recent years that piece of fiction has, amazingly, started to become reality. But in 1988, the year Salinas was elected, Mexican democracy was really a sort of souped-up version of traditional Chicago politics: a one-party system in which votes were bought through patronage, and any shortfall was made up through creative vote counting. The remarkable thing about this system, however, was that the president himself, while very nearly an absolute monarch during his six-year term, could not seek a second term; he would step down, somehow having become wealthy during his tenure, and hand over the reins to a designated successor who would be nominated by the PRI and inevitably win.

By 1988 this system, like Mexico as a whole, was under strain. Salinas faced a real challenger in the general election: Cuauhtémoc Cárdenas, son of a popular former president, who countered Salinas's free-market reformism with a more traditional, anti-capitalist populism. It was a close election, and Cárdenas won. But that was not how the official tally came out. Salinas became president, but now, more than any of his predecessors, he had to deliver the goods. For that, he turned to his Cambridge-trained economic team.

The successes of the Salinas years were built on two crucial policy moves. First was a resolution of the debt crisis. In early 1989, its own presidential election safely past, the U.S. government began showing some unexpected willingness to face up to unpleasant realities. It finally admitted what everyone had long known, that many savings and loan associations had been gambling with taxpayer money and needed to be shut down. Meanwhile, in a surprise speech, Treasury Secretary Nicholas Brady declared that Latin America's debt could not be fully repaid and that some kind of debt forgiveness would have to be worked out. The so-called Brady Plan was more a sentiment than an actual plan—Brady's speech emerged from bureaucratic intrigues worthy of *Yes, Minister*, during which those government officials who might have had the technical expertise to put together a workable blueprint for debt relief were kept in the dark, for fear that they might raise objections. But it gave the extremely competent Mexicans the opening they needed. Within a few months they had devised a scheme that was workable. Mexico ended up replacing much of its outstanding debt with a smaller face value of "Brady bonds."

The overall debt relief from Mexico's Brady deal was modest, but it represented a psychological turning point. Mexicans who had long agitated for debt repudiation were mollified by seeing the foreign bankers give up a pound of flesh; the debt faded as a domestic political issue. Meanwhile foreign investors, who had been afraid to put funds into Mexico for fear that they would be trapped there, saw the deal as putting a period to that phase, and became ready to put in fresh money. The interest rates that Mexico had been forced to pay to keep money from fleeing the country plunged; and because the government no longer had to pay such high interest rates on its debt, the budget deficit quickly faded away. Within a year after the Brady deal, Mexico's financial situation had been transformed.

Nor was a resolution of the debt problem the only trick up Salinas's sleeve. In 1990 he astonished the world by proposing that Mexico establish free trade with the United States and Canada (which had already negotiated a free-trade agreement with each other). In quantitative terms the proposed North American Free Trade Agreement, or NAFTA, would matter less than one might have thought: the U.S. market was already fairly open to Mexican products, and the trade liberalization begun by de la Madrid had moved Mexico itself much, though not all, of the way to free trade. But like the debt reduction package, NAFTA was intended to mark a psychological turning point. By making Mexico's moves to open up to foreign goods and foreign investors not merely a domestic initiative but part of an international treaty, Salinas hoped to make those moves irreversible—and to convince the markets that they were irreversible. He also hoped to guarantee that Mexico's opening would be reciprocated, that the United States would in effect assure Mexico of access to its own market in perpetuity.

George H. W. Bush accepted Salinas's offer. How could he refuse? When the Mexican debt crisis struck in 1982, many in the United States feared that it would lead to a radicalization of Mexican politics, that anti-American forces—perhaps even Communists—would rise in the resulting chaos. Instead, pro-American, free-market types—our kind of people—had miraculously come to power, and offered to take down all the old barriers. To turn them down would be a slap in the face for reform; it would be practically to invite instability and hostility in our neighbor. On compelling foreign-policy grounds, then, American diplomats were enthusiastic about NAFTA. Convincing Congress turned out to be a bit harder, as we will see. But in the first flush of enthusiasm, that was not yet apparent.

Instead, as the reforms in Mexico continued—as state enterprises were sold off, more import restrictions lifted, foreign investors welcomed—enthusiasm for Mexico's prospects accelerated. I personally recall talking to a group of multinational executives—heads of their companies' Latin American operations—in Cancún back in March 1993. I expressed some mild reservations about the Mexican situation, some evidence that the payoff to reform was a bit disappointing. "You're the only person in this room with anything negative to say about this country," I was politely informed. And people like those in the room put their money where their mouths were: in 1993 more than $30 billion in foreign capital was invested in Mexico.

Argentina's Break with the Past

"Rich as an Argentine." That was a common epithet in Europe before World War I, a time when Argentina was viewed by the public, and by investors, as a land of opportunity. Like Australia, Canada, and the United States, Argentina was a resource-rich nation, a favorite destination for both European emigrants and European capital. Buenos Aires was a gracious city with a European feel, hub of a first-rate British-built and -financed railway network, which gathered the wheat and meat of the pampas for export to the world. Linked by trade and investment to the global economy, by telegraph cable to the world capital market, Argentina was a member in good standing of the prewar international system.

True, even then Argentina had a certain tendency now and then to print too much money and to get into difficulties servicing its foreign debt. But then so did the United States. Few could have imagined that Argentina would eventually fall so far behind.

The interwar years were difficult for Argentina, as they were for all resource-exporting countries. The prices of agricultural products were low in the 1920s and crashed in the 1930s. And the situation was made worse by the debt run up in happier years. In effect, Argentina was like a farmer who borrowed heavily when times were good, and finds himself painfully squeezed between falling prices and fixed loan payments. Still, Argentina did not do as badly as one might have expected during the Depression. Its government proved less doctrinaire than those of advanced countries determined to defend the monetary proprieties at all costs. Thanks to a devalued peso, controls on capital flight, and a moratorium on debt repayment, Argentina was actually able to achieve a reasonably strong recovery after 1932; indeed, by 1934 Europeans were once again emigrating to Argentina, because they had a better prospect of finding jobs there than at home.

But the success of heterodox policies during the Depression helped establish governing habits that proved increasingly destructive as time went by. Emergency controls on foreign exchange became a nightmarishly complex set of regulations that discouraged enterprise and fostered corruption. Temporary limitations on imports became permanent barriers behind which astonishingly inefficient industries survived. Nationalized enterprises became sinks for public funds, employing hundreds of thousands of people yet failing to deliver essential services. And deficit spending repeatedly ran amok, leading to ever more disruptive bouts of inflation.

In the 1980s things went from bad to worse. After the debacle of the Falklands War in 1982, Argentina's military government had stepped down, and the civilian government of Raúl Alfonsín took power with the promise of economic revitalization. But the Latin American debt crisis struck Argentina as hard as the rest of the region, and Alfonsín's attempt to stabilize prices by introducing a new currency, the austral, failed dismally. By 1989 the nation was suffering from true hyperinflation, with prices rising at an annual rate of 3,000 percent.

The victor in the 1989 election was Carlos Menem, the Peronist —that is, the candidate of the party founded by Juan Perón, whose nationalistic and protectionist policies had done more than anything else to turn Argentina into a Third World nation. But Menem, it turned out, was prepared to do an economic version of Nixon's trip to China. As finance minister he appointed Domingo Cavallo, a Ph.D. from Harvard (of the same vintage as Pedro Aspe, Mexico's finance minister during the lead-up to its crisis); and Cavallo devised a reform plan even more radical than that of Mexico.

Part of the plan involved opening Argentina up to world markets —in particular, ending the long-standing, destructive habit of treating the country's agricultural exports as a cash cow, to be taxed at prohibitive rates in order to subsidize everything else. Privatization of the country's immense and utterly inefficient state-owned sector also proceeded at a rapid clip. (Unlike Mexico, Argentina even privatized the state-owned oil company.) Because Argentina's initial policies were arguably among the worst in the world, these reforms made a huge difference.

But the distinctive Cavallo touch was the monetary reform. In order to put a definitive end to the country's history of inflation, he resurrected a monetary system that had almost been forgotten in the modern world: a currency board.

Currency boards used to be standard in European colonial possessions. Such possessions would ordinarily be allowed to issue their own currency; but the currency would be rigidly tied in value to that of the mother country, and its soundness would be guaranteed by a law requiring that the domestic currency issue be fully backed by hard-currency reserves. That is, the public would be entitled to convert local currency into pounds or francs at a legally fixed rate, and the central bank would be obliged to keep enough of the mother country's currency on hand to exchange for all of the local notes.

In the postwar years, with the decline of colonial empires and the rise of active economic management, currency boards faded into oblivion. True, in 1983 Hong Kong, faced with a run on its currency, instituted a currency board pegging the Hong Kong dollar at 7.8 to the U.S. dollar. But Hong Kong was itself a sort of colonial relic, albeit a remarkably dynamic one, and the precedent attracted only limited attention.

Argentina's need for credibility, however, was desperate, and so Cavallo reached into the past. The ill-starred austral was replaced with a born-again peso, and this new peso was set at a permanently fixed exchange rate of one peso, one dollar—with every peso in circulation backed by a dollar of reserves. After decades of abusing its money, Argentina had, by law, renounced the ability to print money at all unless someone wanted to exchange a dollar for a peso.

The results were impressive. Inflation dropped rapidly to near zero. Like Mexico, Argentina negotiated a Brady deal and was rewarded with a resumption of capital inflow, though not on the same scale. And the real economy perked up dramatically: after years of decline, GDP increased by a quarter in just three years.

Mexico's Bad Year

At the end of 1993, were there any clouds on Latin America's horizon? Investors were euphoric: it seemed to them that the new free-market orientation of the continent had turned it into a land of opportunity. Foreign businessmen, like those I talked to in Cancún, were almost equally upbeat: the newly liberalized environment had created vast new opportunities for them. Only a few economists had questions, and these were relatively mild.

One question common to both Mexico and Argentina was the appropriateness of the exchange rate. Both countries had stabilized their currencies; both had brought inflation down; but in both cases the slowdown in inflation lagged behind the stabilization of the exchange rate. In Argentina, for example, the peso was pegged against the dollar in 1991; yet over the next two years consumer prices rose 40 percent, compared with only 6 in the United States. A similar, if less stark, process occurred in Mexico. In both cases the effect was to make the country's goods expensive on world markets, leading economists to wonder if their currencies had become overvalued.

A related question involved the trade balance (more accurately, the current account balance, a broader measure that includes services, payment of interest, and so on—but I will use the terms interchangeably). In the early 1990s Mexico's exports grew rather slowly, mainly because the strong peso made their prices uncompetitive. At the same time imports, pulled in both by the removal of import barriers and by a boom in credit, surged. The result was a huge excess of imports over exports: by 1993 Mexico's deficit had reached 8 percent of GDP, a number with few historical precedents. Was this a sign of trouble?

Mexican officials, and many outside the country, argued that it was not. Their argument came straight out of economics text-books. As a sheer matter of accounting, the balance of payments always balances: that is, every purchase that a country makes from foreigners must be matched by a sale of equal value. (Economics students know that there is a small technical qualification to this statement involving unrequited transfers; never mind.) If a country is running a deficit on its *current* account—buying more goods than it sells—it must correspondingly be running an equal surplus on its *capital* account—selling more *assets* than it buys. And the converse is equally true: a country that runs a surplus on capital account must run a deficit on current account. But that meant that Mexico's success in getting foreigners to bring their money, to buy Mexican assets, had a trade deficit as its necessary counterpart—the deficit, in fact, was simply another way of saying that foreigners thought Mexico was a great place to invest. The only reason to be concerned, said the optimists, would be if the capital inflow were somehow artificial—if the government were pulling capital in from abroad by borrowing the money itself (as it did before 1982) or by running budget deficits that created a shortage of domestic savings. Mexico's government, however, was running a balanced budget and was actually building up overseas assets (foreign exchange reserves) rather than liabilities. So why be concerned? If the private sector wanted to pour capital into Mexico, why should the government try to stop it?

And yet there was a disturbing aspect of Mexico's performance: given all the reforms, and all that capital coming in, where was the growth?

Between 1981 and 1989 the Mexican economy had grown at an annual rate of only 1.3 percent, well short of population growth, leaving per capita income far below its 1981 peak. From 1990 to 1994, the years of the "Mexican miracle," things were definitely better: the economy grew 2.8 percent per year. But this was still barely ahead of population growth; as of 1994 Mexico was still, according to its own statistics, far below its 1981 level. Where was the miracle—indeed, where was the payoff to all those reforms, all that foreign investment? In 1993 the MIT economist Rudiger Dornbusch, a longtime observer of the Mexican economy (and the teacher of many of the economists now running Mexico, Aspe included), wrote a caustic analysis of the situation entitled "Mexico: Stabilization, Reform, and No Growth."

Defenders of the Mexican record argued that these numbers failed to reveal the true progress of the economy, especially the transformation from an inefficient, inward-looking industrial base to a highly competitive export orientation. Still, it was certainly disturbing that the huge capital inflows were producing so little measurable result. What was going wrong?

Dornbusch and others argued that the problem lay in the value of the peso: an excessively strong currency was pricing Mexican goods out of world markets, preventing the economy from taking advantage of its growing capacity. What Mexico needed, then, was a devaluation—a onetime reduction in the dollar value of the peso, which would get its economy moving again. After all, in 1992 Britain had been forced by the financial markets (and in particular by George Soros—see Chapter 6) to let the value of the pound decline, and the result was to turn a recession into a boom. Mexico, said some, needed a dose of the same medicine. (Similar arguments were also made for Argentina, whose economy had grown much faster than Mexico's but faced stubbornly high unemployment.)

The Mexicans dismissed such talk, assuring investors that their economic program was on track, that they saw no reason to devalue the peso, and that they had no intention of doing so. It was particularly important to put up a good front because the North American Free Trade Agreement required approval from the U.S. Congress and had run into stiff opposition. Ross Perot had memorably warned of the "great sucking sound" the United States would hear as all its jobs moved south; more respectable voices offered more respectable-sounding arguments. During 1993 the Clinton administration, which had inherited NAFTA from its predecessor, pulled out all the stops and with great difficulty secured passage; but it was a pretty close thing—and just in time.

For during the course of 1994 some important things started to go wrong in Mexico. On New Year's Day there was a peasant uprising in the poor rural state of Chiapas, an area that had gone untouched economically or politically by the changes sweeping through much of Mexico. The stability of the government was not threatened, but the incident was a reminder that bad old habits of corruption, and grinding rural poverty, were still very much a part of the Mexican scene. More serious was the March assassination of Donaldo Colosio, Salinas's designated successor. Colosio was a rare combination of reformer and charismatic popular politician, widely regarded as just the man to truly legitimize the new way of doing things; his assassination both deprived the country of a much needed leader and suggested that dark forces (corrupt political bosses? drug lords?) did not want a strong reformer in charge. The replacement candidate, Ernesto Zedillo, was an American-trained economist whose honesty and intelligence were not in question; but was he a political naïf who would allow himself to be bullied by the dinosaurs? Finally, in the run-up to the election the PRI set about trying to buy support with a moderately large spending spree; some of the pesos it printed were converted into dollars, draining the foreign exchange reserves.

Zedillo won the election, fairly this time, because he managed to convince voters that the populist views of Cárdenas would provoke a financial crisis—as one Mexican friend put it to me, the PRI convinced the voters that unless they voted for Zedillo, "what did happen, would happen." For, alas, the financial crisis came anyway.

The Tequila Crisis

In December 1994, faced with a steady drain on their reserves of foreign exchange, Mexican authorities had to decide what to do. They could stem the loss by raising interest rates, thereby making it attractive for Mexican residents to keep their money in pesos, and perhaps attracting in foreign funds as well. But this rise in interest rates would hurt business and consumer spending, and Mexico was, after several years of disappointing growth, already on the edge of a recession. Or they could devalue the peso—reduce its value in terms of dollars—hoping that this would have the same effect as in Britain sixteen months earlier. That is, a devaluation could in the best scenario not only make Mexico's exports more competitive but also convince foreign investors that Mexican assets were good value, and hence actually allow interest rates to fall.

Mexico chose devaluation. But it botched the job.

What is supposed to happen when a country's currency is devalued is that speculators say, "Okay, that's over," and stop betting on the currency's continued decline. That's the way it worked for Britain and Sweden in 1992. The danger is that speculators will instead view the first devaluation as a sign of more to come, and start speculating all the harder. In order to avoid that, a government is supposed to follow certain rules. First, if you devalue at all, make the devaluation big enough. Otherwise, you will simply set

up expectations of more to come. Second, immediately following
the devaluation, you must give every signal you can that everything
is under control, that you are responsible people who understand
the importance of treating investors right, and so on. Otherwise the
devaluation can crystallize doubts about your economy's soundness and start a panic.

Mexico broke both rules. The initial devaluation was 15 percent,
only half of what economists like Dornbusch had been suggesting.
And the behavior of government officials was anything but reassuring. The new finance minister, Jaime Serra Puche, appeared arro-
gant and indifferent to the opinion of foreign creditors. Worse yet,
it soon became clear that some Mexican businessmen had been
consulted about the devaluation in advance, giving them inside
information denied to foreign investors. Massive capital flight was
now inevitable, and the Mexican government soon had to abandon
fixing the exchange rate at all.

Still, Serra Puche was quickly replaced, and Mexico began making all the right noises. And one might have thought that all the
reforms since 1985 would count for something. But no: foreign
investors were shocked—shocked!—to discover that Mexico was
not the paragon it had seemed, and wanted out at any cost. Soon
the peso had fallen to half its pre-crisis value.

The most pressing problem was the government's own budget.
Governments whose financial credibility is suspect have trouble selling long-term bonds and usually end up with substantial amounts
of short-term debt that must be rolled over at frequent intervals.
Mexico was no exception; and the need to pay high interest rates
on that debt was a major source of fiscal problems in the 1980s.
As we saw, one of the big benefits of the Brady deal of 1989 was
that by making investors more confident, it allowed Mexico to roll

over its short-term debt at much reduced interest rates. Now these gains were lost, and more: by March Mexico was paying investors an interest rate of 75 percent.

Worse yet, in an effort to convince the markets that it would not devalue, Mexico had converted billions of short-term debt into so-called *tesobonos*, which were indexed to the dollar. As the peso plunged, the size of these dollarized debts exploded. And as the *tesobono* problem received wide publicity, it only reinforced the sense of panic.

The government's financial crisis soon spilled over into the private sector. During 1995 Mexico's real GDP would plunge 7 percent, its industrial production 15 percent, far worse than anything the United States has seen since the 1930s—indeed, far worse than the initial slump that followed the 1982 debt crisis. Thousands of businesses went bankrupt; hundreds of thousands of workers lost their jobs. Exactly why the financial crisis had such a devastating effect on the real economy—and why the Mexican government could not, baby-sitting co-op style, act to prevent that slump—is a key question. But let us postpone that discussion until we have a few more crises under our belt.

Most startling of all, the crisis was not confined to Mexico. Instead, the "tequila effect" spread across much of the world, and in particular to other Latin America countries, especially Argentina.

This was an unpleasant surprise. For one thing, Argentina and Mexico are at the opposite ends of Latin America, with few direct trade or financial links. Moreover, Argentina's currency board system was supposed to make the credibility of *its* peso invulnerable. How could it be caught up in Mexico's crisis?

Perhaps Argentina was attacked because to Yanqui investors all Latin American nations look alike. But once speculation against the Argentine peso began, it became clear that the currency board did not provide the kind of insulation its creators had hoped for. True, every peso in circulation was backed by a dollar in reserves, so that in a mechanical sense the country could always defend the peso's value. But what would happen when the public, rationally or not, began to change large numbers of pesos into dollars? The answer, it turned out, was that the country's banks moved quickly to the edge of collapse and threatened to bring the rest of the economy down with them.

Here's how it worked: suppose that a New York loan officer, made nervous by the news from Mexico, decides that he had better reduce his Latin American exposure—and that it is not worth trying to explain to his boss that, as Ronald Reagan once remarked, "they're all different countries." So he tells an Argentine client that his credit line will not be renewed and that the outstanding balance must be repaid. The client withdraws the necessary pesos from his local bank, converting them into dollars with no trouble, because the central bank has plenty of dollars on hand. But the Argentine bank must now replenish its cash reserves; so it calls in a loan to an Argentine businessman.

That's where the trouble starts. To repay its loan, the business must acquire pesos, which will probably be withdrawn from an account at some other Argentine bank—which will itself therefore have to call in some loans, leading to more bank withdrawals, leading to further reductions in credit. The initial reduction in lending from abroad, in other words, will have a *multiplied* effect within Argentina: each dollar of reduced credit from New York leads to several pesos of called loans in Buenos Aires.

And as credit contracts, the business situation in Argentina starts to become dicey. Businesses have trouble repaying their loans on short notice, all the more so because their customers are also under financial pressure. Depositors start to wonder whether banks can really collect from their clients, and start to pull their money out just in case, further tightening credit conditions . . . and we have the beginnings of the sort of vicious circle of credit crunch and bank run that devastated the U.S. economy in 1930–31.

Now, modern nations have defenses against that sort of thing. First of all, deposits are insured by the government, so depositors are not supposed to worry about the solvency of their bank. Second, the central bank is prepared to act as "lender of last resort," rushing cash to banks so they aren't forced into desperate fire-sale methods to meet the demands of depositors. Argentina should thus have been able to nip this process in the bud.

But things weren't that easy. Argentine depositors may have believed that their pesos were safe, but they were less sure that they would preserve their value in dollars. So they wanted to make sure by getting into dollars now, just in case. And the central bank couldn't act as lender of last resort because it was prohibited from printing new pesos except in exchange for dollars! The very rules designed to protect the system from one kind of crisis of confidence left it deeply vulnerable to another.

In early 1995, then, both Mexico and Argentina went suddenly from euphoria to terror. It seemed all too likely that the reformist experiments in both countries would end in disastrous collapse.

The Great Rescue

What Latin America needed, urgently, was dollars: dollars with which Mexico could repay the *tesobonos* as they came due, dollars that would allow Argentina to print pesos and lend them to its banks.

The Mexican package was the larger, more urgent, and politically more difficult of the two. While much of the money came from international agencies like the International Monetary Fund, Europe and Japan saw a Mexican rescue as mainly a U.S. issue, and the United States therefore would have to provide a large chunk of the money itself. Unfortunately, there were powerful political forces arrayed against any such rescue. Those who had bitterly opposed NAFTA saw the Mexican crisis as vindication and were not willing to lay out taxpayers' money on behalf of the Mexicans and their bankers. Meanwhile, conservatives disliked the whole idea of governments intervening to support markets, and particularly disliked the role of the International Monetary Fund, which they regarded as a step on the way toward world government. It soon became clear that the U.S. Congress would not approve any funding for a Mexican rescue.

Luckily, it turned out that the U.S. Treasury can, at its own discretion, make use of the Exchange Stabilization Fund (ESF), a pot of money set aside for emergency intervention in foreign exchange markets. The intent of the legislation that established that fund was clearly to stabilize the value of the *dollar*; but the language didn't actually say that. So with admirable creativity Treasury used it to stabilize the peso instead. Between the ESF and other sources, a remarkable $50 billion credit line was quickly made available to Mexico; and after several heart-pounding months the financial situation did indeed begin to stabilize.

Argentina's lower-profile rescue came via the World Bank, which put up $12 billion to support the nation's banks.

The rescues for Mexico and Argentina did not prevent a very severe economic contraction—it was considerably worse, in fact, than what happened in the first year of the 1980s debt crisis. But by late 1995 investors began to calm down, to believe that maybe the countries were not going to collapse after all. Interest rates came down; spending started to revive; and soon Mexico and Argentina were making a rapid recovery. For thousands of businesses and millions of workers, the crisis had been devastating. But it ended sooner than most had feared or expected.

Learning the Wrong Lessons

Two years after the tequila crisis, it seemed as if everything was back on track. Both Mexico and Argentina were booming, and those investors who had kept their nerve did very well indeed. And so, perversely, what might have been seen as a warning instead became, if anything, a source of complacency. While few people laid out the lessons learned from the Latin crisis explicitly, an informal summary of the post-tequila conventional wisdom might have run as follows:

First, the tequila crisis was not about the way the world at large works: it was a case of Mexico being Mexico. It was caused by Mexican policy errors—notably, allowing the currency to become overvalued, expanding credit instead of tightening it when speculation against the peso began, and botching the devaluation itself in a way that unnerved investors. And the depth of the slump that followed had mainly to do with the uniquely tricky political economy of the Mexican situation, with its still-unresolved legacy of populism and anti-Americanism. In a way you could say that the slump was punishment for the theft of the 1988 election.

The lesson taken, in short, was that Mexico's debacle was of little relevance to the rest of the world. True, the crisis had spilled over to the rest of Latin America, but Argentina's brush with financial collapse somehow did not fully register on the world's attention, perhaps because it was followed by such a strong recovery. And surely the tequila crisis would not be replicated in well-run econo-mies without a history of macroeconomic populism—countries like the miracle economies of Asia.

The other lesson concerned not Mexico but Washington—that is, the International Monetary Fund and the U.S. Treasury Depart-ment. What the crisis seemed to show was that Washington had things under control: that it had the resources and the knowledge to contain even severe financial crises. Huge aid was quickly mobi-lized on Mexico's behalf, and it did the trick. Instead of the seven lean years of the 1980s, the tequila crisis was over in a year and a half. Clearly, it seemed, the people in charge had gotten better at this sort of thing.

Fourteen years after the tequila crisis began, with much of the world, including the United States, experiencing a financial crisis with a distinct resemblance to the events of 1994–95, it's clear that we learned the wrong lessons from Latin America.

What we should have asked was the question posed in many meetings by the economist Guillermo Calvo, of the World Bank and later of the University of Maryland: "Why was so large a pun-ishment imposed for so small a crime?" In the aftermath of the tequila crisis it was all too easy to revisit the policies followed by Mexico in the run-up to that crisis, and find them full of error. But the fact was that at the time they seemed pretty good, and even after the fact it was hard to find any missteps large enough to justify the economic catastrophe of 1995. We should have taken Calvo's question—with its implication that there were mechanisms trans-forming minor policy mistakes into major economic disasters—to heart. We should have looked more closely at the arguments of some commentators that there really were no serious mistakes at all, except for the brief series of fumbles that got Mexico on the wrong side of market perceptions and set in motion a process of self-justifying panic. And we should therefore also have realized that what happened to Mexico could happen elsewhere: that the seeming success of an economy, the admiration of markets and media for its managers, was no guarantee that the economy was immune to sudden financial crisis.

In retrospect it is also clear that we gave far too much credit to "Washington," to the IMF and the Treasury. It was true that they had acted courageously and decisively, and that the results had been a vindication. But on close examination the omens were not all that good for a repeat performance. For one thing, the mobilization of money was achieved through what amounted to a legal sleight of hand, justified mainly by the special significance of Mexico to U.S. interests. Money would not come as quickly or as easily in later crises. The Mexican rescue was also made less complicated by the cooperation of the Mexican government: Zedillo's people had no pride to swallow—not with Mexico's history—and were in complete agreement with Washington about what needed to be done. Dealing with Asian countries that had been accustomed to negotiating from a position of strength, and with Asian leaders accustomed to having things their own way, would be very different.

Perhaps most of all, we failed to understand the extent to which both Mexico and Washington simply got lucky. The rescue wasn't really a well-considered plan that addressed the essence of the crisis: it was an emergency injection of cash to a beleaguered government, which did its part by adopting painful measures less because they were clearly related to the economic problems than because by demonstrating the government's seriousness they might restore market confidence. They succeeded, albeit only after the economy had been punished severely, but there was no good reason to suppose that such a strategy would work the next time.

And so nobody was prepared either for the emergence of a new, tequila-style crisis in Asia a few years later, or for the ineffectiveness of a Mexican-style rescue when that crisis came. We were even less prepared for the global crisis that erupted in 2007. What was odd about our obliviousness was that Asia's biggest economy was already in serious trouble—and was doing a notably bad job taking care of its own business.

3

JAPAN'S TRAP

There was a time, not that long ago, when Americans were obsessed with Japan. The successes of Japanese industry inspired both admiration and fear; you couldn't enter an airport bookstore without encountering rows of dust jackets featuring rising suns and samurai warriors. Some of these books promised to teach the secrets of Japanese management; others prophesied (or demanded) economic warfare. As role models or demons, or both, the Japanese were very much on our minds.

All that is gone now. Japan still makes the headlines now and then, usually when there's bad news—a big fall in the Nikkei, or a disruption of the "carry trade," in which hedge funds borrow cheaply in Japan and lend the money elsewhere. But for the most part we have lost interest. The Japanese weren't that tough after all, the public seems to have concluded, so now we can ignore them.

This is foolish. The failures of Japan are every bit as significant for us as its successes. What happened to Japan is both a tragedy and an omen. The world's second-largest economy is still blessed with well-educated and willing workers, a modern capital stock, and impressive technological know-how. It has a stable government, which has no difficulty collecting taxes. Unlike Latin America, or for that matter smaller Asian economies, it is a creditor nation, not dependent on the goodwill of foreign investors. And the sheer size of its economy, which means that its producers sell mainly to the domestic market, should give Japan—like the United States—a freedom of action denied to lesser nations.

Yet Japan spent most of the 1990s in a slump, alternating brief and inadequate periods of economic growth with ever-deeper recessions. Once the growth champion of the advanced world, in 1998 Japanese industry produced less than it had in 1991. And even worse than the performance itself was the sense of fatalism and helplessness, the loss of faith in the ability of public policy to turn the situation around. This was a tragedy: a great economy like this does not need or deserve to be in a decade-long slump. Japan's woes were never as acute as those of other Asian nations, but they went on far longer, with far less justification. It was also an omen: if it could happen to the Japanese, who was to say that it couldn't happen to us? And sure enough, it did.

How did it happen to Japan?

Japan as Number One

No country—not even the Soviet Union in the days of Stalin's five-year plans—had ever experienced as stunning an economic transformation as Japan did in the high-growth years from 1953 to 1973. In the space of two decades a largely agricultural nation became the world's largest exporter of steel and automobiles, greater Tokyo became the world's largest and arguably most vibrant metropolitan area, and the standard of living made a quantum leap.

Some Westerners took notice. As early as 1969 the futurist Herman Kahn published *The Emerging Japanese Superstate*, predicting that Japan's high growth rates would make it the world's leading economy by the year 2000. But it was not until the late 1970s—around the time that Ezra Vogel wrote his best-seller, *Japan as Number One*—that the realization of just how much Japan had achieved really dawned on the wider public. As sophisticated Japanese products—above all, automobiles and consumer electronics—flooded into Western markets, people began to wonder about the secret of Japan's success.

There was a certain irony in the timing of the great debate about Japan: the truth was that the heroic age of Japanese economic growth ended just about the time Westerners started to take Japan seriously. In the early 1970s, for reasons that are still somewhat mysterious, growth slowed throughout the advanced world. Japan, which had had the highest growth rate, also experienced the biggest slowdown—from 9 percent a year in the 1960s to less than 4 percent after 1973. Although this rate was still faster than that of any other advanced country (half again as fast as that of the United States), at that rate the date of Japan's emergence as the world's leading economy would have to be put off well into the twenty-first century. Still, Japan's growth performance was, literally, the envy of other nations. Many people argued not only that Japan had figured out a better way to run its economy but also that its success came at least partly at the expense of naive Western competitors.

We need not replay here the whole debate over why Japan was successful. Basically, there were two sides. One side explained the growth as the product of good fundamentals, above all excellent basic education and a high savings rate, and—as always—also engaged in a bit of amateur sociology to explain why Japan was so very good at manufacturing high-quality products at low cost. The other side argued that Japan had developed a fundamentally different economic system, a new and superior form of capitalism. The debate over Japan also became a debate over economic philosophy, over the validity of Western economic thought in general and the virtues of free markets in particular.

One element of the supposedly superior Japanese system was government guidance. In the fifties and sixties the Japanese government—both the famed Ministry of International Trade and Industry (MITI) and the quieter but even more influential Ministry of Finance—played a strong role in directing the economy. The economy's growth was at least partly channeled by the government's strategic designs, as bank loans and import licenses flowed to favored industries and firms. By the time the West really focused on Japan, the government's grip had been much loosened, but the image of "Japan Inc.," a centrally directed economy bent on dominating world markets, remained a potent one into the 1990s.

Another element of the distinctive Japanese economic style was the insulation of major companies from short-term financial pressures. Members of Japanese *keiretsu*—groups of allied firms organized around a main bank—typically owned substantial quantities of each other's shares, making management largely independent of the outside stockholders. Nor did Japanese companies worry much about stock prices, or market confidence, since they rarely financed themselves by selling either stocks or bonds. Instead, the main bank lent them the money they needed. So Japanese firms didn't have to worry about short-term profitability, or indeed to worry much about profitability at all. One might have thought that the financial condition of a *keiretsu* bank would in the end discipline corporate investment: if the loans to the bank's affiliates looked unsound, wouldn't the bank start to lose depositors? But in Japan as in most countries, depositors believed that the government would never allow them to lose their savings, so they paid little attention to what banks did with their money.

The result of this system, claimed both those who admired it and those who feared it, was a country able to take the long view. One by one, the Japanese government would target "strategic" industries that could serve as engines of growth. The private sector would be guided into those industries, helped along by an initial period of protection from foreign competition, during which the industry could hone its skills in the domestic market. Then there would be a great export drive, during which firms would ignore profitability while building market share and driving their foreign competitors into the ground. Eventually, its dominance of the industry secured, Japan would move on to the next one. Steel, autos, VCRs, semiconductors—soon it would be computers and aircraft.

Skeptics poked holes in many of the details of this account. But even those who absolved Japan of the charge of predatory behavior, who questioned whether the wizards of MITI were really as all-knowing as advertised, tended to agree that the distinctive characteristics of the Japanese system must have something to do with Japanese success. Only much later would those same distinctive characteristics—the cozy relationship between government and business, the extension of easy credit by government-guaranteed banks to closely allied companies—come to be labeled crony capitalism and seen as the root of economic malaise.

But the weaknesses of the system were actually evident by the late 1980s, to anyone willing to see.

Bubble, Toil and Trouble

At the beginning of 1990 the market capitalization of Japan—the total value of all the stocks of all the nation's companies—was larger than that of the United States, which had twice Japan's population and more than twice its gross domestic product. Land, never cheap in crowded Japan, had become incredibly expensive: according to a widely cited factoid, the land underneath the square mile of Tokyo's Imperial Palace was worth more than the entire state of California. Welcome to the "bubble economy," Japan's equivalent of the Roaring Twenties.

The late 1980s represented a time of prosperity for Japan, of fast growth, low unemployment, and high profits. Nonetheless, nothing in the underlying economic data justified the tripling of both land and stock prices during that period. Even at the time many observers thought that there was something manic and irrational about the financial boom—that traditional companies in slowly growing industries should not be valued like growth stocks, with price-earnings ratios of 60 or more. But as is so often the case in manic markets, the skeptics were without the resources, or the courage, to back their lack of conviction; conventional wisdom found all sorts of justifications for the sky-high prices.

Financial bubbles are nothing new. From tulip mania to Internet mania, even the most sensible investors have found it hard to resist getting caught up in the momentum, to take a long view when everyone else is getting rich. But given the reputation of the Japanese for long-term strategic thinking, the common perception that Japan Inc. was more like a planned economy than a free-market free-for-all, the extent of the bubble remains somewhat surprising.

Now, Japan's reputation for long-sighted, socially controlled investment always exaggerated the reality. Real estate speculators, often getting an extra edge by paying off politicians, and another extra edge through *yakuza* connections, have been a surprisingly important part of the Japanese scene for as long as anyone can remember. Speculative investments in real estate came close to provoking a banking crisis in the 1970s; the situation was saved only through a burst of inflation, which reduced the real value of the speculators' debts and turned bad loans good again. Still, the sheer extent of Japan's bubble was astonishing. Was there some explanation of the phenomenon that ran beyond mere crowd psychology?

Well, it turns out that Japan's bubble was only one of several outbreaks of speculative fever around the world during the 1980s. All of these outbreaks had the common feature that they were financed mainly by bank loans—in particular, that traditionally staid institutions started offering credit to risk-loving, even shady operators in return for somewhat above-market interest rates. The most famous case was that of America's savings and loan associations—institutions whose public image used to be defined by the all-American earnestness of Jimmy Stewart's small-town banker in *It's a Wonderful Life*, but which in the 1980s became identified instead with high-rolling Texas real estate moguls. But similar outbreaks of dubious lending occurred elsewhere, notably in Sweden, another country not usually associated with speculative fever. And economists have long argued that behind all such episodes lies the same economic principle—one, like the basic baby-sitting model of a recession, that will reappear several times in this book. The principle is known as moral hazard.

The term "moral hazard" has its origins in the insurance industry. Very early in the game providers of fire insurance, in particular, noticed that property owners who were fully insured against loss had an interesting tendency to have destructive fires—particularly when changing conditions had reduced the probable market value of their building to less than the insurance coverage. (In the mid-1980s New York City had a number of known "arson-prone" landlords, some of whom would buy a building at an inflated price from a dummy company they themselves owned, use that price as the basis for a large insurance policy, then just happen to have a fire. Moral hazard, indeed.) Eventually the term came to refer to any situation in which one person makes the decision about how much risk to take, while someone else bears the cost if things go badly.

Borrowed money is inherently likely to produce moral hazard. Suppose that I'm a smart guy, but without any capital, and that based on my evident cleverness you decide to lend me a billion dollars, to invest any way I see fit, as long as I promise to repay in a year's time. Even if you charge me a high rate of interest, this is a great deal: I will take the billion, put it into something that *might* make a lot of money, but then again might end up worthless, and hope for the best. If the investment prospers, so will I; if it does not, I will declare personal bankruptcy, and walk away. Heads I win, tails you lose.

Of course, that is why nobody will lend someone without capital of his own a billion dollars to invest as he sees fit, no matter how smart he may seem. Creditors normally place restrictions on what borrowers can do with any money they lend, and borrowers are also normally obliged to put up substantial amounts of their own money, in order to give them a good reason to avoid losses.

Sometimes lenders seem to forget about these rules and lend large sums, no questions asked, to people who put on a good show of knowing what they are doing. We'll get to the amazing story of the hedge funds in Chapter 6. At other times the requirement that the borrower put up enough of his own money can itself be a source of market instability. When assets lose value, those who bought them with borrowed money can be faced with a "margin call": they must either put more of their own money in or repay their creditors by selling the assets, driving the prices down still further, a process that has been central to the current financial crisis. But leaving such market pathologies aside, there is another reason why the rules sometimes get broken: because the moral hazard game is played at taxpayers' expense.

Remember what we said about the main banks of Japanese *keiretsu*: that their depositors believed that their deposits were safe because the government stood behind them. The same is true of almost all banks in the First World, and most banks elsewhere. Modern nations, even if they do not explicitly guarantee deposits, cannot find it in their hearts to let widows and orphans lose their life savings simply because they put them in the wrong bank, just as they cannot bring themselves to stand aside when the raging river sweeps away houses foolishly built in the flood plain. Only the most hard-nosed of conservatives would wish it otherwise. But the result is that people are careless about where they build their houses, and even more careless about where they store their money.

This carelessness offers a tempting opportunity to unscrupulous businessmen: just open a bank, making sure that it has an impressive building and a fancy name. Attract a lot of deposits, by paying good interest if that is allowed, by offering toasters or whatever if it isn't. Then lend the money out, at high interest rates, to high-rolling speculators (preferably friends of yours, or maybe even yourself behind a different corporate front). The depositors won't ask about the quality of your investments since they know that they are protected in any case. And you now have a one-way option: if the investments do well, you become rich; if they do badly, you can simply walk away and let the government clean up the mess.

Okay, it's not that easy, because government regulators aren't entirely stupid. In fact, from the 1930s to the 1980s this kind of behavior was quite rare among bankers because regulators did more or less the same things that a private lender would normally do before handing me a billion dollars to play with. They restricted what banks could do with depositors' money in an effort to prevent excessive risk-taking. They required that the owners of banks put substantial amounts of their own money at stake, through capital requirements. And in a more subtle, perhaps unintentional measure, regulators historically limited the amount of competition among banks, making a banking license a valuable thing in itself, possessed of a considerable "franchise value"; licensees were loath to jeopardize this franchise value by taking risks that could break the bank.

But in the 1980s these restraints broke down in many places. Mainly the cause was deregulation. Traditional banks were safe, but also very conservative; arguably they failed to direct capital to its most productive uses. The cure, argued reformers, was both more freedom and more competition: let banks lend where they thought best, and allow more players to compete for public savings. Somehow reformers forgot that this would give banks more freedom to take bad risks and that by reducing their franchise value it would give them less incentive to avoid them. Changes in the marketplace, notably the rise of alternative sources of corporate finance, further eroded the profit margins of bankers who clung to safe, old-fashioned ways of doing businesses.

And so in the 1980s there was a sort of global epidemic of moral hazard. Few countries can be proud of their handling of the situation—surely not the United States, whose mishandling of the savings and loan affair was a classic case of imprudent, short-sighted, and occasionally corrupt policymaking. But Japan, where all the usual lines—between government and business, between

banks and their clients, between what was and what was not subject to government guarantee—were especially blurry, was peculiarly ill suited to a loosened financial regime. Japan's banks lent
more, with less regard for quality of the borrower, than anyone
else's. In so doing they helped inflate the bubble economy to gro-
tesque proportions.

Sooner or later, bubbles always burst. The bursting of the Japanese bubble wasn't entirely spontaneous: the Bank of Japan, concerned about speculative excess, began raising interest rates in
1990 in an effort to let some of the air out of the balloon. At first
this policy was unsuccessful, but beginning in 1991 land and stock
prices began a steep decline, which within a few years brought
them some 60 percent below their peak.

Initially, and indeed for several years thereafter, Japanese authorities seem to have regarded all of this as healthy—a return to more
sensible, realistic asset valuations. But it gradually became apparent that the end of the bubble economy had brought not economic
health but a steadily deepening malaise.

A Stealthy Depression

Unlike Mexico in 1995, South Korea in 1998, and Argentina in
2002, Japan never went through a year of unmistakable, catastrophic economic decline. In the decade after the bubble burst,
Japan experienced only two years in which real GDP actually fell.

But year after year growth fell short, not just of the economy's
previous experience but of any reasonable estimate of the growth
in its capacity. There was one year in the decade after 1991 in
which Japan grew as fast as it did in an *average* year in the preceding decade. Even if you take a conservative estimate of the growth
in Japan's "potential output," the output the economy could have

produced with full employment of resources, there was also only one year in which actual output grew as rapidly as potential.

Economists have one of their famously awkward phrases for what Japan was experiencing: a "growth recession." A growth recession is what happens when an economy grows but this growth isn't fast enough to keep up with the economy's expanding capacity, so that more and more machines and workers stand idle. Normally growth recessions are rather rare, because both booms and slumps tend to gather momentum, producing either rapid growth or clear-cut decline. Japan, however, essentially experienced a decade-long growth recession, which left it so far below where it should have been that it verged on a new phenomenon: a growth depression.

The slowness with which Japan's economy deteriorated was in itself a source of much confusion. Because the depression crept up on the country, there was never a moment at which the public clamored for the government to do something dramatic. Because Japan's economic engine gradually lost power rather than coming to a screeching halt, the government itself consistently defined success down, regarding the economy's continuing growth as a vindication of its policies even though that growth was well short of what could and should have been achieved. And at the same time, both Japanese and foreign analysts tended to assume that because the economy grew so slowly for so long, it *couldn't* grow any faster.

So Japan's economic policies were marked by an odd combination of smugness and fatalism—and by a noticeable unwillingness to think hard about how things could have gone so very wrong.

Japan's Trap

There is nothing mysterious about the onset of Japan's slump in 1991: sooner or later the financial bubble was bound to burst, and when it did it would bring about a decline in investment, in consumption, and hence in overall demand. The same thing happened in the United States after the U.S. stock market bubble of the 1990s burst, and again after the next decade's housing bubble popped. The question, however, is why Japan's policymakers, in particular its central bank, weren't able to get the economy moving again.

It is time to return to the story of the baby-sitting co-op. Suppose that the U.S. stock market were to crash, undermining consumer confidence. Would this inevitably mean a disastrous recession? Think of it this way: when consumer confidence declines, it is as if for some reason the typical member of the co-op had become less willing to go out, more anxious to accumulate coupons for a rainy day. This could indeed lead to a slump—but need not, if the management were alert and responded by simply issuing more coupons. That is exactly what our head coupon issuer, Alan Greenspan, did in 1987.

Or suppose that the coupon issuer didn't respond quickly enough, and that the economy did indeed fall into a slump. Don't panic: even if the head coupon issuer temporarily gets behind the curve, he can still ordinarily turn the situation around by issuing more coupons— that is, with a vigorous monetary expansion, like the ones that ended the U.S. recessions of 1981–82, 1990–91, and 2001.

What about all the bad investments made during the boom? Well, that was so much wasted capital. But there is no obvious reason why bad investments made in the past require an actual slump in output in the present. Productive capacity may not have risen as much as anticipated, but it has not actually fallen; why not just print enough money to keep spending up so that the economy makes full use of the capacity it has?

Remember, the story of the co-op tells you that economic

slumps are not punishments for our sins, pains that we are fated to suffer. The Capitol Hill co-op didn't get into trouble because its members were bad, inefficient baby-sitters; its troubles did not reveal the fundamental flaws of "Capitol Hill values" or "crony baby-sittingism." It had a technical problem—too many people chasing too little scrip—which could be, and was, solved with a little clear thinking. And so the co-op's story ought to inoculate us against fatalism and pessimism. It seems to imply that recessions are always, and indeed easily, curable.

But in that case why didn't Japan pull up its socks after the bubble burst? How could Japan get stuck in a seemingly intractable slump—one that it didn't appear able to get out of simply by printing coupons? Well, if we extend the co-op's story a little bit, it is not hard to generate something that looks a lot like Japan's problems.

First, we have to imagine a co-op whose members realized that there was an unnecessary inconvenience in their system: there would be occasions when a couple would find itself needing to go out several times in a row, and would run out of coupons—and therefore would be unable to get its babies sat—even though it was entirely willing to do lots of compensatory baby-sitting at a later date. To resolve this problem, we'll suppose the co-op allowed members to *borrow* extra coupons from the management in times of need, repaying with the coupons received from subsequent baby-sitting. (We could move the story a bit closer to the way real economies work by imagining that couples could also borrow coupons from each other; the interest rate in this infant capital market would then play the role the "discount rate" of the co-op management plays in our parable.) To prevent members from abusing this privilege, however, the management would need to impose some penalty, requiring borrowers to repay more coupons than they borrowed.

Under this new system, couples would hold smaller reserves of coupons than before, knowing that they could borrow more if necessary. The co-op's officers would, however, have acquired a new tool of management. If members of the co-op reported that it was easy to find baby-sitters, hard to find opportunities to baby-sit, the terms under which members could borrow coupons could be made more favorable, encouraging more people to go out. If baby-sitters were scarce, those terms could be worsened, encouraging people to go out less.

In other words, this more sophisticated co-op would have a central bank that could stimulate a depressed economy by reducing the interest rate, cool off an overheated one by raising it.

But in Japan interest rates fell almost to zero, and still the economy slumped. Have we finally exhausted the usefulness of our parable?

Well, imagine that there is a seasonality in the demand and supply for baby-sitting. During the winter, when it's cold and dark, couples don't want to go out much but are quite willing to stay home and look after other people's children—thereby accumulating points they can use on balmy summer evenings. If this seasonality isn't too pronounced, the co-op could still keep the supply and demand for baby-sitting in balance by charging low interest rates in the winter months, higher rates in the summer. But suppose that the seasonality is very strong indeed. Then in the winter, even at a zero interest rate, there will be more couples seeking opportunities to baby-sit than there are couples going out, which means that baby-sitting opportunities will be hard to find, which means that couples seeking to build up reserves for summer fun will be even less willing to use those points in the winter, meaning even fewer opportunities to baby-sit . . . and the co-op will slide into a recession even at a zero interest rate.

And the 1990s were the winter of Japan's discontent. Perhaps because of its aging population, perhaps also because of a general nervousness about the future, the Japanese public didn't appear willing to spend enough to use the economy's capacity, even at a zero interest rate. Japan, say the economists, fell into the dread "liquidity trap." And what you have just read is an infantile explanation of what a liquidity trap is and how it can happen.

Japan Adrift

The standard response to a recession is to cut interest rates—to allow people to borrow baby-sitting coupons cheaply so that they will begin going out again. Japan was slow to cut interest rates after the bubble burst, but it eventually cut them all the way to zero, and it still wasn't enough. Now what?

The classic answer, the one that has been associated with the name of John Maynard Keynes, is that if the private sector won't spend enough to maintain full employment, the public sector must take up the slack. Let the government borrow money and use the funds to finance public investment projects—if possible to good purpose, but that is a secondary consideration—and thereby provide jobs, which will make people more willing to spend, which will generate still more jobs, and so on. The Great Depression in the United States was brought to an end by a massive deficit-financed public works program, known as World War II. Why not try to jump-start Japanese growth with a more pacific version of the same?

Japan tried. During the 1990s the government produced a series of stimulus packages, borrowing money to build roads and bridges whether the country needed them or not. These packages created jobs directly and boosted the economy as a whole every time they were tried.

The trouble was that the programs didn't get enough bang for the yen. In 1991 Japan's government was running a fairly hefty budget surplus (2.9 percent of GDP). By 1996 it was running a quite nasty deficit of 4.3 percent of GDP. Yet the economic engine was still sputtering. Meanwhile, the ever-growing deficits were starting to worry Japan's Ministry of Finance, which was concerned about the long-term budget position. The big concern was demographics (which may also have a lot to do with Japan's high savings and low investment demand). Like other countries, Japan had a baby boom followed by a baby bust, and faces the prospect of a rising ratio of retirees to workers. But Japan's problem is extreme: its working-age population is actually declining steadily, even as the number of retirees rapidly grows. And since retired citizens are a heavy fiscal burden on modern governments—recipients of expensive public pensions and health care—standard fiscal principles said that Japan should be building up a trust fund to meet the future bills, not running ever-growing deficits.

In 1997 the voices of fiscal responsibility prevailed, and Prime Minister Ryutaro Hashimoto increased taxes to reduce the budget deficit. The economy promptly plunged into recession.

So it was back to deficit spending. In 1998 Japan introduced a massive new program of public works. But the fiscal issue had now been raised, and it refused to go away. Investors soon noticed that Japan was projecting a deficit of 10 percent of GDP, and that the ratio of government debt to GDP was already above 100 percent. These are the kinds of numbers usually associated with Latin American nations at risk of hyperinflation. Nobody really expected hyperinflation in Japan, but investors were getting at least a bit worried about the long-term soundness of that government's finances. In short, the attempt to jump-start the economy with deficit spending seemed to be reaching its limits.

What other options were there?

If government spending is one standard response to a stalled economy, pumping up the banks is another. One widely held view about the Great Depression is that it persisted so long because the banking crises of 1930–31 inflicted long-term damage to credit markets. According to this view, there were businessmen who would have been willing to spend more if they could have gotten access to credit, and who would in fact have been qualified borrowers. But the bankers who could have made those loans were themselves either out of business or unable to raise funds because the public's confidence in banks had been so shaken. In terms of the baby-sitting co-op, this amounts to saying that there were people who would have been willing to go out in the winter and baby-sit in the summer, but who could not get anybody to lend them the necessary coupons.

Now, Japan's banks made a lot of bad loans in the bubble economy years, and the long stagnation that followed turned many other loans bad as well. So one theory of Japan's slump was that the country was in a liquidity trap mainly because its banks were financially weak; fix the banks and the economy would recover. And in late 1998 Japan's legislature put together a $500 billion bank rescue plan.

Yet another option for Japan was to do whatever it took to get a bit of inflation going. This option needs some explaining.

The truth is that economists didn't think much about the subject of liquidity traps for a very long time. Before Japan's troubles in the 1990s, the last time a major economy appeared to be in such a trap was the United States in the late 1930s. And economic historians have tended to downplay the significance of that experience by arguing either that it wasn't a true liquidity trap—that the Fed could have gotten us out if it had tried hard enough—or that we got into that trap only through extraordinary policy mistakes, unlikely to be repeated. So as the outlines of Japan's trap became clear in the mid-1990s, economists were basically unprepared—and, if I may be critical of my profession, uninterested. I continue to be astonished at how few economists around the world realized just how important a problem Japan's trap was both as a practical matter and as a challenge to our economic doctrines.

But economics is, as the great Victorian economist Alfred Marshall said, "not a body of concrete truth, but an engine for the discovery of concrete truth." Or to put it in less elevated language, old models can be taught to perform new tricks. As we saw in my revised version of the baby-sitting story, a model designed to explain why a central bank can normally cure a recession by cutting interest rates can also illuminate the circumstances under which this over-the-counter remedy does not work. And this revised parable also, it turns out, offers some guidance on ways to get out of a liquidity trap, or at least on how to avoid getting into one in the first place .

Remember, the basic problem with the baby-sitting co-op is that people want to save the credit they earn from baby-sitting in the winter to use in the summer, even at a zero interest rate. But in the aggregate the co-op's members *can't* save up winter baby-sitting for summer use; so individual efforts to do so end up producing nothing but a winter slump.

The answer, as any economist should immediately realize, is to get the price right: to make it clear that points earned in the winter will be devalued if held until the summer—say, to make five hours of baby-sitting credit earned in the winter melt into only four hours by summer. This will encourage people to use their baby-sitting hours sooner, and hence create more baby-sitting opportunities. You might be tempted to think that there is something unfair about this—that it means expropriating people's savings. But the reality is that the co-op as a whole *cannot* bank winter baby-sitting for summer use, so it is actually distorting members' incentives to allow them to trade winter for summer hours on a one-for-one basis.

But what in the non-baby-sitting economy corresponds to our coupons that melt in the summer? The answer is *inflation*, which causes the real value of money to melt away over time. Or to be more precise, one thing that can get an economy out of a liquidity trap is *expected* inflation, which discourages people from hoarding money. Once you take the possibility of a liquidity trap seriously—and the case of Japan makes it clear that we should—it's impossible to escape the conclusion that expected inflation can be a good thing, because it helps you get out of the trap. I have explained the virtues of inflation in terms of the whimsical parable of the baby-sitting co-op, but the same conclusion also pops out from application of any of the standard mathematical models that economists conventionally use to discuss monetary policy. Indeed, there has long been a strand of thought that says that moderate inflation may be necessary if monetary policy is to be able to fight recessions. Still, advocates of inflation have had to contend with a deep-seated sense that stable prices are always desirable, that to promote inflation is to create perverse and dangerous incentives. This belief in the importance of price stability is not based on standard economic models—on the contrary, the usual textbook theory, when applied to Japan's unusual circumstances, points directly to inflation as the natural solution. But conventional economic theory and conventional economic wisdom are not always the same thing—a conflict that would become increasingly apparent as one country after another found itself having to make hard choices in the face of financial crisis.

Japan's Recovery

Japan's economy finally began to show some signs of recovery around 2003. Real GDP started growing at slightly more than 2 percent a year, unemployment came down, and the grinding deflation afflicting the economy (and worsening the liquidity trap) abated, although there was no sign of actual inflation. What went right?

The answer, mainly, was exports. In the middle years of this decade the United States ran huge trade deficits, importing vast quantities of manufactured goods. Some of these goods came from Japan, although the biggest growth came in imports from China and other emerging economies. But Japan benefited from Chinese growth too, because many Chinese manufactured goods contain components made in Japan. One flip side of America's import boom, then, was rising Japanese exports and a recovering Japanese economy.

Japan's escape from its trap remained provisional, however. The call money rate in Japan, the equivalent of the Federal funds rate (the rate set by the Federal Reserve), was only 0.5 percent at the time of writing. This meant that the Bank of Japan had very little room to cut interest rates in the face of the recession that seemed to be looming. And if the recession is deep, Japan will be right back in its trap.

4

ASIA'S CRASH

Thailand isn't really a small country. It has more citizens than Britain or France; Bangkok is a vast urban nightmare whose traffic is every bit as bad as legend has it. Still, the world economy is almost inconceivably huge, and in the commercial scheme of things Thailand is pretty marginal. Despite rapid growth in the 1980s and 1990s, it is still a poor country; all those people have a combined purchasing power no greater than that of the population of Massachusetts. One might have thought that Thai economic affairs, unlike those of an economic behemoth like Japan, were of interest only to the Thais, their immediate neighbors, and those businesses with a direct financial stake in the country.

But the 1997 devaluation of Thailand's currency, the baht, triggered a financial avalanche that buried much of Asia. The crucial questions are why that happened and, indeed, how it even *could* have happened. But before we get to why and how, let's review what: the story of Thailand's boom, its crash, and the spread of that crash across Asia.

The Boom

Thailand was a relative latecomer to the Asian miracle. Traditionally mainly an agricultural exporter, it started to become a major industrial center only in the 1980s, when foreign firms—especially Japanese—began siting plants in the country. But when the economy did take off, it did so very impressively: as peasants moved from the countryside into the new urban jobs, as the good results experienced by the first wave of foreign investors encouraged others to follow, Thailand began growing at 8 percent or more per year. Soon the famed temples of Bangkok lay in the shadow of office and apartment towers. Like its neighbors, Thailand became a place where millions of ordinary people were beginning to emerge from desperate poverty into at least the beginnings of a decent life, and where some people were becoming very rich.

Until the early 1990s, most of the investment associated with this growth came from the savings of the Thais themselves. Foreign money built the big export factories, but the smaller businesses were financed by local businessmen out of their own savings, and the new office and apartment blocks were financed out of the bank deposits of domestic households. In 1991 Thailand's foreign debt was slightly less than its annual exports—not a trivial ratio but one that was well within normal bounds of safety. (In the same year Latin American debt averaged 2.7 times exports.)

During the 1990s, however, Thailand's financial self-sufficiency began to erode. The push mainly came from outside. The resolution of the Latin debt crisis, described in Chapter 2, made investment in the Third World respectable again. The fall of Communism, by

diminishing the perceived threat of radical takeover, made investing outside the safety of the Western world seem less risky than
before. In the early 1990s interest rates in advanced countries were
exceptionally low because central banks were trying to boot their
economies out of a mild recession, and many investors went abroad
in search of higher yields. Perhaps most crucial of all, investment
funds coined a new name for what had previously been called Third
World or developing countries: now they were "emerging markets,"
the new frontier of financial opportunity.

Investors responded in droves. In 1990 private capital flows to
developing countries were $42 billion, and official agencies like the
International Monetary Fund and the World Bank financed more
investment in the Third World than all private investors combined.
By 1997, however, while the flow of official money had actually
slowed, the flow of private capital to developing countries had
quintupled, to $256 billion. At first most of the money went to
Latin America, especially Mexico, but after 1994 it increasingly
went to the apparently safer economies of Southeast Asia.

How did the money get from Tokyo or Frankfurt to Bangkok or
Djakarta? (Most of the lending to Asia was Japanese or European
—through wisdom or luck, U.S. banks mainly stayed on the sidelines.) What did it do when it got there? Let's follow the steps.

Start with a typical transaction: A Japanese bank makes a loan
to a Thai "finance company," an institution whose main purpose is
to act as a conveyor belt for foreign funds. The finance company
now has yen, which it uses to make a loan at a higher interest rate,
to a local real estate developer. But the developer wants to borrow
baht, not yen, since he must buy land and pay his workers in local
currency. So the finance company goes to the foreign exchange
market and exchanges its yen for baht.

Now, the foreign exchange market, like other markets, is governed by the law of supply and demand: increase the demand for something, and its price will normally rise. That is, the demand for baht by the finance company will tend to make the baht rise in value against other currencies. But during the boom years Thailand's central bank was committed to maintaining a stable rate of exchange between the baht and the U.S. dollar. To do this, it would have to offset any increase in the demand for baht by also increasing the supply: selling baht and buying foreign currencies like the dollar or yen. So the indirect result of that initial yen loan would be an increase both in the Bank of Thailand's reserves of foreign exchange and in the Thai money supply. And there would also be an expansion of credit in the economy—not only the loan directly provided by the finance company but also additional credit provided by the banks in which the newly created baht were deposited. And since much of the money lent out would itself end up back in the banks in the form of new deposits, this would finance yet further new loans, and so on, in the classic "money multiplier" process taught in Econ 101. (My description of Argentina's 1995 banking crisis was an example of this same process running in reverse.)

As more and more loans poured in from abroad, then, the result was a massive expansion of credit, which fueled a wave of new investment. Some of this took the form of actual construction, mainly office and apartment buildings, but there was a lot of pure speculation too, mainly in real estate, but also in stocks. By early 1996 the economies of Southeast Asia were starting to bear a strong family resemblance to Japan's "bubble economy" of the late 1980s.

Why didn't the monetary authorities put curbs on the speculative boom? The answer is that they tried but failed. In all the Asian economies, central banks tried to "sterilize" the capital inflows: obliged to sell baht in the foreign exchange market, the Bank of

Thailand would try to buy those baht back elsewhere by selling bonds, in effect borrowing back the money it had just printed. But this borrowing drove up local interest rates, making borrowing from overseas even more attractive and pulling in yet more yen and dollars. The effort to sterilize failed: credit just kept on growing.

The only way the central bank could have prevented money and credit from ballooning would have been to stop trying to fix the exchange rate—to simply let the baht rise. And this is indeed what many Monday-morning quarterbacks now say the Thais should have done. But at the time this seemed like a bad idea: a stronger baht would make Thai exports less competitive on world markets (because wages and other costs would be higher in dollars), and in general the Thais thought that a stable exchange rate was good for business confidence, that they were too small a nation to endure the kind of widely fluctuating exchange rate the United States lives with.

And so the boom was allowed to run its course. Eventually, as an economics textbook would tell you, the expansion of money and credit was self-limiting. Soaring investment, together with a surge of spending by newly affluent consumers, led to a surge in imports, while the booming economy pulled up wages, making Thai exports less competitive (especially because China, an important competitor for Thailand, had devalued its own currency in 1994). So export growth slowed down. The result was a huge trade deficit. Instead of feeding domestic money and credit, those foreign-currency loans started paying for imports.

And why not? Some economists argued—just as Mexico's boosters had argued in the early 1990s—that the trade deficits of Thailand, Malaysia, and Indonesia were a sign not of economic weakness but of economic strength, of markets working the way they were supposed to. To repeat the argument: as a matter of sheer accounting, a country that is attracting net inflows of capital must be running a current account deficit of equal size. So as long as you thought that the capital inflows to Southeast Asia were economically justified, so were the trade deficits. And why wasn't it reasonable for the world to invest a lot of capital in Southeast Asia, given the region's record of growth and economic stability? After all, this wasn't a case of governments on a spending spree: while Malaysia and Indonesia had their share of grandiose public projects, they were being paid for out of current revenue, and budgets were more or less in balance. So these trade deficits were the product of private-sector decisions; why should these decisions be second-guessed?

Still, a growing number of observers started to feel a bit uneasy as the deficits of Thailand and Malaysia grew to 6, 7, 8 percent of GDP—the sorts of numbers Mexico had had before the tequila crisis. The Mexican experience had convinced some economists that international capital flows, even if they represented the undistorted decisions of the private sector, were not necessarily to be trusted. The bullishness of investors about Asian prospects bore a disturbing resemblance to their bullishness about Latin America a couple of years earlier. And the Mexican experience also suggested that a reversal of market sentiment, when it came, would be sharp and hard to deal with.

What we also should have noticed was that the claim that Asian borrowing represented free private-sector decisions was not quite the truth. For Southeast Asia, like Japan in the bubble years, had a moral hazard problem—the problem that would soon be dubbed crony capitalism.

Let's go back to that Thai finance company, the institution that borrowed the yen that started the whole process of credit expansion. What, exactly, were these finance companies? They were not, as it happens, ordinary banks: by and large they had few if any depositors. Nor were they like Western investment banks, repositories of specialized information that could help direct funds to their most profitable uses. So what was their reason for existence? What did they bring to the table?

The answer, basically, was political connections—often, indeed, the owner of the finance company was a relative of some government official. And so the claim that the decisions about how much to borrow and invest represented private-sector judgments, not to be second-guessed, rang more than a bit hollow. True, loans to finance companies were not subject to the kind of formal guarantees that backed deposits in U.S. savings and loans. But foreign banks that lent money to the minister's nephew's finance company can be forgiven for believing that they had a little extra protection, that the minister would find a way to rescue the company if its investments did not work out as planned. And the foreign lenders would have been right: in roughly nine out of ten cases, foreign lenders to finance companies did indeed get bailed out by the Thai government when the crisis came.

Now look at the situation from the point of view of the minister's nephew, the owner of the finance company. Basically, he was in a position to borrow money at low rates, no questions asked. What, then, could be more natural than to lend that money at a high rate of interest to his friend the real estate developer, whose speculative new office tower just might make a killing—but then again might not. If all went well, fine: both men would have made a lot of money. If things did not turn out as hoped, well, not so terrible: the minister would find a way to save the finance company. Heads the nephew wins, tails the taxpayer loses.

One way or another, similar games were being played in all the countries that would soon be caught up in the crisis. In Indonesia middlemen played less of a role: there the typical dubious transaction was a direct loan from a foreign bank to a company controlled by one of the president's cronies. (The quintessential example was the loan that broke Hong Kong's Peregrine Investment Holdings, a loan made directly to Suharto's daughter's taxi company.) In Korea the big borrowers were banks effectively controlled by *chaebol*, the huge conglomerates that have dominated the nation's economy and—until very recently—its politics. Throughout the region, then, implicit government guarantees were helping underwrite investments that were both riskier and less promising than would have been undertaken without those guarantees, adding fuel to what would probably anyway have been an overheated speculative boom.

Given all of this, the development of some kind of crisis was not too surprising. Some of us can even claim to have predicted currency crises more than a year in advance. But nobody realized just how severe the crisis would be.

July 2, 1997

During 1996 and the first half of 1997 the credit machine that had created Thailand's boom began to slip into reverse. Partly this was because of external events: markets for some of Thailand's exports went soft, a depreciation of Japan's yen made Southeast Asian industry a bit less competitive. Mostly, though, it was simply a matter of the house beating the gamblers, which in the long run it always does: a growing number of the speculative investments that had been financed, directly or indirectly, by cheap foreign loans went sour. Some speculators went bust, and some finance companies went out of business. Foreign lenders became increasingly reluctant to lend any more money.

The loss of confidence was to a certain extent a self-reinforcing process. As long as real estate prices and stock markets were booming, even questionable investments tended to look good. As the air began to go out of the bubble, losses began to mount, further reducing confidence and causing the supply of fresh loans to shrink even more. Even before the July 2 crisis, land and stock values had fallen a long way from their peaks.

The slowdown in foreign borrowing also posed problems for the central bank. With fewer yen and dollars coming in, the demand for baht on the foreign exchange market declined; meanwhile, the need to change baht into foreign currencies to pay for imports continued unabated. In order to keep the value of the baht from declining, the Bank of Thailand had to do the opposite of what it had done when capital starting coming in: it went into the market to exchange dollars and yen for baht, supporting its own currency. But there is an important difference between trying to keep your currency down and trying to keep it up: the Bank of Thailand can increase the supply of baht as much as it likes, because it can simply print them; but it cannot print dollars. So there was a limit on its ability to keep the baht up. Sooner or later it would run out of reserves.

The only way to sustain the value of the currency would have been to reduce the number of baht in circulation, driving up interest rates and thus making it attractive once again to borrow dollars to reinvest in baht. But this posed problems of a different sort. As the investment boom sputtered out, the Thai economy had slowed—there was less construction activity, which meant fewer jobs, which meant lower income, which meant layoffs in the rest of the economy. Although it wasn't quite a full-fledged recession, the economy was no longer living in the style to which it had become accustomed. To raise interest rates would be to discourage investment further, and perhaps push the economy into an unambiguous slump.

The alternative was to let the currency go: to stop buying baht and let the exchange rate slide. But this too was an unattractive option, not only because a devaluation of the currency would hurt the government's reputation but also because so many banks, finance companies, and other Thai businesses had debts in dollars. If the value of the dollar in terms of baht were to increase, many of them would find themselves insolvent.

So the Thai government dithered. It wasn't willing to let the baht fall; nor was it willing to take the kind of harsh domestic measures that would have stemmed the loss in reserves. Instead, it played a waiting game, apparently hoping that something would eventually turn up.

All of this was according to the standard script: it was the classic lead-in to a currency crisis, of the kind that economists love to model—and speculators love to provoke. As it became clear that the government did not have the stomach to turn the screws on the domestic economy, it became increasingly likely that eventually the baht would be allowed to fall in value. But since it hadn't happened yet, there was still time to take advantage of the prospective event. As long as the baht-dollar exchange rate seemed likely to remain stable, the fact that interest rates in Thailand were several points higher than in the United States provided an incentive to borrow in dollars and lend in baht. But once it became a high probability that the baht would soon be devalued, the incentive was to go the other way—to borrow in baht, expecting that the dollar value of these debts would soon be reduced, and acquire dollars, expecting that the baht value of these assets would soon increase. Local businessmen borrowed in baht and paid off their dollar loans; wealthy Thais

sold their holdings of government debt and bought U.S. Treasury
bills; and last but not least, some large international hedge funds
began borrowing baht and converting the proceeds into dollars.

All of these actions involved selling baht and buying other currencies, which meant that they required the central bank to buy
even more baht to keep the currency from falling, which depleted
its reserves of foreign exchange even faster—which further reinforced the conviction that the baht was going to be devalued sooner
rather than later. A classic currency crisis was in full swing.

Any money doctor can tell you that once things have reached
that point the government must move decisively, one way or the
other: either make a clear commitment to defend the currency at
all costs, or let it go. But governments usually have a hard time making either decision. Like many governments before and no doubt
many to come, Thailand's waited as its reserves ran down; trying to
convince markets that its position was stronger than it was, it made
those reserves look larger through unannounced "currency swaps"
(in effect, borrowing dollars now for repayment later). But though
the pressure sometimes seemed to abate, it always resumed. By the
beginning of July, it was clear that the game was up. On July 2, the
Thais let the baht go.

Up to this point, nothing all that surprising had happened. The
rundown of reserves, the speculative attack on an obviously weak
currency, were right out of the textbooks. But despite the recent
experience of the tequila crisis, most people thought that the devaluation of the baht would pretty much end the story: a humiliation
for the government, perhaps a nasty shock for some overstretched
businesses, but nothing catastrophic. Surely Thailand looked nothing like Mexico. Nobody could accuse it of having achieved "stabilization, reform, and no growth"; there was no Thai Cárdenas,

waiting in the wings to enforce a populist program. And so there would not be a devastating recession.

They were wrong.

Meltdown

There are two somewhat different questions to ask about the recession that spread across Asia in the wake of the Thai devaluation. The first is one of mechanics: How did this slump happen? Why should a devaluation in one small economy have provoked a collapse of investment and output across so wide an area? The other, in a way deeper, question is, Why didn't governments, or perhaps why couldn't governments, prevent the catastrophe? What happened to macroeconomic policy?

That second question will take some time to answer, at least partly because it is a matter of very sharp disagreement among reasonable people. So let's leave it until the next chapter, and simply try to describe what happened.

When all goes well, nothing terrible happens when a currency is allowed to drop in value. When Britain abandoned its defense of the pound in 1992, the currency dropped about 15 percent, then stabilized: investors figured that the worst was over, that the lower currency would help the country's exports, and that it was therefore a better place to invest than it had been before. Typical calculations suggested that the baht would have to fall something like 15 percent to make Thai industry cost-competitive again, so a decline of roughly that magnitude seemed likely. But instead, the currency went into free fall: the baht price of a dollar soared 50 percent over the next few months, and would have risen even further if Thailand had not sharply raised interest rates.

Why did the baht fall so far? The short answer is "panic"; but there are panics and there are panics. Which was it?

Sometimes a panic is just a panic: an irrational reaction on the part of investors that is not justified by the actual news. An example might be the brief plunge in the dollar in 1981, after a deranged gunman wounded Ronald Reagan. It was a shocking event; but even if Reagan had died, the stability of the U.S. government and the continuity of its policy could hardly have been affected. Those who kept their heads and did not flee the dollar were rewarded for their cool heads.

Much more important in economics, however, are panics that, whatever sets them off, validate themselves—because the panic itself makes panic justified. The classic example is a bank run: when all of a bank's depositors try to withdraw their money at once, the bank is forced to sell its assets at distress prices, causing it to go bankrupt; those depositors who did not panic end up worse off than those who did.

And indeed there *were* some bank runs in Thailand, and even more in Indonesia. But to focus only on these bank runs would be to take the metaphor too literally. What really happened was a circular process—a devastating feedback loop—of financial deterioration and declining confidence, of which conventional bank runs were only one aspect.

The figure on the next page illustrates this process, which occurred in some version in all of the afflicted Asian economies, schematically. Start anywhere in the circle—say, with a decline of confidence in Thailand's currency and economy. This decline in confidence would make investors, both domestic and foreign, want to pull their money out of the country. Other things being the same, this would cause the baht to plunge in value. Since the Thai

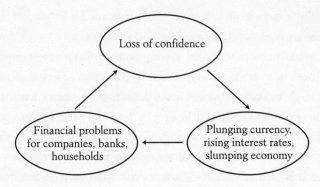

The Vicious Circle of Financial Crisis

central bank could no longer support the value of its currency by buying it on the foreign exchange market (because it no longer had dollars or yen to spend), the only way it could limit the currency's decline was to raise interest rates and pull baht out of circulation. Unfortunately, both the decline in the currency's value and the rise in interest rates created financial problems for businesses, both financial institutions and other companies. On one side, many of them had dollar debts, which suddenly became more burdensome as the number of baht per dollar increased; on the other, many of them also had baht debts, which became harder to service as interest rates soared. And the combination of higher interest rates and troubled balance sheets with a banking system that often found itself unable to make even the safest of loans meant that companies had to slash spending, causing a recession, which in turn meant still worse news for profits and balance sheets. All this bad news from the economy, inevitably, reduced confidence still further—and the economy went into a meltdown.

Leaving aside all the complicated details (which are still being picked over by researchers), this story seems fairly straightforward —especially because something quite similar happened in Mexico in 1995. So why did the disastrous effects of Thailand's devaluation come as such a surprise? The basic answer is that while many economists were aware of the elements of this story—everyone understood that the feedback from confidence, to financial markets, to the real economy, and back again to confidence existed in principle—nobody realized just how powerful that feedback process would be in practice. And as a result nobody realized how explosive the circular logic of crisis could be.

Here's a parallel. A microphone in an auditorium always generates a feedback loop: sounds picked up by the microphone are amplified by the loudspeakers; the output from the speakers is itself picked up by the microphone; and so on. But as long as the room isn't too echoey and the gain isn't too high, this is a "damped" process and poses no problem. Turn the dial a little too far to the right, however, and the process becomes explosive: any little sound is picked up, amplified, picked up again, and suddenly there is an earsplitting screech. What matters, in other words, is not just the qualitative fact of feedback, but its quantitative strength. What caught everyone by surprise was the discovery that the dial was in fact turned up so high.

Indeed, even now there are many people who find it hard to believe that a market economy can really be that unstable, that the feedbacks illustrated in the figure can really be strong enough to create an explosive crisis. But they are—as we can see by looking at the way the crisis spread.

Contagion

There is probably a good reason why important meetings about international finance, especially about international crisis management, tend to take place in rustic resorts—why the postwar monetary system was hammered out at the Mount Washington Hotel at Bretton Woods, why many of the world's finance ministers and central bankers gather each summer at Jackson Lake Lodge in Wyoming. Perhaps the setting helps important people get away from the firefighting of their daily lives and focus at least briefly on the larger issues. In any case, in early October 1997—when the Asian crisis was well underway, but its severity was not yet clear—a number of bankers, officials, and economists converged on Woodstock, Vermont, to take stock.

By then Thailand was already pretty clearly in deep trouble, the currency of its neighbor Malaysia had also been battered, and the Indonesian rupiah had depreciated about 30 percent. The general sense in the room was that Thailand had brought its woes on itself; and there was little sympathy for Malaysia, which like Thailand had been running huge current account deficits in the past several years, and whose prime minister had clearly made things worse with his denunciations of evil speculators. But everyone agreed that while Indonesia had been right to let its currency slide—indeed, many good things were said about Indonesia's economic management— the rupiah's weakness was not really justified. After all, Indonesia's current account deficits had been nowhere near as large relative to GDP as its neighbors'—at less than 4 percent of GDP, Indonesia's 1996 deficit was actually smaller than, say, Australia's. The country's export base—part raw materials, part labor-intensive manufacturing—looked solid; and in general the economy looked fundamentally sound.

Within three months Indonesia was in even worse shape than the rest of Southeast Asia, indeed on its way to one of the worst economic slumps in world history. And the crisis had spread not just across Southeast Asia but all the way to South Korea, a far-away economy whose GDP was twice as large as that of Indonesia, three times as large as that of Thailand.

There are sometimes good reasons for economic contagion. An old line says that when the United States sneezes, Canada catches cold—no wonder, when much of Canada's production is sold in the markets of its giant southern neighbor. And there were some direct links among the afflicted Asian economies: Thailand is a market for Malaysian products and vice versa. A bit of extra traction may have been generated by the tendency of the Asian economies to sell similar products to third parties: when Thailand devalued its currency, the clothing it exports to the West got cheaper, and therefore cut into the profit margins of Indonesian producers of similar items.

But all estimates of this direct, "goods market" spillover among the crisis economies indicate that it just can't have been a major factor in the spread of the crisis. In particular, Thailand's role either as a market for or as a competitor of South Korea was little more than rounding error for the far larger Korean economy.

A more potent source of contagion may have been more or less direct financial linkage. Not that Thais were big investors in Korea, or Koreans in Thailand; but the flows of money into the region were often channeled through "emerging market funds" that lumped all the countries together. When bad news came in from Thailand, money flowed out of these funds, and hence out of all the countries in the region.

Even more important than this mechanical linkage, however, was the way that Asian economies were associated in the minds of investors. The appetite of investors for the region had been fed by the perception of a shared "Asian miracle." When one country's economy turned out not to be all that miraculous after all, it shook faith in all the others. The wise men at Woodstock may have

regarded Indonesia as quite different from Thailand, but the investor in the street was less sure and began to pull back just in case.

And it turned out that whatever the differences among all those
economies, one thing they did have in common was susceptibility to self-validating panic. The wise men at Woodstock were
wrong about Indonesia, and the panicky investors right; this was
not because the wise men had misjudged Indonesia's virtues but
because they had underestimated its vulnerability. In Malaysia,
in Indonesia, in Korea, as in Thailand, the market's loss of confidence started a vicious circle of financial and economic collapse.
It did not matter that these economies were only modestly linked
in terms of physical flows of goods. They were linked in the minds
of investors, who regarded the troubles of one Asian economy as
bad news about the others; and when an economy is vulnerable to
self-validating panic, believing makes it so.

Why Asia? Why 1997?

Why did Asia experience a terrible economic crisis, and why did
it begin in 1997? As Bill Clinton might have put it, the answer
depends on what you mean by "why." You might be asking about
the specific precipitating events, or you might, more importantly,
be asking about the source of Asia's extraordinary vulnerability.

If you insist on placing the blame for the onset of the Asian crisis on some specific event, there is a list of usual suspects. One is
the exchange rate between the yen and the dollar: between 1995
and 1997 the yen, which had rather mysteriously gone to sky-high
levels, fell back to earth. Since most Asian currencies were more or
less pegged to the dollar, this made their exports look more expensive both in Japanese markets and in competition with Japanese
products elsewhere, contributing to an export slowdown. China's

1994 devaluation, and more broadly growing competition from China's cheap labor, likewise cut into Thai and Malaysian exports. And there was a worldwide slump in the demand for electronics in general and semiconductors in particular, an area in which Asia's economies had tended to specialize.

But Asia had shrugged off much bigger shocks before. The 1985 crash in oil prices, for example, was a major blow to oil-exporting Indonesia; yet the economy grew right through the bad news. The 1990–91 recession, which was not very severe but affected much of the industrial world, reduced the demand for Asia's exports but did not slow the region's momentum at all. So the important question is, What had changed about Asia (or perhaps the world) such that *these* pieces of bad news triggered an economic avalanche?

Some of the Asians, notably Malaysia's Prime Minister Mahathir, had a ready answer: conspiracy. Mahathir, indeed, argued not only that the panic in Asia was deliberately engineered by big financial operators like George Soros but also that Soros himself was acting on instructions from the U.S. government, which wanted to cut assertive Asians down to size. As time passed, Mahathir's demonization of hedge funds started to look a bit less silly than it did when he first began his ranting. Indeed, the role of hedge funds now looks important enough to rate a whole chapter in this book (Chapter 6). But that role became important mainly in 1998 (by which time, incidentally, the activities of Soros and others were very much contrary to U.S. policy wishes); as a story about how the crisis began, conspiracy theory doesn't wash.

On the other side, many Westerners have turned the story of Asia's crash into a sort of morality play, in which the economies received their inevitable punishment for the sins of crony capitalism. After the catastrophe, everyone had a story about the excesses and corruption of the region—about those finance companies, about Malaysia's grandiose plans for a "technology corridor," about the fortunes made by Suharto's family, about the bizarre diversification of Korean conglomerates (did you hear the one about the underwear company that bought a ski resort, and eventually had to sell it to Michael Jackson?). But this morality play is problematic on at least two counts.

First, while cronyism and corruption were very real in Asia, they were nothing new. Korea's *chaebol* were essentially family enterprises disguised as modern corporations whose owners had been accustomed to special treatment for decades—preferred access to credit, to import licenses, to government subsidies. And those were decades of spectacular economic growth. It was not a pretty system by Western standards but it functioned very well for thirty-five years. The same may be said, to a lesser extent, of all the countries caught up in the crisis. Why did their flaws become crucial only in 1997?

And a related point: if the crisis was a punishment for the sins of the Asian economies, why did economies that were by no means equally far down the path of development all hit the wall at the same time? Korea in 1997 was not far short of being a developed nation, with per capita income comparable to that of southern European countries, while Indonesia was still a very poor country where progress could be measured in terms of how many calories people managed to consume in a day. How is it that such an ill-matched pair could simultaneously be plunged into crisis?

The only answer that makes sense to me, at least, is that the crisis was *not* (mainly) a punishment for sins. There were real failings in these economies, but the main failing was a vulnerability to self-fulfilling panic.

Back to bank runs: In 1931, about half the banks in the United States failed. These banks were not all alike. Some were very badly run; some took excessive risks, even given what they knew before 1929; others were reasonably well, even conservatively managed. But when panic spread across the land, and depositors everywhere wanted their money immediately, none of this mattered: only banks that had been extremely conservative, that had kept what in normal times would be an excessively large share of their deposits in cash, survived. Similarly, Thailand had a badly run economy; it had borrowed far too much and invested it in very dubious projects. Indonesia, for all its corruption, was much less culpable, and truly had the virtues those wise men imagined, but in the panic those distinctions did not matter.

Were the Asian economies more vulnerable to financial panic in 1997 than they had been, say, five or ten years before? Yes, surely—but not because of crony capitalism, or indeed what would usually be considered bad government policies. Rather, they had become more vulnerable partly because they had opened up their financial markets—because they had, in fact, become better free-market economies, not worse. And they had also grown vulnerable because they had taken advantage of their new popularity with international lenders to run up substantial debts to the outside world. These debts intensified the feedback from loss of confidence to financial collapse and back again, making the vicious circle of crisis more intense. It wasn't that the money was badly spent; some of it was, some of it wasn't. It was that the new debts, unlike the old ones, were in dollars—and that turned out to be the economies' undoing.

Epilogue: Argentina, 2002

Argentina isn't an Asian country. (Duh.) But Argentina had an Asian-style crisis in 2002, one that offered a painfully clear demonstration of how widely praised economic policies can lead a nation into disaster.

I discussed Argentina's monetary history in Chapter 2. After generations of irresponsible use and abuse of the printing press, in 1991 the Argentine government tried to put an end to all that by establishing a currency board that would supposedly provide a permanent link between the Argentine peso and the U.S. dollar. Every peso in circulation was supposed to be backed by a dollar in reserves, with no room for discretion. And this monetary stability, it was hoped, would ensure continued prosperity.

As we saw in Chapter 2, Argentina had a close brush with disaster in 1995, when the backwash from Mexico's crisis came close to bringing down the banking system. But as that crisis ebbed, confidence returned. Foreign observers continued to shower high praise on the Argentine economy and its managers, and foreign capital flowed in, much of it in the form of dollar loans to Argentine businesses and individuals.

In the late 1990s, it all started to go wrong.

At first, the problem was the rigidity of the exchange rate system, which set one peso equal to one U.S. dollar. This might not have been much of a problem if Argentina, like Mexico, did the great bulk of its trade with the United States. But look at a map: Argentina is no closer to the United States than it is to Europe, and in fact Argentina does more trade both with the European Union and with its neighbor Brazil than it does with the United States. And Argentina's currency system did *not* ensure stable exchange rates against either the euro or the *real*, Brazil's currency. On the contrary, the system actually tended to cause gratuitous fluctuations in these exchange rates, and hence in Argentina's trade position. If, for example, the dollar rose against the euro,

for whatever reason the effect was to price Argentine exports out
of European markets.

And that's exactly what happened to Argentina starting in the
late 1990s. On one side, the dollar soared against the euro—at
one point the euro was worth only $0.85, compared with $1.26
at the time of writing. On the other, Brazil, caught in contagion
from Russia's financial crisis (see Chapter 6), sharply devalued the
real. The combined effect of these exchange rate shifts was to leave
Argentina's exports seriously uncompetitive, pushing the country
into a recession.

As Argentina's economy slumped, foreign investors lost faith.
The flow of capital into the country went into reverse, creating a
credit crunch. And as in 1995, the loss of foreign funds also caused
a banking crisis.

Argentine officials tried desperately to contain the growing crisis. They slashed spending, deepening the recession, in the hope
of regaining investor confidence abroad. They limited withdrawals
from the banks, a measure that provoked angry demonstrations outside the presidential palace, with housewives banging pots and pans.
Nothing seemed to work. And in late 2001 the government found
itself unable to maintain the one-peso-one-dollar rule. The value of
an Argentine peso quickly fell from one dollar to about thirty cents.

The initial results of the currency plunge were catastrophic, just
like the currency plunges in Asia. Since many Argentine businesses
and individuals had debts in dollars, the rise in the cost of a dollar
in pesos had a crippling effect on balance sheets, in many cases
leading to bankruptcy. The economy fell into a swoon: real GDP
fell 11 percent in 2002, after falling 4 percent in 2001. Overall, the
size of the Argentine economy declined 18 percent between 1998
and 2002, a Great Depression–scale contraction.

Over the next five years Argentina made a strong recovery, helped by a settlement in which the government paid only about thirty cents on the dollar of its foreign debt. (One of my favorite headlines ever, from a Reuters report on the debt negotiations, was "Argentina to Creditors: So Sue Us.") But the experience was terrifying. And as this book went to press, Argentina was in crisis again.

The Deeper Question

Most commentators on the Asian crisis would probably find some detail of the account in this chapter to quarrel with. Some would argue that the damage done by moral hazard–driven lending was greater than I suggest. Some would argue, on the contrary, that the economies were really in very good shape, and that the crisis was wholly gratuitous. The precise mechanism of crisis—the respective roles of bank failures, real estate prices, exchange rates, interest rates, and so on—will be the subject of much wrangling for years, perhaps decades to come. Nonetheless, in a general sense I believe that this account would receive broad acceptance.

The real controversy—the one that is heated and often personal, because those who criticize the way the crisis was handled are also criticizing those who handled it—concerns policy. Why weren't governments able to do more to limit the damage?

5

POLICY PERVERSITY

In December 1930, just as it started to become obvious that the United States was in no ordinary recession, John Maynard Keynes attempted to explain the causes of the slump to the general public. "We have magneto [alternator] trouble," he declared. It was, in a way, a radical statement, for he was declaring that the economic engine would not restart of its own accord, that it needed a jump start from the government. But in a deeper sense Keynes was being a conservative: he was declaring that the trouble with the engine was not fundamental, that it was amenable to a technical fix. At a time when many of the world's intellectuals were convinced that capitalism was a failed system, that only by moving to a centrally planned economy could the West emerge from the Great Depression, Keynes was saying that capitalism was *not* doomed, that a very limited sort of intervention—intervention that would leave private property and private decision making intact—was all that was needed to make the system work.

Confounding the skeptics, capitalism did survive; but although today's free-market enthusiasts may find this proposition hard to accept, that survival was basically on the terms Keynes suggested. World War II provided the jump start Keynes had been urging for years; but what restored faith in free markets was not just the recovery from the Depression but the assurance that macroeconomic intervention—cutting interest rates or increasing budget deficits to fight recessions—could keep a free-market economy more or less stable at more or less full employment. In effect, capitalism and its economists made a deal with the public: it will be okay to have free markets from now on, because we know enough to prevent any more Great Depressions.

This implicit deal actually has a name: in the 1950s Paul Samuelson, in his famous textbook, called it the "neoclassical synthesis." But I prefer to think of it as the "Keynesian compact."

In the United States and most other advanced countries, that compact is still honored. Oh, there are recessions now and then. However, when they occur, everyone expects the Federal Reserve to do what it did in 1975, 1982, and 1991: cut interest rates to perk up the economy. And we also expect the president and Congress to cut taxes and raise spending if necessary to help the process. We surely do not expect that a recession will be met, Herbert Hoover style, by raising taxes, cutting spending, and increasing interest rates.

But when financial disaster struck Asia, the policies those countries followed in response were almost exactly the reverse of what the United States has done in the face of a slump. Fiscal austerity was the order of the day; interest rates were increased, often to punitive levels. This was not because the policymakers in those countries were stupid or ill informed. On the contrary, for the most part they understood the Keynesian compact very well, indeed had tried to adhere to it in the past. Anyway, once the crisis struck, Asian countries found their policies largely dictated by Washington—that is, by the International Monetary Fund and the U.S. Treasury. And the leadership of those institutions was extremely sophisticated: one could argue that never in history had so many first-rate economists been in positions of so much authority.

Why did these extremely clever men advocate policies for emerging market economies that were completely perverse in terms of standard economic doctrine? The short answer is "fear of speculators." But that short answer makes sense only if put into context—specifically, if we spend some time trying to understand the dilemmas of international money.

How the International Monetary System Didn't Evolve

Once upon a time, the world had a single currency, the globo. It was well managed: the Global Reserve Bank (popularly known as the Glob), under its chairman Alan Globespan, did a reasonably good job of increasing the global money supply when the world threatened to slide into recession, and trimming it when there were indications of inflation. Indeed, in later years some would remember the reign of the globo as a golden age. Businessmen in particular liked the system because they could buy and sell anywhere with a minimum of hassle.

But there was trouble in paradise. You see, although careful management of the globo could prevent a boom-bust cycle *for the world as a whole*, it could not do so for each piece of that whole. Indeed, it turned out that there were often conflicts of interest about monetary policy. Sometimes the Glob would be following an easy-money policy because Europe and Asia were on the edge of recession; but that easy money would fuel a wild speculative boom in North America. At other times the Glob would feel obliged to tighten money to head off inflation in North America, intensifying a developing recession in South America. And because there were no separate continental currencies, there was nothing continental governments could do about these problems.

Eventually there came a time when the frustrations grew too great, and the system broke up. Instead of the globo, each continent introduced its own currency and proceeded to pursue monetary policies tailored to its own needs. When Europe's economy was overheating, it could reduce the supply of euros; when Latin America slumped, it could increase the supply of latinos. The awkwardness of a one-size-fits-all monetary policy was gone.

But it soon turned out that disposing of one problem created another because the exchange rates between continental currencies fluctuated wildly. One might have thought that the exchange rate between, say, the latino and the euro would be determined by the needs of trade: by Latin Americans trading latinos for euros in order to buy European goods, and conversely. It soon became clear, however, that the market was dominated mainly by investors— people buying and selling currencies in order to purchase stocks and bonds. And since these investment demands were highly variable, including a large component of speculation, currency values also proved unstable. Worse yet, people began to speculate on the values of the currencies themselves. The result was that exchange rates bounced around, creating uncertainty for businesses, which could never be sure what their overseas assets and liabilities were really worth.

So some continents tried to stabilize exchange rates—buying

and selling on the foreign exchange market in order to keep the price of a euro in terms of afros, or a gringo in terms of latinos, constant. Central banks reserved the right, however, to change the target exchange rates if necessary—say, by devaluing their currency if this seemed necessary to fight unemployment.

Alas, this "adjustable peg" system turned out to offer speculators too many easy targets: when a continent experienced economic difficulties, and started to look as if it might consider a devaluation, speculators would begin selling its currency in anticipation. This would soon force the continental central bank either to raise interest rates, actually worsening the slump, or to devalue immediately. Or—the one remaining option—it could try to defeat the speculators directly, by placing restrictions on the movement of capital.

And so the world's continents were forced into choosing one of three "currency regimes," each of which had a serious defect. They could opt to maintain an independent monetary policy and let the exchange rate fluctuate as it pleased; this left them free to fight recessions, but introduced disturbing uncertainty into business life. They could fix the value of the exchange rate and attempt to convince markets that they would never devalue; this would make business life simpler and safer but would bring back the problem of one-size-fits-all monetary policy. Or they could continue to maintain an adjustable peg, that is, fix the exchange rate but retain the option of changing it; but this was workable only if they maintained controls on capital movement, which were hard to enforce, imposed extra costs on business, and—like any prohibition on potentially profitable transactions—were a source of corruption.

Okay, okay, it didn't really happen quite that way. There never was a globo; the closest thing to it was the pre-1930s gold standard, which unfortunately was *not* managed so as to prevent worldwide booms and busts. But our imaginary history does illustrate a bit more clearly than the complexities of what actually happened the three-cornered dilemma, or "trilemma," that national economies face in a global economy.

Think of it this way. There are three things that macroeconomic managers want for their economies. They want discretion in monetary policy so that they can fight recessions and curb inflation. They want stable exchange rates so that businesses are not faced with too much uncertainty. And they want to leave international business free—in particular, to allow people to exchange money however they like—in order to get out of the private sector's way.

What the story of the globo and its demise tells us is that countries cannot get all three wishes; at most, they can get two. They can give up on exchange rate stability; this means adopting a floating exchange rate, like the United States and Australia did. They can give up on discretionary monetary policy; this means fixing the exchange rate, the way Argentina did in the 1990s, and possibly even giving up their own currency, like the nations of continental Europe did. Or they can give up on the principle of completely free markets and impose capital controls; this was what most countries did between the 1940s and the 1960s, and what China does right now.

Which of these three imperfect answers is best? There are some people who think that the gains from stable exchange rates are large, the benefits of independent monetary policy overrated. They like to point out that the United States, though spread over a continent, does very well with a single currency, and that some 300 million Europeans have adopted a common currency. So why not the world as a whole? But most economists will point out that the United States has special features that help it live with a single currency: most notably, workers can and do move rapidly from depressed to booming regions, so that one size of monetary policy more or less does fit all. The introduction of the euro, Europe's currency, was in fact quite controversial, with many economists questioning whether Europe is anywhere near as suited to a single money as the United States. But at least the major European economies are rather similar to each other and very closely linked, so that most of the time a monetary policy that is appropriate for France will also be appropriate for Germany, and vice versa. It is hard to see, however, how a suitable monetary policy could be devised that is appropriate for both Japan and the United States, let alone the United States and Argentina. So relatively few economists are nostalgic for the days of the gold standard, or fantasize about the coming of the globo; national, or perhaps regional, monetary independence is still needed.

On the other hand, the capital controls that allowed advanced countries to combine fixed exchange rates with Keynesian policies in the first postwar generation are now very much out of fashion. The fundamental problem with these controls is that the distinction between "good" and "bad" international transactions is a hard one to make. A speculator who pulls his money out of Malaysia because he is trying to profit from a devaluation is engaged in an antisocial act; a Malaysian exporter who wins customers abroad in part by letting them buy now, pay later is helping the country earn its way in world markets. But suppose that the exporter, suspecting that the ringgit will soon be devalued, asks his customers to pay in dollars and encourages them to take a long time before settling. The effect is the same as if he took ringgit and bought dollars on the black market. And there are dozens of other ways in which the line between productive business and currency speculation can be blurred. What this means is either that attempts to control speculation will be easily evaded or that the government can limit speculation only by imposing onerous restrictions on ordinary transactions (e.g., limiting the credit exporters can give their customers). Fifty years ago most governments regarded these restrictions as a price worth paying. Today, however, we live in a world that has relearned the virtues of free markets, is suspicious of government intervention, and is particularly aware that the more things are prohibited, the greater the scope for bribery and cronyism.

Which leaves freely floating exchange rates, which by the mid-1990s most economists had come to regard as the lesser of three evils. True, exchange rates have repeatedly proved to be far more volatile than they "should" be, given economic fundamentals (over the past fifteen years the dollar-yen rate has gone from 120, to 80, to nearly 150, then back below 110, all with relatively little measurable change in fundamentals); and even those who are generally pro-floating agree that tightly integrated regions that form "optimal currency areas" should adopt the ultimate form of fixed exchange rates, a common currency. (Whether Europe constitutes such an area is another question.) But as a general rule, the preferred alternative of most economists—and, in particular, the one most consistent with the Keynesian compact, because it leaves countries free to pursue both free-market and full-employment policies—is a floating exchange rate.

The virtues of such free floating, when it works, are not hard to demonstrate. The United States is well served by its general policy of benign neglect toward the foreign exchange value of the dollar; while the dollar-yen and dollar-euro rates may go through annoying gyrations, this annoyance is surely a small thing compared with the freedom of action the absence of an exchange rate commitment gives to the Federal Reserve—the ability to cut interest rates sharply and immediately when recession or financial crisis looms.

Better yet, consider the example of Australia during the Asian crisis. In 1996 an Australian dollar was worth almost eighty cents in U.S. currency. By the late summer of 1998 it had fallen to little more than sixty cents. No surprise there: most of Australia's exports went either to Japan or to the troubled tigers. But Australia, except for a brief period in the summer of 1998 when it seemed to be facing a coordinated attack by hedge funds (more on that in the next chapter), did not try to prop up its currency, either by buying it on the foreign exchange market or by raising interest rates. Instead, the currency's fall proved self-limiting: when the Aussie dollar fell, investors regarded it as an opportunity to invest cheaply in what they continued to regard as a solid economy. And this confidence appeared justified by the "Australian miracle": despite its dependence on Asian markets, Australia actually boomed amidst Asia's crisis.

But if Australia could so easily avoid getting caught up in its neighbors' economic catastrophe, why couldn't Indonesia or South Korea do the same?

The Speculative Threat

Imagine an economy that isn't perfect. (What economy is?) Maybe the government is running a budget deficit that, while not really threatening its solvency, is coming down more slowly than it should, or maybe banks with political connections have made too many loans to questionable borrowers. But, as far as anyone can tell from the numbers, there are no problems that cannot be dealt with given goodwill and a few years of stability.

Then, for some reason—perhaps an economic crisis on the other side of the world—investors become jittery and start pulling their money out en masse. Suddenly the country is in trouble—its stock market is plunging, its interest rates are soaring. You might think that savvy investors would see this as an opportunity to buy. After all, if the fundamentals haven't changed, doesn't this mean that assets are now undervalued? But, as we saw in Chapter 4, the answer is "not necessarily." The crash in asset values may cause previously sound banks to collapse. Economic slump, high interest rates, and a devalued exchange rate may cause sound companies to go bankrupt. At worst, economic distress may cause political instability. Maybe buying when everyone else is rushing for the exits isn't such a good idea after all; maybe it's better to run for the exit yourself.

Thus it is possible in principle that a loss of confidence in a country can produce an economic crisis that justifies that loss of confidence—that countries may be vulnerable to what economists call "self-fulfilling speculative attacks." And while many economists used to be skeptical about the importance of such self-fulfilling crises, the experience of the 1990s in Latin America and Asia settled those doubts, at least as a practical matter.

The funny thing is that once you take the possibility of self-fulfilling crises seriously, market psychology becomes crucial—so crucial that within limits, the expectations, even the prejudices of investors, become economic fundamentals—because believing makes it so.

Suppose, for example, that everyone is convinced that despite its remarkably high dependence on foreign capital (it has run large current account deficits of more than 4 percent of GDP for decades), Australia is basically a sound country—it can be counted on to be politically and economically stable. Then the market response to a decline in the Australian dollar is in effect to say, "Good, that's over, let's buy Australian," and the economy actually benefits. The market's good opinion is therefore confirmed.

On the other hand, suppose that despite twenty years of remarkable progress people are not quite convinced that Indonesia is no longer the country of *The Year of Living Dangerously*. Then when the rupiah falls they may say, "Oh, my God, they're reverting to the bad old days"; the resulting capital flight leads to financial, economic, and political crisis, and the market's bad opinion is similarly confirmed.

It seems, in other words, that the Keynesian compact is a sometime thing. The common view among economists that floating rates are the best, if imperfect, solution to the international monetary trilemma was based on the experience of countries like Canada, Britain, and the United States. But during the 1990s a series of countries—Mexico, Thailand, Indonesia, Korea—discovered that they were subject to different rules. Again and again, attempts to engage in moderate devaluations led to a drastic collapse in confidence. It is this problem of confidence that ultimately explains why the Keynesian compact has been broken.

The Confidence Game

In the summer of 1998 Brazil was already suffering an economic slowdown; unemployment was rising, while inflation—Brazil's traditional ailment—had given way to price stability, and some were even talking of deflation. Then the collapse of economic reform in Russia triggered an attack on Brazil's *real* (why? See Chapter 6), and the country went to the United States and the IMF for help. What Brazil wanted was both money and, even more important, a sort of Good Housekeeping seal on its policies, something that would persuade nervous investors to stop running. In return, it promised to implement a program of economic "stabilization."

So what did the program—intended, remember, for a country with a slowing economy and no inflation to speak of—involve? Higher taxes, reduced government spending, and a continuation of extremely high interest rates (Brazil had raised rates to nearly

50 percent when the crisis began). In other words, the Brazilian government implemented extremely tight monetary and fiscal policies, which guaranteed that the country would experience a nasty recession in 1999.

The program for Brazil was peculiarly extreme; it was almost like a caricature of the policies that had been introduced in Asia the preceding year. But like many caricatures, it emphasized the distinctive features of its subject. At the core of the policies imposed by Washington on many of the crisis countries was an almost perfect inversion of the Keynesian compact: faced with an economic crisis, countries were urged to raise interest rates, slash spending, and increase taxes.

Why, sixty years after Keynes, would anybody think that it was a good idea to break so profoundly with the Keynesian compact? The answer lay in the perceived need to win market confidence at all costs.

First of all, the Australian solution—just letting the currency slide—was ruled out. The fixed exchange rate between Brazil's *real* and the dollar had been a centerpiece of the country's reform program, the program that had brought price stability after generations of high inflation. To give up that fixed rate, both Brazil and Washington feared, would be devastating for investor confidence. True, one could make a good case that the *real* was, say, 20 percent overvalued and that a 20 percent devaluation would do the country far more good than harm. But nobody believed that a 20 percent devaluation was a realistic strategy: as one U.S. official put it, "For developing countries, there are no small devaluations."

How was a devaluation of the *real* to be avoided? The IMF could supply money, which together with the country's own foreign exchange reserves could be used to support the currency in the markets. But this money would soon be gone unless something could be done to stop capital flight. The only tool immediately at hand was to impose very high interest rates, high enough to persuade people to keep money in Brazil even though they suspected that its currency might end up devalued after all.

Nor was that all. When the markets decided that Brazil was a bad risk, they also decided that at the core of Brazil's problems was its large budget deficit. Now, you could question that assessment. Brazil's government actually didn't have all that much debt—considerably less, as a share of national income, than many European countries or Japan. And much of the deficit was actually a consequence of the crisis: high interest rates had driven up the government's interest payments, while the slumping economy depressed tax revenue. (At "normal" levels of employment and interest rates, Brazil's budget deficit would have been quite modest.) But what was the use of arguing? Investors believed that Brazil would have a disastrous crisis unless the deficit was quickly reduced, and they were surely right, because they themselves would generate that crisis. (And indeed they did, in January 1999.)

The point is that because speculative attacks can be self-justifying, following an economic policy that makes sense in terms of the fundamentals is not enough to assure market confidence. In fact, the need to win that confidence can actually prevent a country from following otherwise sensible policies and force it to follow policies that would normally seem perverse.

Now, consider the situation from the point of view of those clever economists who were making policy in Washington. They found themselves dealing with economies whose hold on investor confidence was fragile. Almost by definition a country that has come to the United States and/or the IMF for help is one that has already experienced a devastating run on its currency and is at risk of another. The overriding objective of policy must therefore be to mollify market sentiment. But because crises can be self-fulfilling, sound economic policy is not sufficient to gain market confidence—one must cater to the perceptions, the prejudices, the whims of the market. Or, rather, one must cater to what one *hopes* will be the perceptions of the market.

And that is how the Keynesian compact got broken: international economic policy ended up having very little to do with economics. It became an exercise in amateur psychology, in which the IMF and the Treasury Department tried to persuade countries to do things they hoped would be perceived by the market as favorable. No wonder the economics textbooks went right out the window as soon as the crisis hit.

Unfortunately, the textbook issues did not go away. Suppose that Washington was right, that a country threatened with an investor panic must raise interest rates, cut spending, and defend its currency to avoid devastating crisis. It still remains true that tight monetary and fiscal policies, together with an overvalued currency, produce recessions. What remedy does Washington offer? None. The perceived need to play the confidence game supersedes the normal concerns of economic policy. It sounds pretty crazy, and it is.

And so now we have solved the mystery with which Chapter 4 ended: why did policy fail to oppose the devastating feedback process that caused one economy after another to melt down? The answer is that those making policy believed that they had to play the confidence game, and that this meant following macroeconomic policies that exacerbated slumps instead of relieving them.

But was it really necessary to play this game?

Did the IMF Make the Situation Worse?

Nobody likes the International Monetary Fund; if anyone did, it would be a bad sign. For the IMF is a "lender of last resort" for national governments: it is the place they go for money when they are in trouble. And lenders of last resort are supposed to practice tough love: to give you what you need rather than what you want, and to force you to pull yourself together in the process. A warm, cuddly IMF wouldn't be doing its job.

But the converse isn't necessarily true: just because people hate the IMF doesn't mean that it is doing its job well. And since the onset of the Asian crisis there have been many complaints about the IMF's role. Quite a few people think that the IMF (and the U.S. Treasury Department, which de facto largely dictates the IMF's policies) actually caused the crisis, or that it mishandled the crisis in a way that made it far worse than it needed to be. Are they right?

Let's start with the easy part: two things that the IMF clearly did do wrong.

First, when the IMF was called in to Thailand, Indonesia, and Korea, it quickly demanded that they practice fiscal austerity—that they raise taxes and cut spending in order to avoid large budget deficits. It was hard to understand why this was part of the program, since in Asia (unlike in Brazil a year later) nobody but the IMF seemed to regard budget deficits as an important problem. And the attempt to meet these budget guidelines had a doubly negative effect on the countries: where the guidelines were met, the effect was to worsen the recession by reducing demand; where they were not met, the effect was to add, gratuitously, to the sense that things were out of control, and hence to feed the market panic.

Second, the IMF demanded "structural" reform—that is, changes that went well beyond monetary and fiscal policy—as a condition for loans to afflicted economies. Some of these reforms, like closing bad banks, were arguably relevant to the financial crisis. Others, like demanding that Indonesia eliminate the practice of giving presidential cronies lucrative monopolies in some businesses, had little if anything to do with the IMF's mandate. True, the monopoly on cloves (which Indonesians like to put in their cigarettes) was a bad thing, a glaring example of crony capitalism at work. But what did it have to do with the run on the rupiah?

If you had asked IMF officials at the time what they thought they were doing, they would have answered that it was all part of the business of rebuilding confidence. Budget deficits were not a market concern at the moment, but they thought they soon would be. And they also thought that it was important for countries to make a highly visible show of combating cronyism and corruption, to convince markets that they really had changed their ways. One might almost describe this as the view that governments had to show their seriousness by inflicting pain on themselves—whether or not that pain had any direct relevance to the immediate problems—because only thus could they regain the market's trust.

If that was the theory, it turns out to have been quite wrong. The budget guidelines were eventually relaxed, and nobody minded; markets became bullish once again on Korea, even though structural reform had stalled. Meanwhile, the sheer breadth of IMF demands, aside from raising suspicions that the United States was trying to use the crisis to impose its ideological vision on Asia, more or less guaranteed a prolonged period of wrangling between Asian governments and their rescuers, a period during which the crisis of confidence steadily worsened.

So the IMF bungled two important pieces of the rescue. But the really big issues involved interest rates and exchange rates. Did it bungle these too?

Here's what the IMF did: In Asia (as opposed to Brazil, which as I said was a sort of caricature of the Asian programs) it did not tell countries to defend the values of their currencies at all cost. But it did tell them to raise interest rates, initially to very high levels, in an attempt to persuade investors to keep their money in place. Some vociferous critics of the IMF—most notably Harvard's Jeffrey Sachs—said that this was very much the wrong thing to do. Sachs believed, in effect, that Asian countries could and should have behaved like Australia, simply letting their currencies decline until they started to look cheap to investors, and that if they had done so, the great slump would never have happened.

What the IMF said in response is that Asia is not Australia: that to let the currencies fall unchecked would have led to "hyperdevaluations," and that the result would have been both massive financial distress (because so many businesses had debt denominated in dollars) and soaring inflation. The trouble with this rationale is, of course, that the massive financial distress happened anyway, thanks to high interest rates and the recession they helped cause. So the IMF at best avoided one vicious circle only by starting another.

This same observation undermines the argument made by many right-wing critics of the IMF, that it *should* have told countries to defend their original exchange rates at all cost. This could indeed have avoided the collapse of confidence in Asian *currencies*; but it would have done nothing to prevent the collapse of confidence in Asian *economies*, and the economic meltdown would probably still have happened.

Would simply letting the currencies fall have worked better? Sachs argued that by *not* raising interest rates, governments would have avoided feeding the financial panic; the result would have been modest, tolerable devaluations and a far better economic outcome. This argument, which seemed implausible to many people (myself included) at the time of the Asian crisis, gained a bit more credibility in January 1999, when Washington quite clearly bungled Brazil—but more about that in Chapter 7.

Surely, however, the bottom line is that there were no good choices. The rules of the international financial system, it seemed, offered many countries no way out. And so it was really nobody's fault that things turned out so badly.

Which is not to say that there were no villains in the plot.

6

MASTERS OF THE UNIVERSE

In the bad old days, before the triumph of capitalism, the figure of the evil speculator—the malefactor of great wealth who manipulates markets to the detriment of honest workers—was a staple of popular culture. But with the fall of Communism, the successes of globalization, and the general revival of faith in free markets, the evil speculator went the way of witches and warlocks: serious people stopped believing in his existence. Oh, nobody but the most extreme defenders of laissez-faire denied that there were cases in which people traded on inside information and maybe even manipulated the price of a stock here, a commodity there. But surely this was petty crime; the big financial events, those that shaped the destiny of nations, involved markets far too large for conspiracy theories to be plausible. No individuals or small groups could really affect the currency value of even a middle-sized economy, could they?

Well, maybe they could. One of the most bizarre aspects of the economic crisis of the 1990s was the prominent part played by "hedge funds," investment institutions that are able to take temporary control of assets far in excess of their owners' wealth. Without question hedge funds, in both their success and their failure, rocked world markets. And in at least a few cases, the evil speculator staged a comeback.

The Nature of the Beast

Hedge funds don't hedge. Indeed, they do more or less the opposite. To hedge, says *Webster's*, is "to try to avoid or lessen loss by making counterbalancing bets, investments, etc." That is, one hedges in order to make sure that market fluctuations do *not* affect one's wealth.

What hedge funds do, by contrast, is precisely to try to make the most of market fluctuations. The way they do this is typically to go short in some assets—that is, promise to deliver them at a fixed price at some future date—and go long in others. Profits come if the price of the shorted asset falls (so that they can be delivered cheaply) or the value of the purchased asset rises, or both.*

* The terminology of "short" versus "long" positions is jargon, but too useful a shorthand to be avoided in this book. Basically, to go long in something is to put yourself in a position to gain if its price rises—which is what the ordinary investor does when buying stock, real estate, or anything else. To go short in something is to put yourself in a position to gain if its price *falls*. To sell a stock short, one borrows the stock from its owner with a promise to return it later—then one sells it. This means that the stock must be repurchased before the due date; the short-seller is betting that its price will have fallen by then. Meanwhile, the short-seller has acquired extra cash, which can be invested in something else—that is, he takes a long position in some other asset.

Of course, the owners of the borrowed assets have to be reassured that the short-seller will actually have enough cash to buy the asset back, so they will want some kind

The advantage of this kind of financial play is that it can deliver a very high return to the hedge fund's investors. The reason is that the fund can take a position much larger than the amount of money its owners put in, since it buys its "long" position mainly with the cash raised from creating its "short" position. Indeed, the only reason it needs to have any capital at all is to persuade the counterparties to its asset shorts that it will be able to deliver on its promises. Hedge funds with good reputations have been able to take positions as much as a hundred times as large as their owners' capital; that means that a 1 percent rise in the price of their assets, or decline in the price of their liabilities, doubles that capital.

The downside, of course, is that a hedge fund can also lose money very efficiently. Market movements that might not seem all that large to ordinary investors can quickly wipe out a hedge fund's capital, or at least cause it to lose its shorts—that is, induce those who have lent it stocks or other assets to demand that they be returned.

How big are hedge funds? Nobody really knows because until quite recently nobody thought it was necessary to find out. Indeed, despite occasional warnings from concerned economists, and even despite the events I'll describe shortly, hedge funds have been left virtually untouched by regulation. Partly that's because hedge funds—needing only a limited amount of capital, from a small number of people—can and do operate "offshore," establishing legal residence in accommodating jurisdictions to free themselves

---

of reassurance that he has enough wealth to deliver on his promise. When investors who engage in a lot of short-selling suffer heavy losses, they typically find that they are no longer able to borrow as much as they could before. When such investors play a large role in the market, this can have interesting consequences, as we will see shortly.

from annoying interference. To police their operations wouldn't be impossible, but it would be difficult. Moreover, for a long time the general consensus, at least in the United States, was that there was no need.

But in a way that was a strange attitude, because as early as 1992 one famous hedge fund gave an impressive demonstration of just how much influence a highly leveraged investor can have.

The Legend of George Soros

George Soros, a Hungarian refugee turned American entrepreneur, founded his Quantum Fund in 1969. By 1992 he was a billionaire, already famous as the "world's greatest investor," and already celebrated for the generosity and creativity of his philanthropic activities. But Soros—who is a man with intellectual as well as financial ambitions, who would like the world to take his philosophical pronouncements as seriously as it takes his business acumen—wanted more. As he himself says, he went in search of a business coup that would not only make money but generate publicity for himself, publicity that he could use to promote his nonbusiness ventures.

He found his opportunity in Britain that summer. In 1990 Britain had joined the European Monetary System's Exchange Rate Mechanism (ERM), a system of fixed exchange rates that was intended as a way station en route to a unified European currency. Like the unhappy continents in our globo parable, however, Britain found that it did not like the monetary policy it was forced to follow. At the time Europe did not have a European Central Bank; while there was a legal fiction of symmetry among nations, in practice everyone matched the monetary policy of Germany's Bundesbank. And Germany was, literally, in a different place from the rest of Europe: having just reunified, it was compelled to spend large sums on the attempted reconstruction of East Germany. Fearing that this expenditure would be inflationary, the Bundesbank maintained high interest rates to prevent its own economy from overheating. Meanwhile Britain, which probably entered the ERM at too high an exchange rate, was in a deep recession, and its government was facing growing popular dissatisfaction. Officials strenuously denied that they would consider dropping out of the ERM; but there was a nagging doubt about whether they really meant it.

It was a situation ready-made for a currency crisis, and Soros decided not only to bet on such a crisis but also to provoke one.

The mechanics of the bet were conceptually simple, if extremely complex in detail. The first stage had to be low profile, even secretive, as the Quantum Fund quietly established credit lines that would allow it to borrow about $15 billion worth of British pounds and to convert that sum into dollars at will. Then, once the fund was already substantially long in dollars and short in pounds, the attack had to turn noisy: Soros would be as ostentatious as possible about short-selling the pound, give interviews to financial newspapers declaring his belief that the pound would soon be devalued, and so on. If all went well, this would generate a run on the pound by other investors, a run that would force the British government to give in and devalue it.

It worked. Soros's high-profile assault on the pound began in August. Within weeks Britain had spent nearly $50 billion in the foreign exchange markets to defend the pound, to no avail. In mid-September the government raised interest rates to defend the currency, but this proved politically unacceptable. After only three days Britain dropped out of the ERM, and the pound was set afloat (where it remains to this day). Soros not only made roughly a billion dollars in quick capital gains but also established himself as perhaps the most famous speculator of all time.

But what did Soros actually do? There are three questions here.

First, did Soros undermine a currency that would otherwise have maintained its value? Probably not. The fact is that pressures on the pound were building steadily, and many economists (though not many market participants) already suspected that Britain was not long for the ERM. Nobody can prove this assertion, but my strong belief is that Britain's attempt to join the continental monetary club was doomed, Soros or no Soros.

But in that case, did Soros at least move up the timetable, causing the pound to devalue sooner than it otherwise would have? Almost surely yes, but the question is, by how much? Again, one cannot prove this one way or the other, but my own guess is that economic conditions were moving Britain in the direction of a near-term exit from the ERM in any case and that Soros moved up the timetable by only a few weeks.

Finally, did Soros do his victims any harm? The government of Prime Minister John Major never recovered from the humiliation. But it is actually possible to argue that Soros did the British nation as a whole a favor. The decline of the pound did not create an economic crisis: the currency stabilized spontaneously at about 15 percent below its previous value. Freed of the need to support the pound, the British government was able to reduce interest rates. (Chancellor of the Exchequer Norman Lamont declared that he had been "singing in the bath" with relief over the end of a currency peg he had declared absolutely inviolable only a few days before. His relief was premature—most Britons gained from the devaluation, but he himself was soon forced to resign.) The combination of lower interest rates and a more competitive exchange rate soon led to a strong recovery in the British economy, which within a few years had brought unemployment down to levels its neighbors regarded as unreachable. For the ordinary Briton, Soros's attack on the pound brought mainly good things.

So it wasn't such a terrible story, after all. True, Europeans who were deeply committed to the cause of monetary union regarded the events of 1992 as a tragedy. The French, who basically fought off the speculative attacks of 1992 and 1993 (they briefly allowed the franc to float, but soon brought it back into the ERM band), were heard to mutter old-fashioned denunciations of currency speculators as agents of evil. But in the dominant Anglo-Saxon world of policy discussion, the story of Soros and the pound was not regarded as any sort of worrisome omen.

All that changed when the Asian crisis hit, and it turned out that the results of speculation could be considerably less benign.

The Madness of Prime Minister Mahathir

Try to imagine how it must have felt. He had managed his country's awkward ethnic politics with consummate skill: he pacified the country's Malay majority with the *bumiputra* ("son of the soil") program offering that majority preferential economic treatment, yet did so without driving out the commercially crucial Chinese minority. He had made the nation a favorite site for multinational branch plants even while pursuing an independent, somewhat anti-Western foreign policy that played well with a mostly Islamic populace. And under his leadership the country had shared fully in the Asian miracle: as its economy surged, foreign businessmen, from Bill Gates on down, came courting, and in the summer of 1997 *Time* declared him one of the world's top one hundred "technology leaders."

Oh, there were a few criticisms. Some of his friends and family members seemed to have gotten rich rather easily. Some foreigners accused him of grandiosity, with his insistence on building the world's tallest building and on constructing a new capital and a massive new "technology corridor." But on the whole he had every reason to feel well satisfied with his achievements.

Then, with shocking suddenness, things went sour. His undisciplined neighbors had a currency crisis—well, that was their problem. But then money started flooding out of his country too. He was faced with the humiliating choice between letting the currency plunge or raising interest rates, either of which would put many of those hard-built businesses in severe financial straits.

So in a way we should not blame Mahathir Mohamad, prime minister of Malaysia, for his susceptibility to conspiracy theories. After all, it was common knowledge that George Soros had engineered the run on the pound five years earlier, and Quantum Fund had certainly been speculating in Southeast Asian currencies over the past several years. What was more natural than to blame the famous speculator for his woes? One might even call it a bit of poetic justice: Soros, by his own account, had attacked the pound as much for the notoriety as the money; now he was being hoisted by his own petard.

Nonetheless, Mahathir clearly should have kept his mouth shut. At a time when confidence in his economy was already plunging, the sight of the prime minister raving about an American conspiracy against Asia—and broadly hinting that it was in fact, yes, a *Jewish* conspiracy—was not what the money doctors would have prescribed.

And it also happened not to be true. Quantum Fund had speculated against Thailand, but then so had lots of people. The speculative flight of capital from Malaysia, it turns out, was carried out largely by Malaysians themselves—in particular, some of the very same businessmen who had gotten rich thanks to Mahathir's favor.

Nonetheless, Mahathir continued to press his case, attacking Soros in press conferences and speeches. Only after several months had gone by, and the state of the Malaysian economy began to look truly alarming, did he become relatively quiet, afraid to disturb the markets. Perhaps he also became aware that most of the world thought his complaints were silly. Conspiracies like that just don't happen in the real world.

And then one did.

The Attack on Hong Kong

Hong Kong has long had a special place in the hearts of free-market enthusiasts. At a time when most Third World countries believed that protectionism and government planning were the way to develop, Hong Kong had free trade and a policy of letting entrepreneurs rip—and showed that such a wide-open economy could grow at rates development theorists had never imagined possible. The city-state also led the revival of currency boards, which some conservatives liked to imagine constituted the first step on the road back to the gold standard. Year after year the conservative Heritage Foundation gave Hong Kong top ranking on its "index of economic freedom."

But Hong Kong suffered from the Asian crisis. It is hard to find any fault in the city's own management: more than any other in the region, its economy was run according to the rule of law, with well-regulated banks and conservative budget policies. There was little sign of rampant cronyism before the crisis, nor was there, in the first year, any panicky flight of capital. Still, the city was clearly in the wrong place at the wrong time. As its neighbors slumped, business suffered: Japanese stopped popping over for shopping trips, Southeast Asian firms stopped buying the services of Hong Kong banks. Worse yet, Hong Kong's strict currency board system meant that the exchange rate was fixed solidly at 7.8 to the U.S. dollar, even as much of the rest of Asia's currencies were devalued, and suddenly Hong Kong was far more expensive than Bangkok or even Tokyo. The result was a deepening recession, the worst in memory.

Inevitably, nagging doubts began to surface. Would Hong Kong really defend its exchange rate at all costs? Some Hong Kong businessmen openly urged the Monetary Authority to devalue the currency, to make their costs competitive again. Such demands were dismissed, and the government declared the rate inviolate; but then so had the government of Britain in 1992. Also, what about China? Asia's giant largely escaped the first wave of the crisis, thanks mainly to its currency controls. But by the summer of 1998 signs of an economic slowdown were emerging, and with them rumors that China's currency, too, might be devalued, putting Hong Kong under far greater strain.

Some might have seen all of this as bad news; but some hedge funds saw it as an opportunity.

There are, for obvious reasons, no hard numbers on just what happened in August and September of 1998, but here is the way the story is told, both by Hong Kong officials and by market players. A small group of hedge funds—rumored to include Soros's Quantum Fund and Julian Robertson's less famous but equally influential Tiger Fund, although officials named no names—began a "double play" against Hong Kong. They sold Hong Kong stocks short—that is, they borrowed stocks from their owners, then sold them for Hong Kong dollars (with a promise to those owners to buy the stocks back and return them, of course—as well as a "rental fee" for the use of the stocks in the meantime). Then they traded those Hong Kong dollars for U.S. dollars. In effect, they were betting that one of two things would happen. Either the Hong Kong dollar would be devalued, so that they would make money on their currency speculation; or the Hong Kong Monetary Authority would defend its currency by raising interest rates, which would drive down the local stock market, and they would make money off their stock market short position.

But in the view of Hong Kong officials, the hedge funds weren't just betting on these events: like Soros in 1992, they were doing their best to make them happen. The sales of Hong Kong dollars were ostentatious, carried out in large blocks, regularly timed, so as to make sure that everyone in the market noticed. Again without naming names, Hong Kong officials also claimed that the hedge funds paid reporters and editors to run stories suggesting that the Hong Kong dollar or the Chinese renminbi, or both, were on the verge of devaluation. In other words, they were deliberately trying to start a run on the currency.

Did the hedge funds actually conspire together? It's possible: while an explicit agreement to manipulate the price of, say, Microsoft stock would land you in jail, a comparable conspiracy against the Hong Kong stock market (which had about the same capitalization in 1998) apparently falls through the legal cracks. It's also possible there was no contact at all. But more likely there were hints and winks, a few generalities over a round of golf or an expensive bottle of wine. After all, there weren't that many players, and they all knew how the game worked.

Indeed, some observers saw the shadow of a still wider plot. The

Hong Kong Four (or Five, or whatever) had other plays going at the same time. They were short in yen—because interest rates in Japan were low, and they thought the yen might well plunge along with the Hong Kong dollar—as well as Australian dollars, Canadian dollars, and so on. And they became big, ostentatious sellers of some of these other currencies too. So you could think of Hong Kong as only the centerpiece of a play against much of the Asia-Pacific region, indeed quite possibly the largest market conspiracy of all time.

And it all looked quite likely to succeed. After all, what could Hong Kong do? Its stock market was large compared with that of most developing countries but not compared with the resources of the hedge funds. There were reports that the combined short position of the alleged conspirators was about $30 billion, which would be the equivalent of short-selling roughly $1.5 *trillion* in the U.S. stock market. Moreover, the Hong Kong market was wide open and likely to remain so: a city whose livelihood depended precisely on its reputation as a place where people could do as they liked with their money, free from arbitrary government interference, would not even dare to flirt with controls on capital flight. All in all, it looked like a brilliant plan, with very high chances of success.

Unexpectedly, Hong Kong fought back.

The main weapon in that fight was a novel, unconventional use of the Hong Kong Monetary Authority's funds. The HKMA, as it happened, had huge resources. Remember, Hong Kong had a currency board, so that every 7.8 Hong Kong dollars of money in circulation was backed by one U.S. dollar in reserves; but it turned out that the HKMA had actually banked far more dollars than it needed for that purpose. How could this wealth be deployed as a defense against the hedge funds? By using it to buy local stocks—

thereby driving their prices up and causing the hedge funds, which had sold those stocks short, to lose money. Of course, in order to be effective these purchases would have to be on a large scale, comparable to or even greater than the hedge funds' short sales. But the authorities certainly had the resources to make such purchases.

Why, then, hadn't the hedge funds expected this response? Because they didn't think the Hong Kong government would be willing to risk the inevitable reaction from conservatives horrified that such a free-market paragon would try to manipulate market prices. And the reaction was fierce indeed. The government's actions were "insane," thundered Milton Friedman. The Heritage Foundation formally removed the city-state's designation as a bastion of economic freedom; newspaper stories linked Hong Kong with Malaysia, which had just imposed draconian capital controls. Finance Secretary Donald Tsang began touring the world, trying to explain the actions to investors and reassure them that his government was as pro-capitalism as ever. But it was an uphill fight.

For a time the hedge funds expected that the reaction would force the Hong Kong authorities to back down. They rolled over their short positions (i.e., paid the original owners of the stock additional fees for the right to put off their return) and settled in to wait the government out. The government then upped the ante, instituting new rules that restricted short-selling, thereby forcing the Hong Kong investors who had rented out their stocks to call them in; this forced the hedge funds to unwind their positions, but raised further howls of outrage.

And then the whole Hong Kong issue faded away, as a bizarre series of events around the world forced the hedge funds themselves to curtail their activities.

The Potemkin Economy

In 1787, the empress Catherine of Russia toured her empire's southern provinces. According to legend, her chief minister, Grigori Aleksandrovich Potemkin, stayed one day ahead, setting up false fronts that made wretched villages look prosperous, then dismantling the props and leapfrogging them to the next destination. Ever since, the term "Potemkin village" has been used to refer to apparently happy scenes that are in reality nothing but facades, bearing no relation to what really lies behind them.

It is entirely appropriate, then, that in the second half of the 1990s Russia itself became a sort of Potemkin economy.

Nobody found the transition from socialism to capitalism easy, but Russia found it harder than most. For years after the fall of Communism its economy seemed caught in a sort of limbo, having lost whatever guidance central planning used to provide, yet without having managed to achieve a working market system either. Even the things that used to work to some extent no longer functioned: factories that used to produce low-quality goods produced nothing at all, collective farms became even less productive than they were before, and the dreary Brezhnev years began to seem like a golden age. There were hundreds of thousands of highly skilled programmers, engineers, scientists, mathematicians, but they couldn't find decent work.

It was a sorry state of affairs, but Russia had one last asset: as the heir of the Soviet Union, it still had a massive arsenal of nuclear weapons. It didn't explicitly threaten to sell nukes to the highest bidder, but the risk that it might conditioned Western policy, making the U.S. government anxious to put the best face on things. Long after most informed people had become thoroughly cynical, the United States continued to hope that Russia's reformers would somehow manage to complete the stalled transition, that the oligarchs would stop being so selfish or at least so shortsighted. So the U.S. government bullied the International Monetary Fund into lending money to Russia to buy time for stabilization plans that somehow never materialized. (*The Medley Report*, an international economic newsletter, commented that the United States was not, as some said, throwing money down a rathole. Instead, it was throwing money down a missile silo.)

The apparent ability of Russia to use its nuclear arms as collateral, in turn, encouraged high-rolling foreign investors to take a risk and put money into Russia. Everyone knew that the ruble might well be devalued, perhaps massively, or that the Russian government might simply default on its debts. But it seemed a good bet that before that happened, the West would step in with yet another emergency cash injection. Since Russian government debt was offering extremely high interest rates, eventually reaching 150 percent, the bet was an appealing one to investors with a high tolerance for risk—notably hedge funds.

However, it turned out that the bet wasn't that good after all. In the summer of 1998 Russia's financial situation unraveled faster than expected. In August, George Soros (!) suggested publicly that Russia devalue the ruble and then establish a currency board. His remarks triggered a run on the currency, an inadequate Mexican-style devaluation, and then a combination of currency collapse and debt moratorium. And the West had apparently had enough: there was no rescue this time. Suddenly claims on Russia could be sold, if at all, for a fraction of their face value, and billions of dollars had been lost. (What happened to that nuclear collateral? Good question; let's not think about it.)

In sheer dollar terms the money lost in Russia was quite trivial— no more than is lost when, for example, the U.S. stock market falls by a fraction of a percent, which it does almost every other day. But these losses fell heavily on a small group of highly leveraged financial operators, which meant that they had almost ridiculously large effects on the rest of the world. Indeed, for a few weeks it looked as if Russia's financial collapse would drag down the whole world.

The Panic of 1998

In the summer of 1998 the balance sheets of the world's hedge funds were not only huge but also immensely complex. Still, there was a pattern. Typically these funds were short in assets that were safe— not likely to plunge in value—and liquid—that is, easy to sell if you needed cash. At the same time, they were long in assets that were risky and illiquid. Thus a hedge fund might be short in German government debt, which is safe and easy to sell, and long in Danish mortgage-backed securities (indirect claims on houses), which are a bit more risky and a lot harder to sell at short notice. Or they might be short in Japanese bonds and long in Russian debt.

The general principle here was that historically markets have tended to place a rather high premium on both safety and liquidity, because small investors were risk-averse and never knew when they might need to cash out. This offered an opportunity to big operators, who could minimize the risk by careful diversification (buying a mix of assets so that gains on one would normally offset losses on another), and who would not normally find themselves suddenly in need of cash. It was largely by exploiting these margins that hedge funds made so much money, year after year.

By 1998, however, many people understood this basic idea, and competition among the hedge funds themselves had made it increasingly difficult to make money. Some hedge funds actually started returning investors' money, declaring that they could not find enough profitable opportunities to use it. But they also tried to find new opportunities by stretching even further, taking complex positions that appeared on the surface to be hugely risky but that supposedly were cunningly constructed to minimize the chance of losses.

What nobody realized until catastrophe struck was that the competition among hedge funds to exploit ever narrower profit opportunities had created a sort of financial doomsday machine.

Here's how it worked. Suppose that some hedge fund—call it Relativity Fund—has taken a big bet in Russian government debt. Then Russia defaults, and it loses a billion dollars or so. This makes the investors who are the counterparts of Relativity's short positions—the people who have lent it stocks and bonds, to be returned in the future—nervous. So they demand their assets back. However, Relativity doesn't actually have those assets on hand; it must buy them back, which means that it must sell other assets to get the necessary cash. And since it is such a big player in the markets, when it starts selling, the prices of the things it has invested in go down.

Meanwhile, Relativity's rival, the Pussycat Fund, has also invested in many of the same things. So when Relativity is forced into sudden large sales, this means big losses for Pussycat as well; it too finds itself forced to "cover its shorts" by selling, driving the prices of other assets down. In so doing, it creates a problem for the Elizabethan Fund, and so on down the line.

If all this reminds you of the story of Asia's financial meltdown, as I told it in Chapter 4, it should: at a fundamental level it was the same kind of process, involving plunging prices and imploding balance sheets—a vicious cycle of deleveraging. Nobody thought that such a thing could happen in the modern world, but it did, and the consequences were startling.

You see, it turned out that the hedge funds had been so assid-
uous about arbitraging away liquidity and risk premia that for
many illiquid assets they *were* the market; when they all tried to
sell at once, there were no alternative buyers. And so after years
of steadily narrowing, liquidity and risk premia suddenly surged
to unheard-of levels as hedge funds were forced to unwind their
positions. Twenty-nine-year U.S. government bonds—a perfectly
safe asset, in the sense that if the U.S. government goes, so does
everything else—were offering significantly higher interest rates
than thirty-year bonds, which are traded in a larger market and
are therefore slightly easier to sell. Corporate bonds normally offer
higher returns than U.S. government debt, but the spread had
suddenly widened by several percentage points. And commercial
mortgage-backed securities—the financial instruments that indirectly fund most nonresidential real estate construction—could not
be sold at all. At one meeting I attended, participants asked a Federal Reserve official who had described the situation what could be
done to resolve it. "Pray," he replied.

In fact, luckily, the Fed did more than that. First of all, it engineered the rescue of the most famous casualty among the hedge
funds: Connecticut-based Long Term Capital Management.

The saga of LTCM is even more remarkable than the legend
of George Soros. Soros is a figure in a long tradition, that of the
swashbuckling financial raider—not that different, when you get
to essentials, from Jim Fisk or Jay Gould. The managers at Long
Term Capital, however, were quintessentially modern types: nerd
savants using formulas and computers to outsmart the market.
The firm boasted two Nobel laureates, and many of their best students, on its payroll. They believed that by carefully studying the
historical correlations between assets, they could construct clever
portfolios—long in some assets, short in others—that yielded high

returns with much less risk than people imagined. And year after year they delivered, with such regularity that, it turned out, people who lent them money stopped even asking whether the firm really had enough capital to be a safe partner.

Then the markets went crazy.

It is still unclear whether the losses that LTCM suffered were the result of once-in-a-lifetime shocks that could not have been anticipated, or whether the computer models they used were naive in not allowing for the occasional large market disturbance. (And also whether this naïveté, if that was what it was, was deliberate— moral hazard again.) Whatever the cause, by September the company was facing margin calls—demands that it either put more cash on deposit with the lenders or pay up in full—that it could not meet. And suddenly it became clear that LTCM had become so large a player in the markets that if it failed, and its positions were liquidated, it might precipitate a full-scale panic.

Something had to be done. In the end, no public money was required: the New York Fed was able to persuade a group of investors to take over majority ownership of LTCM in return for a desperately needed injection of cash. As it turned out, once markets had calmed down again, the banks actually made a profit on the deal.

Even with the rescue, however, it was by no means a foregone conclusion that the crisis would be surmounted. When the Federal Reserve cut interest rates by only 0.25 percent at its regularly scheduled September meeting, the size of the cut disappointed the markets, and the already troubled financial situation started to look like a runaway panic. Suddenly people were starting to draw analogies between the financial crisis and the bank runs that plunged the United States into the Great Depression; J.P. Morgan even went so far as to flatly predict a severe recession in 1999.

But the Fed had a trick up its sleeve. Normally interest rate changes take place only when the Federal Open Market Committee meets, roughly every six weeks. In that September meeting, however, the committee had granted Alan Greenspan the discretionary power to cut interest rates a further quarter point whenever necessary. On October 15 he surprised the markets by announcing that cut—and, miraculously, the markets rallied. When the Fed cut rates yet again at its next meeting, the panic turned into euphoria. By the end of 1998 all the unusual liquidity premia had vanished, and the stock market was once again setting new records.

It is important to realize that even now Fed officials are not quite sure how they pulled this rescue off. At the height of the crisis it seemed entirely possible that cutting interest rates would be entirely ineffectual—after all, if nobody can borrow, what difference does it make what the price would be if they could? And if everyone had believed that the world was coming to an end, their panic might—as in so many other countries—have ended up being a self-fulfilling prophecy. In retrospect Greenspan seemed to have been like a general who rides out in front of his demoralized army, waves his sword and shouts encouragement, and somehow turns the tide of battle: well done, but not something you would want to count on working next time.

Indeed, some Fed officials fretted that the public was overrating their abilities—a new form of moral hazard, said one Greenspan adviser, based on the belief that the Fed could bail the economy and the markets out of any crisis. Sure enough, the limits of the Fed's power were graphically demonstrated when the crisis of 2008 hit.

Before we get to that, however, let's talk about the legend of Alan Greenspan, and how it all went wrong.

7

GREENSPAN'S BUBBLES

For more than eighteen years, from May 1987 to January 2006, Alan Greenspan was the chairman of the Federal Reserve's Board of Governors. The position, in itself, made him one of the world's most powerful financial officials. But Greenspan's influence went far beyond his formal powers: he was the Maestro, the Oracle, the senior member of the Committee to Save the World, as a 1999 cover story in *Time* put it.

When Greenspan left office, he did so trailing clouds of glory. Alan Blinder of Princeton University pronounced him possibly the greatest central banker in history. When Greenspan made one of his final appearances before Congress, he was hailed virtually as a monetary messiah: "You have guided monetary policy through stock-market crashes, wars, terrorist attacks and natural disasters," declared one congressman. "You have made a great contribution to the prosperity of the U.S. and the nation is in your debt."

Almost three years later, Greenspan's name was mud.

The story of the rise and fall of Alan Greenspan's reputation is more than a personal morality tale. It's also the story of how the makers of economic policy convinced themselves that they had everything under control, only to learn, to their horror—and the country's pain—that they didn't.

The Age of Greenspan

How did Greenspan become such a legend? In large part because he presided over a period of generally good economic news. The 1970s and early 1980s were an era of nasty shocks—of inflation and unemployment rates that went into double digits, of the worst economic slumps since the Great Depression. By contrast, the Greenspan era was relatively serene. Inflation stayed low throughout, and the two recessions during his tenure were brief, eight-month affairs, at least according to the official chronology (more on that later). Jobs were relatively plentiful: in the late 1990s and again in the middle of the next decade, the unemployment rate fell to levels not seen since the 1960s. And for financial investors, the Greenspan years were heavenly: the Dow soared past 10,000, and stock prices on average rose more than 10 percent a year.

How much credit did Greenspan deserve for this good performance? Less than he received, surely. It was Greenspan's predecessor, Paul Volcker, who brought inflation under control, achieving that goal with tight-money policies that caused a severe economic slump but finally broke the back of inflationary psychology. After Volcker did the hard, unpopular work, Greenspan was able to bask in the payoff.

Much of the good economic news also had little to do with

monetary policy. During the Greenspan years American businesses finally figured out how to use information technology
effectively. When a new technology is introduced, it often takes
a while before the economic benefits become apparent, because
it takes time for businesses to rearrange their structure to take
proper advantage of the innovation. The classic example is elec-
tricity. Although electrical machinery became widely available in
the 1880s, at first businesses continued to build factories the old
way: multistory buildings with machines crammed into narrow
spaces, a design dictated by the need to have a big steam engine
in the basement run all the shafts and pulleys. It wasn't until after
World War I that businesses began taking advantage of the fact
that they no longer needed a central power source, by switching
to one-story, open-plan factories with plenty of room to move
materials around.

The same thing happened with information technology. The
microprocessor was invented in 1971, and personal computers
were widespread by the early 1980s. But for a long time offices
continued to be run the way they had been in the age of carbon
paper. It wasn't until the mid-1990s that businesses really began
taking advantage of the new technology to create networked
offices, continuous-time updates of inventory, and so on. When
they did, there was a sharp acceleration in the growth rate of U.S.
productivity—the amount an average worker produces in an hour.
This lifted profits and helped control inflation, contributing to the
good economic news under Greenspan; but the Fed chairman had
nothing to do with it.

Although Greenspan didn't beat inflation or create the productivity revolution, he did have a distinctive approach to monetary
management that seemed to work well at the time. The operative

word here may be "seemed," but before we get to that, let's look at what was distinctive about Greenspan's reign as chairman.

America's Designated Driver

Alan Greenspan wasn't the longest-serving Fed chairman ever. That honor went to William McChesney Martin Jr., who ran the Fed from 1951 to 1970. The two men's monetary philosophies couldn't have been more different.

Martin famously declared that the Fed's job was "to take away the punch bowl just as the party gets going." By that he mainly meant that the Fed should raise interest rates to prevent a booming economy from overheating, which could cause inflation. But his remark was also interpreted to mean that the Fed should try to prevent "irrational exuberance"—Greenspan's phrase—in the financial markets.

While Greenspan warned against excessive exuberance, however, he never *did* much about it. He used the phrase "irrational exuberance" in a 1996 speech in which he suggested, without quite saying it, that there was a bubble in stock prices. But he didn't raise interest rates to curb the market's enthusiasm; he didn't even seek to impose margin requirements on stock market investors. Instead, he waited until the bubble burst, as it did in 2000, then tried to clean up the mess afterward.

As an article in Reuters caustically but accurately put it, Greenspan acted like a parent who sternly warns teenagers against overdoing it but doesn't actually stop the party, and stands ready to act as designated driver when the fun is over.

To be fair to Greenspan, many economists, from both sides of the political spectrum, agreed with this policy doctrine. And the truth is that Greenspan's willingness to let the good times roll served the

U.S. economy well in at least one respect: the spectacular job creation during the Clinton years probably wouldn't have been quite as spectacular if someone else had been in charge at the Fed.

The figure below, which shows the U.S. unemployment rate since the beginning of 1987, tells the tale.* Official recession dates are indicated by the shaded bars. The dominating feature of this graph is the extraordinary decline in unemployment from 1993 to 2000, a decline that brought the unemployment rate below 4 percent for the first time since 1970. Now, Greenspan didn't cause this decline, but he did let it happen. And his benign neglect toward the unemployment decline was both unorthodox and, it turned out, the right thing to do.

In the early to mid-1990s the conventional view (which I shared myself) was that inflation would start accelerating if the unemployment rate fell below about 5.5 percent. That seemed to be

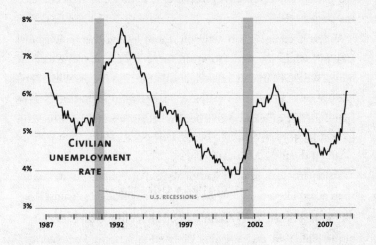

* Source: 2008 Federal Reserve Bank of St. Louis. Civilian unemployment rate from U.S. Department of Labor's Bureau of Labor Statistics; data on U.S. recessions from NBER.

the lesson of the previous couple of decades. In fact, inflation had accelerated right on cue in the late 1980s when the unemployment rate closed in on 5 percent. When the unemployment rate fell through the traditional red line in the mid-1990s, a chorus of economists urged Greenspan to raise interest rates to prevent a resurgence of inflation.

Greenspan, however, refused to fire before he saw the whites of inflation's eyes. He speculated publicly that the acceleration of productivity growth might have changed the historic relationship between low unemployment and accelerating inflation, and used this argument to put off any interest rate increase until there was clear evidence that inflation actually was on the rise. And it turned out that something had, in fact, changed in the economy. (Economists are still arguing about what.) Unemployment fell to levels not seen in decades, yet inflation remained quiescent. And the nation felt a sense of prosperity it hadn't experienced since the sixties.

When it came to job creation, then, letting the punch bowl stay out while the party went on turned out to be an excellent move. When it came to irrational exuberance in the asset markets, however, Greenspanism was less successful. Only after Greenspan had left office would it become clear just *how* unsuccessful he had been.

Greenspan's Bubbles

As I've just noted, Greenspan warned about irrational exuberance, but he didn't do anything about it. And in fact, the Fed chairman holds what I believe is a unique record among central bankers: he presided over not one but two enormous asset bubbles, first in stocks, then in housing.

The graph on this page shows the timing and size of these two bubbles. One line shows the ratio of stock prices to corporate earnings, a commonly used indicator of whether stocks are reasonably priced. The other shows a comparable measure for housing prices, the ratio of average U.S. home prices to average rents, expressed as an index, with 1987 equaling 100. You can clearly see the stock bubble of the 1990s, followed by the housing bubble of the next decade.* Overall, housing prices never got quite as far out of line with historical norms as stock prices did. But that's misleading, in several respects. First, housing is a bigger deal than the stock market, especially for middle-class families, whose houses are usually their main asset. Second, the boom in housing prices was uneven:

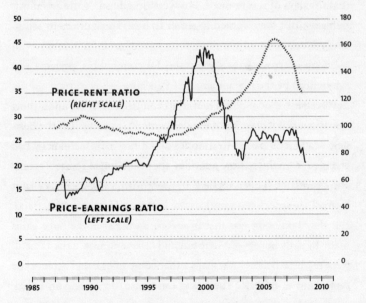

* The price-earnings ratio in the figure is from Robert Shiller of Yale University, who compares stock prices with average earnings over the previous decade—to smooth out short-run fluctuations in profits due to booms and slumps. The house price index is the Case-Shiller national index, while rents are taken from the Bureau of Economic Analysis.

in the central part of the United States, where land is abundant, housing prices never rose much more than overall inflation, but in coastal areas, especially Florida and southern California, prices soared to well over twice their normal ratio to rents. Finally, the financial system turned out to be much more vulnerable to the side effects of falling home prices than it was to the side effects of a stock bust, for reasons that I'll explain in Chapter 9.

How did these bubbles happen?

The stock bubble of the 1990s probably mainly reflected two things. One of them, extreme optimism about the profit potential of information technology, has received a lot of attention. The other, the growing sense of security about the economy, the belief that the days of severe recessions were over, hasn't gotten as much publicity. But they worked together to push stock prices to astonishing levels.

Today, everyone knows about the dot-com bubble, perhaps best symbolized by the phenomenon of Pets.com, which turned a dubious business model plus a clever ad campaign into an astonishing valuation. But it wasn't just the dot-coms. Across much of the business sector, companies told stories about how new technology had changed everything, how old rules about the limits to their profits and growth no longer applied. In more than a few cases, we later learned, these feel-good stories were buttressed by accounting fraud. But the main point was that investors, having seen the huge gains made by early buyers of Microsoft and other entrants in the IT field, were ready to believe that many other companies could achieve the same kind of miracle. There was, of course, an adding-up fallacy in all of this: there wasn't room in the economy for all the future Microsofts people thought they saw. But hype springs eternal, and people were willing to suspend their rational faculties.

There also seemed to be more serious reasons to buy stocks.

It was well known among economists and financial experts that stocks had, historically, been very good investments, at least for people who were willing to buy and hold. There was even an extensive literature in economics about the puzzle of the "equity premium": stocks consistently did so much better than alternative investments like bonds that it was hard to understand why people didn't put all their money into equities. The answer, probably, was fear: the big stock losses of the 1930s, and the more recent memory of how stocks swooned in the face of stagflation during the 1970s—the real value of stocks fell about 7 percent a year between 1968 and 1978—kept investors cautious. But as the Great Moderation persisted, with inflation low and no severe recessions, the fear gradually ebbed. Books like *Dow 36,000*, which was based on a garbled version of the equity premium literature (the authors did the calculation all wrong, but hey, who was counting?), became best-sellers.

And as stock prices rose, they began to feed on themselves. Never mind the more or less reasonable arguments in favor of stock investing; by 1998 or so, what people saw was that anyone who bought stocks had made lots of money, while anyone who waited on the sidelines was being left behind. So more and more funds poured into the stock market, prices rose ever higher, and the bubble expanded, seemingly without limit.

But there was, of course, a limit. As Robert Shiller, the author of *Irrational Exuberance*, has pointed out, an asset bubble is a sort of natural Ponzi scheme in which people keep making money as long as there are more suckers to draw in. But eventually the scheme runs out of suckers, and the whole thing crashes. In the case of stocks, the peak came in the summer of 2000. Over the next two years, stocks lost on average about 40 percent of their value.

The next bubble began inflating shortly thereafter.

The housing bubble was, in some sense, even less justified than the stock bubble of the previous decade. Yes, it was foolish to get so excited over Pets.com and all that, but the truth was that there was an exciting new technological universe opening up for exploitation. Add to that the fact that macroeconomic performance really had improved—stagflation had receded as a threat, and the business cycle seemed to have moderated—and there was a case for believing that some old rules no longer applied.

But what justified a bubble in housing? We know why home prices started rising: interest rates were very low in the early years of this decade, for reasons I'll explain shortly, which made buying houses attractive. And there's no question that this justified some rise in prices.

It did not, however, justify the belief that all the old rules no longer applied. Houses are houses; Americans have long been in the habit of buying houses with borrowed money, but it's hard to see why anyone should have believed, circa 2003, that the basic principles of such borrowing had been repealed. From long experience, we knew that home buyers shouldn't take on mortgages whose payments they couldn't afford, and that they should put enough money down so that they can sustain a moderate drop in home prices and still have positive equity. Low interest rates should have changed the mortgage payments associated with a given amount of borrowing, but not much else.

What actually happened, however, was a complete abandonment of traditional principles. To some extent this was driven by the irrational exuberance of individual families who saw house prices rising ever higher and decided that they should jump into the market, and not worry about how to make the payments. But it was driven to a greater extent by a change in lending practices. Buyers were given loans requiring little or no down payment, and with monthly bills that were well beyond their ability to afford—or at least would be unaffordable once the initial low, teaser interest rate reset. Much though not all of this dubious lending went under the heading of "subprime," but the phenomenon was much broader than that. And it wasn't just low-income or minority home buyers who were taking on more than they could handle; it was happening across the board.

Why did lenders relax their standards? First, they came to believe in ever-rising home prices. As long as home prices only go up, it doesn't matter much from the lender's point of view whether a borrower can make his or her payments: if the payments are too high, well, the buyer can either take out a home equity loan to get more cash or, if worst comes to worst, just sell the home and pay off the mortgage. Second, the lenders didn't concern themselves with the quality of their loans because they didn't hold on to them. Instead, they sold them to investors, who didn't understand what they were buying.

"Securitization" of home mortgages—assembling large pools of mortgages, then selling investors shares in the payments received from borrowers—isn't a new practice. In fact, it was pioneered by Fannie Mae, the government-sponsored lending agency, which dates back to the 1930s. Until the great housing bubble, however, securitization was more or less completely limited to "prime" mortgages: loans to borrowers who could make a substantial down payment and had enough income to meet the mortgage payments. Such borrowers still defaulted now and then, in the wake of job loss or medical emergency, but default rates were low, and buyers of mortgage-backed securities more or less knew what they were buying.

The financial innovation that made securitization of subprime mortgages possible was the collateralized debt obligation, or CDO.

A CDO offered shares in the payments from a mortgage pool—but not all shares were created equal. Instead, some shares were "senior," receiving first claim on the payments from the mortgagees. Only once those claims were satisfied was money sent to less senior shares. In principle, this was supposed to make the senior shares a very safe investment: even if some mortgagees defaulted, how likely was it that enough would default to pose problems for the cash flow to these senior shares? (Quite likely, it turned out—but that wasn't understood at the time.) And so the rating agencies were willing to classify senior shares in CDOs as AAA, even if the underlying mortgages were highly dubious. This opened up large-scale financing of subprime lending, because there are many institutional investors, such as pension funds, that won't buy anything except AAA securities but were quite willing to buy AAA-rated assets that yielded significantly higher returns than ordinary bonds.

As long as housing prices kept rising, everything looked fine and the Ponzi scheme kept rolling. There were few defaults, mortgage-backed securities yielded high returns, and funds continued to pour into the housing market. Some economists, including yours truly, warned that there was a major housing bubble, and that its bursting would pose serious risks to the economy. But authoritative figures declared otherwise. Alan Greenspan, in particular, declared that any major decline in home prices would be "most unlikely." There might, he conceded, be some "froth" in local housing markets, but there wasn't a national bubble.

But there was, and it began deflating in 2006—slowly at first, then with increasing speed. By that time Greenspan was no longer chairman of the Fed, having been succeeded by Ben Bernanke. But Greenspanism still held sway: the Fed (and the Bush administration) believed that the effects of the housing bust could be "contained," that Bernanke, like Greenspan, could serve as America's designated driver.

Yet the experience after the stock bubble popped should have been a clear warning that this confidence was misplaced.

When Bubbles Burst

The story of the aftermath of the 1990s stock bubble is usually told this way: After the bubble burst, the U.S. economy fell into recession. But Greenspan aggressively cut interest rates and quickly turned the situation around. The recession was shallow, with no big declines in GDP, and short, ending after only eight months.

The real story is this: Officially the recession was short, but the job market kept deteriorating long after the recession had officially been declared over. You can see this in the figure on p. 143: the unemployment rate rose steeply during the recession (the shaded bar) but continued to rise in the months that followed. The period of deteriorating employment actually lasted two and a half years, not eight months.

You might ask why, in this case, the recession was declared over so soon. Well, in the United States the official starting and ending dates of recessions are determined by an independent committee of economists associated with the National Bureau of Economic Research. The committee looks at a variety of indicators— employment, industrial production, consumer spending, GDP. If all these indicators are going down, a recession is declared. If several of them turn up again, the recession is declared over. By late 2001, industrial production and GDP were rising, though slowly, so that indicated the end of the official recession. But as we've seen, the job market was still getting worse.

And the Fed was deeply worried about the weakness of the job market and the general sluggishness of the economy, which seemed all too reminiscent of Japan in the 1990s. Greenspan would later write that he was concerned about the possibility of "corrosive deflation." So he kept cutting rates, eventually bringing the Federal funds rate down to just 1 percent.

When monetary policy finally did get traction, it was through the housing market. Cynics said that Greenspan had succeeded only by replacing the stock bubble with a housing bubble—and they were right. And the question everyone should have been asking (but few were) was, What will happen when the housing bubble bursts? The Fed was barely able to pull the economy out of its post-stock-bubble slump, and even then it was able to do so only because it was lucky enough to have another bubble come along at the right time. Would the Fed be able to pull off the feat again?

In the event, the consequences when the housing bubble burst were worse than almost anyone imagined. Why? Because the financial system had changed in ways that nobody fully appreciated.

8

BANKING IN THE SHADOWS

B anks are wonderful things, when they work. And they usually do. But when they don't, all hell can break loose—as it has in the United States and much of the world over the course of the past year.

But wasn't the age of banking crises supposed to have ended seventy years ago? Aren't banks regulated, insured, guaranteed up the wazoo? Yes and no. Yes for traditional banks; no for a large part of the modern, de facto banking system.

To understand the problem, it helps to run through a brief, selective history of banking and bank regulation.

The History of Banking, Simplified

Modern banks are supposed to have originated with goldsmiths, whose primary business was making jewelry but who developed a profitable sideline as keepers of other people's coin: since gold-smiths' shops had good safes, they provided more secure places for the wealthy to stash their cash than, say, a strongbox under the bed. (Think of Silas Marner.)

At some point goldsmiths discovered that they could make their sideline as keepers of coin even more profitable by taking some of the coin deposited in their care and lending it out at interest. You might think this would get them in trouble: what if the own-ers of the coin showed up and demanded it right away? But what the goldsmiths realized was that the law of averages made this unlikely: on any given day some of their depositors would show up and demand their coin back, but most would not. So it was enough to keep a fraction of the coin in reserve; the rest could be put to work. And thus banking was born.

Every once in a while, however, things would go spectacularly wrong. There would be a rumor—maybe true, maybe false—that a bank's investments had gone bad, that it no longer had enough assets to repay its depositors. The rumor would cause a rush by depositors to get their money out before it was all gone—what we call "a run on the bank." And often such a run would break the bank even if the original rumor was false: in order to raise cash quickly, the bank would have to sell off assets at fire-sale prices, and sure enough, at those prices it *wouldn't* have enough assets to pay what it owed. Since runs based even on false rumors could break healthy institutions, bank runs became self-fulfilling prophe-cies: a bank might collapse, not because there was a rumor about its investments having gone bad, but simply because there was a rumor that it was about to suffer from a run.

And one thing that could cause such a rumor is the fact that other banks had already suffered from bank runs. The history of the U.S. financial system before the Great Depression is punctuated by "panics": the Panic of 1873, the Panic of 1907, and so on. These panics were, for the most part, series of contagious bank runs in which each bank's collapse undermined confidence in other banks, and financial institutions fell like a row of dominoes.

By the way, any resemblance between this description of pre-Depression panics and the financial contagion that swept Asia in the late 1990s is not at all coincidental. All financial crises tend to bear a family resemblance to one another.

The problem of banking panics led to a search for solutions. Between the Civil War and World War I the United States did not have a central bank—the Federal Reserve was created in 1913—but it did have a system of "national banks" that were subject to a modest degree of regulation. Also, in some locations bankers pooled their resources to create local clearinghouses that would jointly guarantee a member's liabilities in the event of a panic, and some state governments began offering deposit insurance on their banks' deposits.

The Panic of 1907, however, showed the limitations of this system (and eerily prefigured our current crisis). The crisis originated in institutions in New York known as "trusts," bank-like institutions that accepted deposits but were originally intended to manage only inheritances and estates for wealthy clients. Because they were supposed to engage only in low-risk activities, trusts were less regulated and had lower reserve requirements and lower cash reserves than national banks. However, as the economy boomed during the first decade of the twentieth century, trusts began speculating in real estate and the stock market, areas from which national banks were prohibited. Because they were less regulated than national banks, trusts were able to pay their depositors higher returns. Meanwhile, trusts took a free ride on national banks' reputation for soundness, with depositors considering them equally safe. As a result, trusts grew rapidly: by 1907, the total value of the assets in the trusts in New York City was as high as the total in the national banks. Meanwhile, the trusts declined to join the New York Clearinghouse, a consortium of New York City national banks that guaranteed each other's soundness, because that would have required the trusts to hold higher cash reserves, reducing their profits.

The Panic of 1907 began with the demise of the Knickerbocker Trust, a large New York City trust that failed when it financed an unsuccessful large-scale speculation in the stock market. Quickly, other New York trusts came under pressure, with frightened depositors queuing in long lines to withdraw their funds. The New York Clearinghouse declined to step in and lend to the trusts, and even healthy ones came under serious assault. Within two days a dozen major trusts had gone under. Credit markets froze, and the stock market fell dramatically as stock traders were unable to get credit to finance their trades and business confidence evaporated.

Fortunately, New York City's wealthiest man, a banker by the name of J. P. Morgan, quickly stepped in to stop the panic. Understanding that the crisis was spreading and would soon engulf healthy institutions, trusts and banks alike, he worked with other bankers, wealthy men such as John D. Rockefeller, and the U.S. secretary of the treasury to shore up the reserves of banks and trusts so they could withstand the onslaught of withdrawals. Once people were assured that they could withdraw their money, the panic ceased. While the panic itself lasted little more than a week, it and the stock market collapse decimated the economy. A four-year recession ensued, with production falling 11 percent and unemployment rising from 3 to 8 percent.

Although disaster had been narrowly avoided, counting on J. P. Morgan to save the world a second time didn't seem like a good idea, even in the Gilded Age. So the Panic of 1907 was followed by banking reform. In 1913 the national banking system was eliminated, and the Federal Reserve System was created with the goal of compelling all deposit-taking institutions to hold adequate reserves and open their accounts to inspection by regulators. Although the new regime standardized and centralized the holding of bank reserves, it didn't eliminate the threat of bank runs—and the most severe banking crisis in history emerged in the early 1930s. As the economy slumped, commodity prices plunged; this hit highly indebted American farmers hard, precipitating a series of loan defaults followed by bank runs in 1930, 1931, and 1933, each of which started at Midwestern banks and then spread throughout the country. There's more or less unanimous agreement among economic historians that the banking crisis is what turned a nasty recession into the Great Depression.

The response was the creation of a system with many more safeguards. The Glass-Steagall Act separated banks into two kinds: commercial banks, which accepted deposits, and investment banks, which didn't. Commercial banks were sharply restricted in the risks they could take; in return, they had ready access to credit from the Fed (the so-called discount window), and, probably most important of all, their deposits were insured by the taxpayer. Investment banks were much less tightly regulated, but that was considered acceptable because as nondepository institutions they weren't supposed to be subject to bank runs.

This new system protected the economy from financial crises for almost seventy years. Things often went wrong—most notably, in the 1980s a combination of bad luck and bad policy led to the failure of many savings and loans, a special kind of bank that had become the dominant source of housing loans. Since S&L deposits were federally insured, taxpayers ended up footing the bill, which ended up being about 5 percent of GDP (the equivalent of more than $700 billion now). The fall of the S&Ls led to a temporary credit crunch, which was one major cause of the 1990–91 recession, visible in the figure on p. 143. But that was as bad as it got. The age of banking crises, we were told, was over.

It wasn't.

The Shadow Banking System

What is a bank?

That can sound like a stupid question. We all know what a bank looks like: it's a big marble building—okay, these days it might also be a storefront in a shopping mall—with tellers accepting and handing out cash, and an "FDIC insured" sign in the window.

But from an economist's point of view, banks are defined not by what they look like but by what they do. From the days of those enterprising goldsmiths to the present day, the essential feature of banking is the way it promises ready access to cash for those who place money in its care, even while investing most of that money in assets that can't be liquidated on a moment's notice. Any institution or arrangement that does this is a bank, whether or not it lives in a big marble building.

Consider, for example, an arrangement known as an auction-rate security, which was invented at Lehman Brothers in 1984 and became a preferred source of funding for many institutions, ranging from the Port Authority of New York and New Jersey to New York's Metropolitan Museum of Art. The arrangement worked like this: Individuals would lend money to the borrowing institution on a long-term basis; legally, the money might be tied up for thirty years. At frequent intervals, however, often once a week, the institution would hold a small auction in which potential new investors would bid for the right to replace investors who wanted to get out. The interest rate determined by this bidding process would apply to all funds invested in the security until the next auction was held, and so on. If the auction failed—if there weren't enough bidders to let everyone who wanted out to leave—the interest rate would rise to a penalty rate, say 15 percent; but that wasn't expected to happen. The idea of an auction-rate security was that it would reconcile the desire of borrowers for secure long-term funding with the desire of lenders for ready access to their money.

But that's exactly what a bank does.

Yet auction-rate securities seemed to offer everyone a better deal than conventional banking. Investors in auction-rate securities were paid higher interest rates than they would have received on bank deposits, while the issuers of these securities paid lower rates than they would have on long-term bank loans. There's no such thing as a free lunch, Milton Friedman told us, yet auction-rate securities seemed to offer just that. How did they do that?

Well, the answer seems obvious, at least in retrospect: Banks are highly regulated; they are required to hold liquid reserves, maintain substantial capital, and pay into the deposit insurance system. By raising funds via auction-rate securities, borrowers could bypass these regulations and their attendant expense. But that also meant that auction-rate securities weren't protected by the banking safety net.

And sure enough, the auction-rate security system, which contained $400 billion at its peak, collapsed in early 2008. One after another, auctions failed, as too few new investors arrived to let existing investors get their money out. People who thought they had ready access to their cash suddenly discovered that their money was, instead, tied up in decades-long investments they couldn't get out of. And each auction failure led to another: having seen the perils of these too-clever investment schemes, who wanted to put fresh money into the system?

What happened to auction-rate securities was, in all but name, a contagious series of bank runs.

The parallel to the Panic of 1907 should be obvious. In the early years of the twentieth century, the trusts, the bank-like institutions that seemed to offer a better deal because they were able to operate outside the regulatory system, grew rapidly, only to become the epicenter of a financial crisis. A century later, the same thing happened.

Today, the set of institutions and arrangements that act as "nonbank banks" are generally referred to either as the "parallel banking system" or as the "shadow banking system." I think the latter term is more descriptive as well as more picturesque. Conventional banks, which take deposits and are part of the Federal Reserve system, operate more or less in the sunlight, with open books and regulators looking over their shoulders. The operations of nondepository institutions that are de facto banks, by contrast, are far more obscure. Indeed, until the crisis hit, few people seem to have appreciated just how important the shadow banking system had become.

In June 2008 Timothy Geithner, the president of the New York Federal Reserve Bank, gave a speech at the Economic Club of New York in which he tried to explain how the end of the housing bubble could have done as much financial damage as it did. (Geithner didn't know this, but the worst was yet to come.) Even though the speech was, necessarily, written in centralbankerese, with a hefty dose of jargon, Geithner's shock at how out of control the system had gotten comes through:

The structure of the financial system changed fundamentally during the boom, with dramatic growth in the share of assets outside the traditional banking system. This non-bank financial system grew to be very large, particularly in money and funding markets. In early 2007, asset-backed commercial paper conduits, in structured investment vehicles, in auction-rate preferred securities, tender option bonds and variable rate demand notes, had a combined asset size of roughly $2.2 trillion. Assets financed overnight in triparty repo grew to $2.5 trillion. Assets held in hedge funds grew to roughly $1.8 trillion. The combined balance sheets of the then five major investment banks totaled $4 trillion.

In comparison, the total assets of the top five bank holding companies in the United States at that point were just over $6 trillion, and total assets of the entire banking system were about $10 trillion.

Geithner, then, considered a whole range of financial arrangements, not just auction-rate securities, to be part of the "non-bank financial system": things that weren't banks from a regulatory point of view but were nonetheless performing banking functions. And he went on to point out just how vulnerable the new system was:

The scale of long-term risky and relatively illiquid assets financed by very short-term liabilities made many of the vehicles and institutions in this parallel financial system vulnerable to a classic type of run, but without the protections such as deposit insurance that the banking system has in place to reduce such risks.

Indeed, several of the sectors he described have already collapsed: auction-rate securities have vanished, as already described;

asset-backed commercial paper (short-term debt issued by funds that invested the money in long-term assets, including mortgage-backed securities) has withered; two of the five major investment banks have failed and another has merged with a conventional bank; and so on. And it turns out that Geithner was missing some additional major points of vulnerability: the government in effect had to nationalize AIG, the world's largest insurance company, and the carry trade—an international financial arrangement that transferred funds from Japan and other low-interest-rate nations to higher-yielding investments elsewhere in the world—imploded as this new edition was going to press.

But let's postpone discussion of the crisis until the next chapter, and instead ask about the buildup to the crisis: why was the system allowed to become so vulnerable?

Malign Neglect

The financial crisis has, inevitably, led to a hunt for villains.

Some of the accusations are entirely spurious, like the claim, popular on the right, that all our problems were caused by the Community Reinvestment Act, which supposedly forced banks to lend to minority home buyers who then defaulted on their mortgages; in fact, the act was passed in 1977, which makes it hard to see how it can be blamed for a crisis that didn't happen until three decades later. Anyway, the act applied only to depository banks, which accounted for a small fraction of the bad loans during the housing bubble.

Other accusations have a grain of truth, but are more wrong than right. Conservatives like to blame Fannie Mae and Freddie Mac, the government-sponsored lenders that pioneered securitization, for the housing bubble and the fragility of the financial system. The grain of truth here is that Fannie and Freddie, which had grown enormously between 1990 and 2003—largely because they were filling the hole left by the collapse of many savings and loans—did make some imprudent loans, and suffered from accounting scandals besides. But the very scrutiny Fannie and Freddie attracted as a result of those scandals kept them mainly out of the picture during the housing bubble's most feverish period, from 2004 to 2006. As a result, the agencies played only a minor role in the epidemic of bad lending.

On the left, it's popular to blame deregulation for the crisis—specifically, the 1999 repeal of the Glass-Steagall Act, which allowed commercial banks to get into the investment banking business and thereby take on more risks. In retrospect, this was surely a move in the wrong direction, and it may have contributed in subtle ways to the crisis—for example, some of the risky financial structures created during the boom years were the "off balance sheet" operations of commercial banks. Yet the crisis, for the most part, hasn't involved problems with deregulated institutions that took new risks. Instead, it has involved risks taken by institutions that were never regulated in the first place.

And that, I'd argue, is the core of what happened. As the shadow banking system expanded to rival or even surpass conventional banking in importance, politicians and government officials should have realized that we were re-creating the kind of financial vulnerability that made the Great Depression possible—and they should have responded by extending regulation and the financial safety net to cover these new institutions. Influential figures should have proclaimed a simple rule: anything that does what a bank does, anything that has to be rescued in crises the way banks are, should be regulated like a bank.

In fact, the Long Term Capital Management crisis, described in

Chapter 6, should have served as an object lesson of the dangers posed by the shadow banking system. Certainly many people were aware of just how close the system had come to collapse.

But this warning was ignored, and there was no move to extend regulation. On the contrary, the spirit of the times—and the ideology of the George W. Bush administration—was deeply antiregulation. This attitude was symbolized by a photo-op held in 2003, in which representatives of the various agencies that play roles in bank oversight used pruning shears and a chainsaw to cut up stacks of regulations. More concretely, the Bush administration used federal power, including obscure powers of the Office of the Comptroller of the Currency, to block state-level efforts to impose some oversight on subprime lending.

Meanwhile, the people who should have been worrying about the fragility of the system were, instead, singing the praises of "financial innovation." "Not only have individual financial institutions become less vulnerable to shocks from underlying risk factors," declared Alan Greenspan in 2004, "but also the financial system as a whole has become more resilient."

So the growing risks of a crisis for the financial system and the economy as a whole were ignored or dismissed. And the crisis came.

9

THE SUM OF ALL FEARS

On July 19, 2007, the Dow Jones Industrial Average rose above 14,000 for the first time. Two weeks later the White House released a "fact sheet" boasting about the economy's performance on the Bush administration's watch: "The President's Pro-Growth Policies Are Helping Keep Our Economy Strong, Flexible, and Dynamic," it declared. What about the problems already visible in the housing market and in subprime mortgages? They were "largely contained," said Treasury Secretary Henry Paulson in an August 1 speech in Beijing.

On August 9 the French bank BNP Paribas suspended withdrawals from three of its funds—and the first great financial crisis of the twenty-first century had begun.

I'm tempted to say that the crisis is like nothing we've ever seen before. But it might be more accurate to say that it's like everything we've seen before, all at once: a bursting real estate bubble comparable to what happened in Japan at the end of the 1980s; a wave of bank runs comparable to those of the early 1930s (albeit mainly involving the shadow banking system rather than conventional banks); a liquidity trap in the United States, again reminiscent of Japan; and, most recently, a disruption of international capital flows and a wave of currency crises all too reminiscent of what happened to Asia in the late 1990s.

Let's tell the tale.

The Housing Bust and Its Fallout

The great U.S. housing boom began to deflate in the fall of 2005—but it took a while for most people to notice. As prices rose to the point where purchasing a home became out of reach for many Americans—even with no-down-payment, teaser-rate loans—sales began to slacken off. There was, as I wrote at the time, a hissing sound as air began to leak out of the bubble.

Yet housing prices kept rising for a while. This was to be expected. Houses aren't like stocks, with a single market price that changes minute by minute. Each house is unique, and sellers expect to wait a while before actually finding a buyer. As a result, prices tend to be based on what other houses have sold for in the recent past: sellers don't start cutting prices until it becomes painfully obvious that they aren't going to get a full-price offer. In 2005, after an extended period during which home prices had been rising sharply each year, sellers expected the trend to continue, so asking prices actually continued to rise for a while even as sales dropped.

By the late spring of 2006, however, the weakness of the market was starting to sink in. Prices began dropping, slowly at first, then with growing speed. By the second quarter of 2007, according to the widely used Case-Shiller home price index, prices were only down about 3 percent from their peak a year earlier. Over the course of the next year they fell more than 15 percent. The price declines were, of course, much larger in the regions that had experienced the biggest bubbles, like coastal Florida.

Even the gradual initial decline in home prices, however, undermined the assumptions on which the boom in subprime lending was based. Remember, the key rationale for this lending was the belief that it didn't really matter, from the lender's point of view, whether the borrower could actually make the mortgage payments: as long as home prices kept rising, troubled borrowers could always either refinance or pay off their mortgage by selling the house. As soon as home prices started falling instead of rising, and houses became hard to sell, default rates began rising. And at that point another ugly truth became apparent: foreclosure isn't just a tragedy for the homeowners, it's a lousy deal for the lender. Between the time it takes to get a foreclosed home back on the market, the legal expenses, the degradation that tends to happen in vacant homes, and so on, creditors seizing a house from the borrower typically get back only part, say half, of the original value of the loan.

In that case, you might ask, why not make a deal with the current homeowner to reduce payments and avoid the costs of foreclosure? Well, for one thing, that also costs money, and it requires staff. And subprime loans were not, for the most part, made by banks that held on to the loans; they were made by loan originators, who quickly sold the loans to financial institutions, which, in turn, sliced and diced pools of mortgages into collateralized debt obligations (CDOs) sold to investors. The actual management of the loans was left to loan servicers, who had neither the resources nor, for the most part, the incentive to engage in loan restructuring. And one more thing: the complexity of the financial engineering supporting subprime lending, which left ownership of mortgages dispersed among many investors with claims of varying seniority, created formidable legal obstacles to any kind of debt forgiveness.

So restructuring was mostly out, leading to costly foreclosures. And this meant that securities backed by subprime mortgages turned into very bad investments as soon as the housing boom began to falter.

The first moment of truth came early in 2007, as the trouble with subprime loans first became apparent. Recall that collateralized debt obligations established a seniority ranking for shares: owners of the more senior shares, the ones rating agencies declared to be AAA, had first dibs on payments, with those holding the less senior shares, which were given lower ratings, being paid only after the senior-share holders had received their due. Around February 2007 the realization sank in that the lower-rated shares were probably going to take serious losses, and prices of those shares plunged. This more or less put an end to the whole process of subprime lending: because nobody would buy the junior shares, it was no longer possible to repackage and sell subprime loans, and financing disappeared. This in turn, by removing an important source of housing demand, worsened the housing slump.

Still, for a long time investors believed that the senior shares in those CDOs were reasonably well protected. As late as October 2007, AAA-rated shares in subprime-backed mortgage pools were still trading at close to their face value. Eventually, however, it became clear that nothing related to housing was safe—not senior shares, not even loans made to borrowers with good credit ratings who made substantial down payments.

Why? Because of the sheer scale of the housing bubble. Nationally, housing was probably overvalued by more than 50 percent by the summer of 2006, which meant that to eliminate the overvaluation, prices would have to fall by a third. In some metropolitan areas, the overvaluation was much worse. In Miami, for example, home prices appeared to be at least twice as high as the fundamentals could justify. So in some areas prices could be expected to fall by 50 percent or more.

This meant that practically anyone who bought a house during the peak bubble years, even if he or she put 20 percent down, was going to end up with negative equity—with a mortgage worth more than the house. Indeed, there are probably around 12 million American homeowners with negative equity as this book goes to press. And homeowners with negative equity are prime candidates for default and foreclosure, no matter what their background. For one thing, some of them may simply choose to "walk away"—to walk out on their mortgage, figuring that they will end up ahead financially even after losing the house. It's never been clear how important a phenomenon walking away really is, but there are plenty of other routes to default. Job loss, unexpected medical expenses, divorce—all of these can leave a homeowner unable to make mortgage payments. And if the house is worth less than the mortgage, there is no way to make the lender whole.

As the severity of the housing bust sank in, it became clear that lenders would lose a lot of money, and so would the investors who bought mortgage-backed securities. But why should we cry for these people, as opposed to the homeowners themselves? After all, the end of the housing bubble will probably, when the final reckoning is made, have wiped out about $8 trillion of wealth. Of that, around $7 trillion will have been losses to homeowners, and only about $1 trillion losses to investors. Why obsess about that $1 trillion?

The answer is, because it has triggered the collapse of the shadow banking system.

The Non-Bank Banking Crisis

As we've seen, there were some serious financial tremors in the first half of 2007, but as late as early August the official view was that the problems posed by the housing slump and subprime loans were contained—and the strength of the stock market suggested that markets agreed with the official position. Then, not to put too fine a point on it, all hell broke loose. What happened?

In Chapter 8 I quoted Tim Geithner of the New York Federal Reserve Bank about the risks posed by the rise of the shadow banking system: "The scale of long-term risky and relatively illiquid assets financed by very short-term liabilities made many of the vehicles and institutions in this parallel financial system vulnerable to a classic type of run, but without the protections such as deposit insurance that the banking system has in place to reduce such risks." In that same speech, given in June 2008, he described—in surprisingly vivid language for a central banker—how that run had actually happened. It began with subprime-related losses, which undermined confidence in the shadow banking system. And this led to a vicious cycle of deleveraging:

Once the investors in these financing arrangements—many conservatively managed money funds—withdrew or threatened to withdraw their funds from these markets, the system became vulnerable to a self-reinforcing cycle of forced liquidation of assets, which further increased volatility and lowered prices across a variety of asset classes. In response, margin requirements were increased, or financing was withdrawn altogether from some customers, forcing more de-leveraging. Capital cushions eroded as assets were sold into distressed markets. The force of this dynamic was exacerbated by the

poor quality of assets—particularly mortgage-related assets—
that had been spread across the system. This helps explain
how a relatively small quantity of risky assets was able to
undermine the confidence of investors and other market participants across a much broader range of assets and markets.

Notice Geithner's emphasis on how declining asset values
damaged balance sheets, forcing further asset sales in a self-
reinforcing process. This is, at a fundamental level, the same logic
of deleveraging that led to the self-fulfilling financial crises in Asia
in 1997 and 1998, described in Chapter 4. Highly leveraged players in the economic system suffered losses, which forced them into
actions that led to further losses, and so on. In this case the losses
occurred through the collapsing value of risky financial assets rather
than through the collapsing value of the domestic currency, as in
Indonesia or Argentina, but the story was essentially the same.

And the result of this self-reinforcing process was, in effect, a
massive bank run that caused the shadow banking system to shrivel
up, much as the conventional banking system did in the early 1930s.
Auction-rate securities, in effect a banking sector providing $330 bil-
lion worth of credit, disappeared. Asset-backed commercial paper,
another de facto banking sector, dropped from providing $1.2 trillion
in credit to providing only $700 billion. And so on down the line.

Crazy things began happening in the financial markets. Interest
rates on U.S. Treasury bills—that is, short-term debt—dropped
close to zero. That was because investors were fleeing to safety,
and as one commentator put it, the only things they were willing
to buy were T-bills and bottled water. (U.S. government debt is as
safe as anything on the planet, not because the United States is
the most responsible nation on earth but because a world in which
the U.S. government collapses would be one in which pretty much

everything else collapses too—hence the demand for bottled water.) On a few occasions the interest rates on T-bills actually went negative, because they were the only thing people would accept as collateral in financial deals, and there was a scramble for the limited available supply.

Some borrowers were able to make up for the collapse of the shadow banking system by turning back to conventional banks for credit. One of the seemingly perverse aspects of the crisis has been an expansion of bank credit, which has confused some observers: where's the credit crunch, they ask? But the expansion of old-fashioned bank lending came nowhere near to making up for the collapse in shadow banking.

Consumer credit was the last to go, but by October 2008 there was growing evidence that credit cards were also on the chopping block, with credit limits cut, more applicants turned down, and the whole ability of American consumers, already feeling nervous, to charge things being undermined.

All across the economy, some businesses and individuals were losing access to credit, while others found themselves paying higher interest rates even as the Federal Reserve was trying to push rates down. And that brings us to the emergence of a Japan-style trap for U.S. monetary policy.

The Fed Loses Traction

By the time the financial crisis hit, Alan Greenspan was no longer running the Federal Reserve. In his place—and obliged to deal with the mess he left behind—was Ben Bernanke, a former economics professor at Princeton. (Bernanke was head of the Princeton economics department before leaving for the Fed, and hired me when I moved to Princeton from MIT.)

If you had to choose one individual to be in charge of the Fed during this crisis, that person would be Bernanke. He's a scholar of the Great Depression. His research on the way the banking crisis intensified the Depression led him to make a major theoretical contribution to monetary economics, focusing on the role of credit availability and balance sheet problems in restricting investment (mumble "Bernanke-Gertler" to a group of economists worriedly discussing the crisis, and they'll nod their heads knowingly). And he did extensive research on Japan's troubles in the 1990s. Nobody was more prepared, intellectually, for the mess we're in.

Yet as the crisis has unfolded, the Bernanke Fed has had a very hard time achieving any traction on either the financial markets or the economy as a whole.

The Fed is set up to do two main things: manage interest rates and, when necessary, provide cash to banks. It manages interest rates by buying Treasury bills from banks, thereby increasing their reserves, or selling T-bills to banks, thereby reducing their reserves. It provides cash to specific banks in times of need by lending them money directly. And it has used these tools aggressively since the crisis began. The Fed has cut the Federal funds rate—the overnight rate at which banks lend reserves to one another, which is the normal instrument of monetary policy—from 5.25 percent on the eve of the crisis to just 1 percent at the time of writing. "Total borrowings of depository institutions from the Federal Reserve," a measure of direct lending, have gone from near-zero before the crisis to more than $400 billion.

In normal times, these moves would have led to much easier credit. A fall in the Federal funds rate normally translates into reduced interest rates across the spectrum—lower interest rates on commercial credit, lower interest rates on corporate borrowing, lower mortgage rates. Meanwhile, lending to banks has historically been enough to ease any shortage of liquidity in the financial system. But these are not normal times, and historical precedents haven't applied.

The Fed's lack of traction is most apparent when it comes to riskier borrowers. Most obviously, there aren't any subprime loans being made now, shutting one whole class of potential home buyers out of the market. Businesses without a top credit rating are paying higher interest rates for short-term credit now than they did before the crisis, even though the interest rates the Fed controls have fallen by more than four percentage points. The interest rate on Baa-rated corporate bonds at the time of writing was above 9 percent, compared with about 6.5 percent before the crisis. Down the line, the interest rates that matter for spending and investment decisions have risen or at least failed to fall, in spite of the Fed's attempt to drive rates down.

Even prime mortgage borrowers have been hit: the thirty-year mortgage rate is still roughly where it was in the summer of 2007. That's because the crisis in the financial system more or less knocked private lenders out of the market, leaving only Fannie Mae and Freddie Mac, the government-sponsored lenders, still in business. And Fannie and Freddie found themselves in trouble too: they hadn't made as many bad loans as the private sector, but they had made some, and they had very thin capital bases. In September 2008 the federal government took control of Fannie and Freddie, which should have eased concerns about their debt and reduced mortgage rates. But the Bush administration made a point of denying that Fannie/Freddie debt was backed by the full faith of the U.S. government, so that even after nationalization they continued to have trouble raising funds.

What about all the loans the Federal Reserve made to the banks? They have probably helped, but not as much as one might have expected, because conventional banks aren't at the heart of the crisis. Here's an example: if auction-rate security arrangements had been part of the conventional banking system, the issuers would have been able to borrow from the Fed when too few private investors showed up at the auctions; as a result, the auctions wouldn't have failed and the sector wouldn't have collapsed. Because they weren't part of conventional banks, however, the auctions did fail and the sector did collapse, and no amount of Fed loans to Citibank or Bank of America could do anything to halt the process.

In effect, then, the Fed found itself presiding over a Japan-style liquidity trap, in which conventional monetary policy had lost all traction over the real economy. True, the Fed funds rate hadn't been cut all the way to zero, but there was little reason to think that cutting one more percentage point would have much impact.

What else could the Fed do? In 2004, in scholarly work, Bernanke had argued that monetary policy could be effective, even in a liquidity trap, if one were willing to "alter the composition of the central bank's balance sheet." Instead of only holding Treasury bills and loans to conventional banks, the Fed could make loans to other players: investment banks, money-market funds, maybe even nonfinancial businesses. And over the course of 2008 the Fed introduced an alphabet soup of special lending "facilities" to do just that: the TSLF, the PDCF, and so on. In October 2008 the Fed announced that it would begin buying commercial paper too, in effect proposing to do the lending the private financial system wouldn't or couldn't do.

It remains possible, at the time of writing, that these schemes will eventually bear fruit. What one has to say, however, is that their effects so far have been disappointing. Why? I'd argue that the problem is one of substitution and scale. When the Fed acts to increase the quantity of bank reserves, it's doing something no other institution can do: only the Fed can create monetary base, which can be used as cash in circulation or held as bank reserves. Furthermore, its actions tend to be large relative to the scale of the asset classes involved, since the monetary base is "only" $800 billion. When the Fed tries to support the credit market more broadly, by contrast, it's doing something private actors also do—which means that the credit it pumps into the system may be partly offset by private withdrawals—and it's also trying to move a much bigger beast, the $50 trillion or so credit market.

The Bernanke Fed has also suffered from the problem of being, again and again, behind the curve. The financial crisis keeps developing new dimensions, which few people—including the very smart people at the Fed—see coming. And that brings me to the international dimension of the crisis.

The Mother of All Currency Crises

After the financial crises of 1997 and 1998, the governments of the affected countries tried to protect themselves against a repeat performance. They avoided the foreign borrowing that had made them vulnerable to a cutoff of overseas funding. They built up huge war chests of dollars and euros, which were supposed to protect them in the event of any future emergency. And the conventional wisdom was that the "emerging markets"—Brazil, Russia, India, China, and a host of smaller economies, including the victims of the 1997 crisis—were now "decoupled" from the United States, able to keep growing despite the mess in America. "Decoupling is no myth," *The Economist* assured its readers back in March. "Indeed, it may yet save the world economy."

Unfortunately, that doesn't seem likely. On the contrary, says Stephen Jen, the chief currency strategist at Morgan Stanley, the

"hard landing" in emerging markets may become the "second epicenter" of the global crisis (U.S. financial markets were the first).

What happened? Alongside the growth of the shadow banking
system, there was another transformation in the character of the
financial system over the past fifteen years, with much of it taking
place after the Asian crisis—namely, the rise of financial globalization, with investors in each country holding large stakes in other
countries. In 1996, on the eve of the Asian crisis, the United States
had assets overseas equal to 52 percent of GDP, and liabilities
equal to 57 percent of GDP. By 2007, these numbers were up to
128 percent and 145 percent, respectively. The United States had
moved deeper into net debtor status; but the net is less impressive
than the vast increase in cross-holdings.

Like much of what happened to the financial system over the past
decade or two, this change was supposed to reduce risk: because
U.S. investors held much of their wealth abroad, they were less
exposed to a slump in America, and because foreign investors held
much of their wealth in the United States, they were less exposed
to a slump overseas. But a large part of the increase in financial
globalization actually came from the investments of highly leveraged financial institutions, which were making various sorts of
risky cross-border bets. And when things went wrong in the United
States, these cross-border investments acted as what economists
call a "transmission mechanism," allowing a crisis that started with
the U.S. housing market to drive fresh rounds of crises overseas.
The failure of hedge funds associated with a French bank is generally considered to have marked the beginning of the crisis; by the
fall of 2008, the troubles of housing loans in places like Florida had
destroyed the banking system of Iceland.

In the case of the emerging markets, there was a special point
of vulnerability, the so-called carry trade. This trade involves bor-

rowing in countries with low interest rates, especially but not only Japan, and lending in places with high interest rates, like Brazil and Russia. It was a highly profitable trade as long as nothing went wrong; but eventually something did.

The triggering event seems to have been the fall of Lehman Brothers, the investment bank, on September 15, 2008. When Bear Stearns, another of the original five major investment banks, got in trouble in March 2008, the Fed and the Treasury moved in—not to rescue the firm, which disappeared, but to protect the firm's "counterparties," those to whom it owed money or with whom it had made financial deals. There was a widespread expectation that Lehman would receive the same treatment. But the Treasury Department decided that the consequences of a Lehman failure would not be too severe, and allowed the firm to go under without any protection for its counterparties.

Within days it was clear that this had been a disastrous move: confidence plunged further, asset prices fell off another cliff, and the few remaining working channels of credit dried up. The effective nationalization of AIG, the giant insurer, a few days later, failed to stem the panic.

And one of the casualties of the latest round of panic was the carry trade. The conduit of funds from Japan and other low-interest nations was cut off, leading to a round of self-reinforcing effects all too familiar from the crisis of 1997. Because capital was no longer flowing out of Japan, the value of the yen soared; because capital was no longer flowing into emerging markets, the value of emerging-market currencies plunged. This led to large capital losses for whoever had borrowed in one currency and lent in another. In some cases that meant hedge funds—and the hedge fund industry, which had held up better than expected until the demise of Lehman Brothers, began shrinking rapidly. In other cases it meant firms in emerging markets, which had borrowed cheaply abroad, suddenly faced big losses.

For it turned out that the efforts of emerging-market governments to protect themselves against another crisis had been undone by the private sector's obliviousness to risk. In Russia, for example, banks and corporations rushed to borrow abroad because foreign interest rates were lower than ruble rates. So while the Russian government was accumulating an impressive $560 billion hoard of foreign exchange, Russian corporations and banks were running up an almost equally impressive $460 billion foreign debt. Then, suddenly, these corporations and banks found their credit lines cut off, and the ruble value of their debts surging. And nobody was safe: for example, major Brazilian banks avoided taking on a large foreign exposure but nonetheless found themselves in trouble because their domestic clients hadn't been equally careful.

It all bore a strong resemblance to previous currency crises—Indonesia 1997, Argentina 2002. But it was on a far larger scale. This, truly, is the mother of all currency crises, and it represents a fresh disaster for the world's financial system.

A Global Slump

Most of this chapter has been taken up with the financial aspects of the crisis. What does all this portend for the "real economy," the economy of jobs, wages, and production? Nothing good.

The United States, Britain, Spain, and several other countries probably would have suffered recessions when their housing bubbles burst even if the financial system hadn't broken down. Falling home prices have a direct negative effect on employment through the decline in construction, and they tend to lead to reduced consumer spending because consumers feel poorer and lose access to home equity loans; these negatives have a multiplier effect as falling employment leads to further declines in spending. That said, the U.S. economy actually held up fairly well at first in the face of the housing bust, mainly because the weakness of the dollar led to rising exports, which helped offset the decline in construction.

But the financial collapse seems certain to turn what might have been a run-of-the-mill recession—the U.S. employment rate began to drop at the end of 2007, but until September 2008 the decline was fairly modest—into something much, much worse. The intensification of the credit crisis after the fall of Lehman Brothers, the sudden crisis in emerging markets, a collapse in consumer confidence as the scale of the financial mess hit the headlines, all point to the worst recession in the United States, and in the world as a whole, since the early 1980s. And many economists will be relieved if it's only that bad.

And what's really worrying is the loss of policy traction. The recession of 1981–82, which drove the unemployment rate above 10 percent, was a terrible thing, but it was also more or less a deliberate choice: the Fed pursued a tight-money policy to break the back of inflation, and as soon as Fed Chairman Paul Volcker decided the economy had suffered enough, he undid the screws, and the economy came roaring back. Economic devastation turned into "morning in America" with startling speed.

This time, by contrast, the economy is stalling despite repeated efforts by policymakers to get it going again. This policy helplessness is reminiscent of Japan in the 1990s. It's also reminiscent of the 1930s. We're not in a depression now, and despite everything, I don't think we're heading into one (although I'm not as sure of that as I'd like to be). We are, however, well into the realm of depression economics.

10

THE RETURN OF
DEPRESSION ECONOMICS

The world economy is not in depression; it probably won't fall into depression, despite the magnitude of the current crisis (although I wish I was completely sure about that). But while depression itself has not returned, depression economics—the kinds of problems that characterized much of the world economy in the 1930s but have not been seen since—has staged a stunning comeback. Fifteen years ago hardly anybody thought that modern nations would be forced to endure bone-crushing recessions for fear of currency speculators, and that major advanced nations would find themselves persistently unable to generate enough spending to keep their workers and factories employed. The world economy has turned out to be a much more dangerous place than we imagined.

How did the world become this dangerous? More important, how do we get out of the current crisis, and what can we do to prevent such crises from happening in the first place? In this book I have told many stories; now it is time to try to draw some morals.

What Is Depression Economics?

What does it mean to say that depression economics has returned? Essentially it means that for the first time in two generations, failures on the demand side of the economy—insufficient private spending to make use of the available productive capacity—have become the clear and present limitation on prosperity for a large part of the world.

We—by which I mean not only economists but also policymakers and the educated public at large—weren't ready for this. The specific set of foolish ideas that has laid claim to the name "supply-side economics" is a crank doctrine that would have had little influence if it did not appeal to the prejudices of editors and wealthy men. But over the past few decades there has been a steady drift in emphasis in economic thinking away from the demand side to the supply side of the economy.

This drift was partly the result of theoretical disputes within economics that—as they so often do—gradually filtered out, in somewhat garbled form, into wider discourse. Briefly, the source of the theoretical disputes was this: in principle, shortfalls of overall demand would cure themselves if only wages and prices fell rapidly in the face of unemployment. In the story of the depressed baby-sitting co-op, one way the situation could have resolved itself would have been for the price of an hour of baby-sitting in terms of coupons to fall, so that the purchasing power of the existing supply of coupons would have risen, and the co-op would have returned to "full employment" without any action by its management. In reality prices don't fall quickly in the face of recession, but economists have been unable to agree about exactly why. The result has been a series of bitter academic battles that have made the whole subject of recessions and how they happen a sort of professional minefield in which ever fewer economists dare to tread. And the public has understandably concluded either that economists don't understand recessions or that demand-side remedies have been discredited. The truth is that good old-fashioned demand-side macroeconomics has a lot to offer in our current predicament—but its defenders lack all conviction, while its critics are filled with a passionate intensity.

Paradoxically, if the theoretical weaknesses of demand-side economics are one reason we were unready for the return of depression-type issues, its practical successes are another. During all the decades that economists have argued with one another over whether monetary policy can actually be used to get an economy out of a recession, central banks have repeatedly gone ahead and used it to do just that—so effectively in fact that the idea of a prolonged economic slump due to insufficient demand became implausible. Surely the Federal Reserve and its counterparts in other countries could always cut interest rates enough to keep spending high; except in the very short run, then, the only limitation on economic performance was an economy's ability to produce—that is, the supply side.

Even now, many economists still think of recessions as a minor issue, their study as a faintly disreputable subject. Robert Lucas's presidential address, which I quoted in Chapter 1, explicitly made the case that the business cycle was no longer an important subject, and that economists should shift their attention to technological progress and long-run growth. These are fine, important issues, and in the long run they are what really matter—but as Keynes pointed out, in the long run we are all dead.

Meanwhile, in the short run the world is lurching from crisis to crisis, all of them crucially involving the problem of generating sufficient demand. Japan from the early 1990s onward, Mexico in 1995, Mexico, Thailand, Malaysia, Indonesia, and Korea in 1997, Argentina in 2002, and just about everyone in 2008—one country after another has experienced a recession that at least temporarily undoes years of economic progress, and finds that the conventional policy responses don't seem to have any effect. Once again, the question of how to create enough demand to make use of the economy's capacity has become crucial. Depression economics is back.

What to Do: Dealing with the Emergency

What the world needs right now is a rescue operation. The global credit system is in a state of paralysis, and a global slump is building momentum as I write this. Reform of the weaknesses that made this crisis possible is essential, but it can wait a little while. First, we need to deal with the clear and present danger. To do this, policymakers around the world need to do two things: get credit flowing again and prop up spending.

The first task is the harder of the two, but it must be done, and soon. Hardly a day goes by without news of some further disaster wreaked by the freezing up of credit. As I wrote this draft, for example, reports were coming in of the collapse of letters of credit, the key financing method for world trade. Suddenly, buyers of imports, especially in developing countries, can't carry through on their deals, and ships are standing idle: the Baltic Dry Index, a widely used measure of shipping costs, has fallen 89 percent this year.

What lies behind the credit squeeze is the combination of reduced trust in and decimated capital at financial institutions. People and institutions, including the financial institutions, don't want to deal with anyone unless they have substantial capital to back up their promises, yet the crisis has depleted capital across the board.

The obvious solution is to put in more capital. In fact, that's a standard response in financial crises. In 1933 the Roosevelt administration used the Reconstruction Finance Corporation to recapitalize banks by buying preferred stock—stock that had seniority over common stock in terms of its claims on profits. When Sweden experienced a financial crisis in the early 1990s, the government stepped in and provided the banks with additional capital equal to 4 percent of the country's GDP—the equivalent of about $600 billion for the United States today—in return for a partial ownership. When Japan moved to rescue its banks in 1998, it purchased more than $500 billion in preferred stock, the equivalent relative to GDP of around a $2 trillion capital injection in the United States. In each case, the provision of capital helped restore the ability of banks to lend, and unfroze the credit markets.

A financial rescue along similar lines is now underway in the United States and other advanced economies, although it was late in coming, thanks in part to the ideological tilt of the Bush administration. At first, after the fall of Lehman Brothers, the Treasury Department proposed buying up $700 billion in troubled assets from banks and other financial institutions. Yet it was never clear how this was supposed to help the situation. (If the Treasury paid market value, it would do little to help the banks' capital position, while if it paid above-market value it would stand accused of throwing taxpayers' money away.) Never mind: after dithering for three weeks, the United States followed the lead already set first by Britain and then by continental European countries, and turned the plan into a recapitalization scheme.

It seems doubtful, however, that this will be enough to turn things around, for at least three reasons. First, even if the full $700 billion is used for recapitalization (so far only a fraction has been committed), it will still be small, relative to GDP, compared with the Japanese bank bailout—and it's arguable that the severity of the financial crisis in the United States and Europe now rivals that of Japan. Second, it's still not clear how much of the bailout will reach the shadow banking system, the core of the problem. Third, it's not clear whether banks will be willing to lend out the funds, as opposed to sitting on them (a problem encountered by the New Deal seventy-five years ago).

My guess is that the recapitalization will eventually have to get bigger and broader, and that there will eventually have to be more assertion of government control—in effect, it will come closer to a full temporary nationalization of a significant part of the financial system. Just to be clear, this isn't a long-term goal, a matter of seizing the economy's commanding heights: finance should be reprivatized as soon as it's safe to do so, just as Sweden put banking back in the private sector after its big bailout in the early nineties. But for now the important thing is to loosen up credit by any means at hand, without getting tied up in ideological knots. Nothing could be worse than failing to do what's necessary out of fear that acting to save the financial system is somehow "socialist."

The same goes for another line of approach to resolving the credit crunch: getting the feds, temporarily, into the business of lending directly to the nonfinancial sector. The Federal Reserve's willingness to buy commercial paper is a major step in this direction, but more will probably be necessary.

All these actions should be coordinated with other advanced countries. The reason is the globalization of finance, described in Chapter 9. Part of the payoff to U.S. rescues of the financial system is that they help loosen up access to credit in Europe; part of the payoff to European rescue efforts is that they loosen up credit here. So everyone should be doing more or less the same thing; we're all in this together.

And one more thing: the spread of the financial crisis to emerging markets makes a global rescue for developing countries part of the solution to the crisis. As with recapitalization, parts of this were already in place at the time of writing: the International Monetary Fund was providing loans to countries with troubled economies like Ukraine, with less of the moralizing and demands for austerity that it engaged in during the Asian crisis of the 1990s. Meanwhile, the Fed provided swap lines to several emerging-market central banks, giving them the right to borrow dollars as needed. As with recapitalization, the efforts so far look as if they're in the right direction but too small, so more will be needed.

Even if the rescue of the financial system starts to bring credit markets back to life, we'll still face a global slump that's gathering momentum. What should be done about that? The answer, almost surely, is good old Keynesian fiscal stimulus.

Now, the United States tried a fiscal stimulus in early 2008; both the Bush administration and congressional Democrats touted it as a plan to "jump-start" the economy. The actual results were, however, disappointing, for two reasons. First, the stimulus was too small, accounting for only about 1 percent of GDP. The next one should be much bigger, say, as much as 4 percent of GDP. Second, most of the money in the first package took the form of tax rebates, many of which were saved rather than spent. The next plan should focus on sustaining and expanding government spending—sustaining it by providing aid to state and local governments, expanding it with spending on roads, bridges, and other forms of infrastructure.

The usual objection to public spending as a form of economic stimulus is that it takes too long to get going—that by the time the boost to demand arrives, the slump is over. That doesn't seem to be a major worry now, however: it's very hard to see any quick economic recovery, unless some unexpected new bubble arises to replace the housing bubble. (A headline in the satirical newspaper *The Onion* captured the problem perfectly: "Recession-Plagued Nation Demands New Bubble to Invest In.") As long as public spending is pushed along with reasonable speed, it should arrive in plenty of time to help—and it has two great advantages over tax breaks. On one side, the money would actually be spent; on the other, something of value (e.g., bridges that don't fall down) would be created.

Some readers may object that providing a fiscal stimulus through public works spending is what Japan did in the 1990s—and it is. Even in Japan, however, public spending probably prevented a weak economy from plunging into an actual depression. There are, moreover, reasons to believe that stimulus through public spending would work better in the United States, if done promptly, than it did in Japan. For one thing, we aren't yet stuck in the trap of deflationary expectations that Japan fell into after years of insufficiently forceful policies. And Japan waited far too long to recapitalize its banking system, a mistake we hopefully won't repeat.

The point in all of this is to approach the current crisis in the spirit that we'll do whatever it takes to turn things around; if what has been done so far isn't enough, do more and do something different, until credit starts to flow and the real economy starts to recover.

And once the recovery effort is well underway, it will be time to turn to prophylactic measures: reforming the system so that the crisis doesn't happen again.

Financial Reform

We have magneto trouble, said John Maynard Keynes at the start of the Great Depression: most of the economic engine was in good shape, but a crucial component, the financial system, wasn't working. He also said this: "We have involved ourselves in a colossal muddle, having blundered in the control of a delicate machine, the working of which we do not understand." Both statements are as true now as they were then.

How did this second great colossal muddle arise? In the aftermath of the Great Depression, we redesigned the machine so that we *did* understand it, well enough at any rate to avoid big disasters. Banks, the piece of the system that malfunctioned so badly in the 1930s, were placed under tight regulation and supported by a strong safety net. Meanwhile, international movements of capital, which played a disruptive role in the 1930s, were also limited. The financial system became a little boring but much safer.

Then things got interesting and dangerous again. Growing international capital flows set the stage for devastating currency crises in the 1990s and for a globalized financial crisis in 2008. The growth of the shadow banking system, without any corresponding extension of regulation, set the stage for latter-day bank runs on a massive scale. These runs involved frantic mouse clicks rather than frantic mobs outside locked bank doors, but they were no less devastating.

What we're going to have to do, clearly, is relearn the lessons our grandfathers were taught by the Great Depression. I won't try to lay out the details of a new regulatory regime, but the basic principle should be clear: anything that has to be rescued during a financial crisis, because it plays an essential role in the financial mechanism, should be regulated when there *isn't* a crisis so that it doesn't take excessive risks. Since the 1930s commercial banks have been required to have adequate capital, hold reserves of liquid assets that can be quickly converted into cash, and limit the types of investments they make, all in return for federal guarantees when things go wrong. Now that we've seen a wide range of non-bank institutions create what amounts to a banking crisis, comparable regulation has to be extended to a much larger part of the system.

We're also going to have to think hard about how to deal with financial globalization. In the aftermath of the Asian crisis of the 1990s, there were some calls for long-term restrictions on international capital flows, not just temporary controls in times of crisis. For the most part these calls were rejected in favor of a strategy of building up large foreign exchange reserves that were supposed to stave off future crises. Now it seems that this strategy didn't work. For countries like Brazil and Korea, it must seem like a nightmare: after all that they've done, they're going through the 1990s crisis all over again. Exactly what form the next response should take isn't clear, but financial globalization has definitely turned out to be even more dangerous than we realized.

The Power of Ideas

As readers may have gathered, I believe not only that we're living in a new era of depression economics, but also that John Maynard Keynes—the economist who made sense of the Great Depression—is now more relevant than ever. Keynes concluded his masterwork, *The General Theory of Employment, Interest and Money*, with a famous disquisition on the importance of economic ideas: "Soon or late, it is ideas, not vested interests, which are dangerous for good or evil."

We can argue about whether that's always true, but in times like these, it definitely is. The quintessential economic sentence is supposed to be "There is no free lunch"; it says that there are limited resources, that to have more of one thing you must accept less of another, that there is no gain without pain. Depression economics, however, is the study of situations where there *is* a free lunch, if we can only figure out how to get our hands on it, because there are unemployed resources that could be put to work. The true scarcity in Keynes's world—and ours—was therefore not of resources, or even of virtue, but of understanding.

We will not achieve the understanding we need, however, unless we are willing to think clearly about our problems and to follow those thoughts wherever they lead. Some people say that our economic problems are structural, with no quick cure available; but I believe that the only important structural obstacles to world prosperity are the obsolete doctrines that clutter the minds of men.

PENGUIN CLASSICS

THE WEALTH OF NATIONS
ADAM SMITH

Edited with an introduction and notes by Andrew Skinner

'It is not from the benevolence of the butcher, the brewer, or the baker that we expect our dinner, but from their regard to their own interest'

With this landmark treatise on political economy, Adam Smith paved the way for modern capitalism, arguing that a truly free market – fired by competition yet guided as if by an 'invisible hand' to ensure justice and equality – was the engine of a fair and productive society. *The Wealth of Nations* examines the 'division of labour as the key to economic growth, by ensuring the interdependence of individuals within society. Smith's work laid the foundations of economic theory in general and 'classical' economics in particular, but the real sophistication of his analysis derives from the fact that it also encompasses a combination of ethics, philosophy and history to create a vast panorama of society.

Published in two volumes (Books I-III and Books IV-V), this edition contains an in-depth discussion of Smith as an economist and social scientist, as well as a preface, further reading and explanatory notes.

PENGUIN POLITICS / ECONOMICS

**THE TRUTH ABOUT MARKETS: WHY SOME NATIONS ARE RICH
BUT MOST REMAIN POOR**
JOHN KAY

'Readers of this illuminating book will better understand what has gone wrong
with the market economy and what should be done about it' Joseph Stiglitz,
author of *Globalization and Its Discontents*

'Ambitious and brilliantly executed ... accessible and witty ... John Kay exposes
the flaws of the American business model' *The Times*

Capitalism faltered at the end of the 1990s as corporations were rocked by fraud
and the state of the stock-market, and the American business model – unfettered
self-interest, privatization and low tax – faced a storm of protest. But what are the
alternatives to the mantras of market fundamentalism?

Leading economist John Kay unravels the truth about markets, from Wall Street to
Switzerland, from Russia to Mumbai, examining why some nations are rich and
some poor, why 'one-size-fits-all' globalization hurts developing countries and
why markets *can* work – but only in a humane social and cultural context. His
answers offer a radical new blueprint for the future.

'Profound ... a landmark work' Will Hutton

'Kay shows how markets really work – everything you wanted to know about
economics but were afraid to ask' Mervyn King, Governor of the Bank of
England

'Written with wit and subtlety ... An important contribution to the post-1990s
reassessment of capitalism' Martin Vander Weyer, *Daily Telegraph*

'The big idea of the moment ... offers one of the most truthful and fruitful ways
in years of looking at the relationship between modern government and the
modern economy' Martin Kettle, *Guardian*

PENGUIN POLITICS

**THE ROARING NINETIES: WHY WE'RE PAYING THE PRICE FOR
THE GREEDIEST DECADE IN HISTORY**
JOSEPH STIGLITZ

'One of the most important economic and political thinkers of our time'
Independent on Sunday

His previous book revealed the shocking truth about globalization. Now, Joseph
Stiglitz blows the whistle on the devastation wrought by the free market mantra in
the nineties – and shows how Bush is ignoring the lessons from what happened.

This is the explosive story of how capitalism US-style got its comeuppance: how
excessive deregulation, government pandering to big business and exorbitant CEO
salaries all fed the bubble that burst so dramatically amid corporate scandal and
anti-globalization protest.

As Chief Economic Advisor to the President at the time, Stiglitz exposes the
inside story of what went wrong, but also reveals how Bush's administration is
now making things worse – much worse – for the economy, the US and the rest of
the world. Stiglitz takes us one step further, showing how a more balanced
approach to the market and government can lead not only to a better economy, but
a better society.

'Stiglitz's dissection of the follies of the "Roaring Nineties" is as good as it gets'
Will Hutton

'An iconic figure … Stiglitz's book will encourage those who wish to halt the
partial Americanization that has already taken place in Europe' *Daily Telegraph*

'Stiglitz has become a hero to the anti-globalization movement' *Economist*

Penguin Economics

THE ECONOMICS OF INNOCENT FRAUD: TRUTH FOR OUR TIME
JOHN KENNETH GALBRAITH

'A prophet whose warnings have come to pass ... Galbraith is an iconoclast'
Independent

John Kenneth Galbraith, lifelong critic of unbridled corporate power and one of the most renowned economists of the twentieth century, delivers a scathing polemic on today's economics, politics and public morality.

Sounding the alarm on the gap between 'conventional wisdom' and reality, Galbraith distils years of expertise in this radical critique of our society. He shows the danger of the private sector's unprecedented and unbridled control over public life – from government to the military to the environment. And he reveals how politicians and the media have colluded in the myths of a benign 'market': that big business always knows best, that minimal intervention stimulates the economy, that obscene pay gaps and unrestrained self-enrichment are an inevitable by-product of the system. The result, he shows, is that we have given ourselves over to a lie and come to accept legal, legitimate, innocent fraud.

Galbraith's taut, wry and incisive analysis shows that the gulf between truth and illusion has never been wider. It is essential reading for anyone who cares about the economic and political future of the world.

John Kenneth Galbraith is Paul M. Warburg Professor of Economics, Emeritus, at Harvard University. He has worked in economics for over seventy years, and his many books include *A History of Economics*, *The Great Crash, 1929*, *The Age of Uncertainty* and *The Culture of Contentment*.

'The scourge of contemporary economics ... he has always been superb at attacking "conventional wisdom" *Observer*

'America's leading public intellectual' *Guardian*

'The most widely read economist in the world' Amartya Sen, Nobel Prize-winner for Economics

---

Penguin Economics

THE ACCIDENTAL THEORIST AND OTHER DISPATCHES FROM THE DISMAL SCIENCE
PAUL KRUGMAN

'Probably the most creative economist of his generation' *Economist*

'Everything Mr Krugman has to say is smart, important and even fun to read…he is one of a handful of very bright, relatively young economists who do everything well' Peter Passell, *New York Times Book Review*

Paul Krugman has made a reputation for himself by telling us the truth about economics, however unlikely it may seem and however little we want to believe it.

In this wonderfully cohesive set of sharp, witty essays, Krugman tackles bad economic ideas from across the political spectrum, giving us clear-eyed insights into unemployment, globalization, economic growth and financial speculation among other topics. The writing here brilliantly combines the acerbic style and clever analysis that has made Krugman famous. Some of the articles have been written in response to particular economic events, but there is no particular orthodoxy in them, only rational common sense.

'Paul Krugman is the heir apparent to Galbraith. Some of these essays will make you smile, some will make you wince, all will make you think. Krugman's words are as sharp as his mind' Alan S. Blinder, Princeton University

'You can learn a great deal, about economics and otherwise, by reading these delightful essays' Robert M. Solow, Nobel Laureate, Massachusetts Institute of Technology

'[Paul Krugman] writes better than any economist since John Maynard Keynes' Rob Norton, *Fortune*

PENGUIN HISTORY

THE CASH NEXUS : MONEY AND POWER IN THE MODERN WORLD 1700–2000
NIALL FERGUSON

Money : the root of all evil, or the stuff that makes the world go round?

Modern history shows that a nation's success largely depends on the way it manages its money. In times of war, finance has been just as crucial to victory as firepower. But where do money and politics meet? Starting in 1700 and ending at the present day, Niall Ferguson offers a bold and dazzling analysis of the evolution of today's economic and political landscape. Far from being driven by the profit motive alone, our recent history, as Ferguson makes brilliantly clear, has also been made by potent and often conflicting human impulses – sex, violence and the desire for power.

'A marvellous combination of persuasion and provocation…*The Cash Nexus* has enough ideas for a dozen books' Martin Daunton, *History Today*

'Niall Ferguson is probably the most brilliant of the up-and-coming generation of British historians…*The Cash Nexus* is…packed with intriguing arguments and controversial propositions…[an] outstanding book' Frank McLynn, *Independent*

'Combining scholarly research with trenchant analysis of contemporary issues, Ferguson explores the interaction between economics and politics from a variety of angles…he brings to these questions an encyclopaedic knowledge of economic history, and an array of unexpected anecdotes' Geoffrey Owen, *Sunday Telegraph*

'Ferguson is one of the most technically accomplished historians writing today…*The Cash Nexus* offers an important corrective to the naïve story of economic growth' Robert Skidelsky, *New York Review of Books*

ECONOMICS

FREAKONOMICS

STEVEN D. LEVITT & STEPHEN J. DUBNER

'A sensation … you'll be stimulated, provoked and entertained. Of how many books can that be said?' *Sunday Telegraph*

'The book is a delight; it educates, surprises and amuses … dazzling' *Economist*

'Prepare to be dazzled' Malcolm Gladwell

What do estate agents and the Ku Klux Klan have in common?

Why do drug dealers live with their mothers?

How can your name affect how well you do in life?

The answer: Freakonomics. It's at the heart of everything we do and the things that affect us daily, from sex to crime, parenting to politics, fat to cheating, fear to traffic jams. And it's all about using information about the world around us to get to the heart of what's *really* happening under the surface of everyday life.

'If Indiana Jones were an economist he'd be Steven Levitt' *Wall Street Journal*

PENGUIN ECONOMICS

THE BLACK SWAN
THE IMPACT OF THE HIGHLY IMPROBABLE
NASSIM NICHOLAS TALEB

'Mindblowing … a masterpiece' Chris Anderson, author of *The Long Tail*

What have the invention of the wheel, Pompeii, the Wall Street Crash, Harry Potter and the internet got in common?

Why should you never run for a train or read a newspaper?

What can Catherine the Great's lovers tell us about probability?

Why are almost all forecasters con-artists?

This book is all about Black Swans: the random events that underlie our lives, from bestsellers to world disasters. Their impact is huge; they're nearly impossible to predict; yet after they happen we always try to rationalize them. A rallying cry to ignore the 'experts', *The Black Swan* shows us how to stop trying to predict everything and take advantage of uncertainty.

'A deeply intelligent, provocative book' *Economist*

'An idiosyncratically brilliant new book' Niall Ferguson

'Great fun … brash, stubborn, entertaining, opinionated, curious, cajoling' Stephen J. Dubner, author of *Freakonomics*

He just wanted a decent book to read ...

Not too much to ask, is it? It was in 1935 when Allen Lane, Managing Director of Bodley Head Publishers, stood on a platform at Exeter railway station looking for something good to read on his journey back to London. His choice was limited to popular magazines and poor-quality paperbacks – the same choice faced every day by the vast majority of readers, few of whom could afford hardbacks. Lane's disappointment and subsequent anger at the range of books generally available led him to found a company – and change the world.

'We believed in the existence in this country of a vast reading public for intelligent books at a low price, and staked everything on it'
Sir Allen Lane, 1902–1970, founder of Penguin Books

The quality paperback had arrived – and not just in bookshops. Lane was adamant that his Penguins should appear in chain stores and tobacconists, and should cost no more than a packet of cigarettes.

Reading habits (and cigarette prices) have changed since 1935, but Penguin still believes in publishing the best books for everybody to enjoy. We still believe that good design costs no more than bad design, and we still believe that quality books published passionately and responsibly make the world a better place.

So wherever you see the little bird – whether it's on a piece of prize-winning literary fiction or a celebrity autobiography, political tour de force or historical masterpiece, a serial-killer thriller, reference book, world classic or a piece of pure escapism – you can bet that it represents the very best that the genre has to offer.

Whatever you like to read – trust Penguin.

MAJ SJÖWALL (1935–) and PER WAHLÖÖ (1926–1975) were husband and wife. They were both committed Marxists and, between 1965 and 1975, they collaborated on ten mysteries featuring Martin Beck, including *The Terrorists*, *The Fire Engine that Disappeared* and *The Locked Room*. Four of the books have been made into films, most famously *The Laughing Policeman*, which starred Walter Matthau.

From the reviews of the *Martin Beck* series:

'First class'   *Daily Telegraph*

'One of the most authentic, gripping and profound collections of police procedural ever accomplished'

MICHAEL CONNELLY

'Hauntingly effective storytelling'   *New York Times*

'There's just no question about it: the reigning King and Queen of mystery fiction are Maj Sjöwall and her husband Per Wahlöö'   *The National Observer*

'Sjöwall/Wahlöö are the best writers of police procedural in the world'   *Birmingham Post*

Also by Maj Sjöwall and Per Wahlöö

Roseanna
The Man Who Went Up in Smoke
The Man on the Balcony
The Laughing Policeman
Murder at the Savoy
The Fire Engine that Disappeared
The Abominable Man
The Locked Room
Cop Killer
The Terrorists

MAJ SJÖWALL
AND PER WAHLÖÖ

The Abominable Man

Translated from the Swedish by Thomas Teal

HARPER PERENNIAL
London, New York, Toronto and Sydney

Harper Perennial
An imprint of HarperCollins*Publishers*
77–85 Fulham Palace Road
Hammersmith
London W6 8JB

www.harperperennial.co.uk

This edition published by Harper Perennial 2007
1

This translation first published by Random House Inc,
New York, in 1972
Originally published in Sweden by P. A. Norstedt & Söners Forlag

A catalogue record for this book is available from the British Library

ISBN 978-0-00-724297-9

Set in Minion by Palimpsest Book Production Limited,
Grangemouth, Stirlingshire

Printed and bound in Great Britain by Clays Ltd, St Ives plc

1

Just after midnight he stopped thinking.

He'd been writing something earlier, but now the blue ball-point pen lay in front of him on the newspaper, exactly in the right-hand column of the crossword puzzle. He was sitting erect and utterly motionless on a worn wooden chair in front of a low table in the cramped little attic room. A round yellowish lamp-shade with a long fringe hung above his head. The fabric was pale with age, and the light from the feeble bulb was hazy and uncertain.

It was quiet in the house. But the quiet was relative – inside there were three people breathing, and from outside came an indistinct, pulsating, barely discernible murmur. As if from traffic on far-off roads, or from a distant boiling sea. The sound of a million human beings. Of a large city in its anxious sleep.

The man in the attic room was dressed in a beige lumber jacket, grey ski pants, a machine-knit black turtleneck jumper and brown ski boots. He had a large but well-tended moustache, just a shade lighter than the hair combed smoothly back at an angle across his head. His face was narrow, with a clean profile and finely chiselled features, and behind the rigid mask of resentful accusation and obstinate purpose there was an almost childlike expression, weak and perplexed and appealing, and nevertheless a little bit calculating.

His clear blue eyes were steady but vacant.

He looked like a little boy grown suddenly very old.

The man sat stock still for almost an hour, the palms of his hands resting on his thighs, his eyes staring blankly at the same spot on the faded flowered wallpaper.

Then he stood up, walked across the room, opened a closet door, reached up with his left hand and took something from the shelf. A long thin object wrapped in a white kitchen towel with a red border.

The object was a carbine bayonet.

He drew it and very carefully wiped off the yellow gun grease before sliding it into its steel-blue scabbard.

In spite of the fact that he was tall and rather heavy, his movements were quick and lithe and economical, and his hands were as steady as his gaze.

He unbuckled his belt and slid it through the leather loop on the sheath. Then he zipped up his jacket, put on a pair of gloves and a chequered tweed cap and left the house.

The wooden stairs creaked beneath his weight, but his footsteps themselves were inaudible.

The house was small and old and stood on the top of a little hill above the main road. It was a chilly, starlit night.

The man in the tweed cap swung around the corner of the house and moved with the sureness of a sleepwalker towards the driveway behind.

He opened the left front door of his black Volkswagen, climbed in behind the wheel and adjusted the bayonet, which rested against his right thigh.

Then he started the engine, turned on the headlights, backed out on to the main road and drove north.

The little black car hurtled forward through the darkness

precisely and implacably, as if it were a weightless craft in space.

The buildings tightened along the road and the city rose up beneath its dome of light, huge and cold and desolate, stripped of everything but hard naked surfaces of metal, glass and concrete.

Not even in the central city was there any street life at this hour of the night. With the exception of an occasional taxi, two ambulances and a patrol car, everything was dead. The police car was black with white sides and rushed quickly past on its own bawling carpet of sound.

The traffic lights changed from red to yellow to green to yellow to red with a meaningless mechanical monotony.

The black car drove strictly in accordance with traffic regulations, never exceeded the speed limit, slowed at all cross streets and stopped at all red lights.

It drove along Vasagatan past the Central Station and the newly completed Sheraton-Stockholm, swung left at Norra Bantorget and continued north on Torsgatan.

In the square was an illuminated tree and bus 591 waiting at its stop. A new moon hung above St Eriksplan and the blue neon hands on the Bonnier Building showed the time. Twenty minutes to two.

At that instant, the man in the car was precisely thirty-six years old.

Now he drove east along Odengatan, past deserted Vasa Park with its cold white streetlamps and the thick, veined shadows of ten thousand leafless tree limbs.

The black car made another right and drove one hundred and twenty-five yards south along Dalagatan. Then it braked and stopped.

With studied negligence, the man in the lumber jacket and the tweed cap parked with two wheels on the pavement right in front of the stairs to the Eastman Institute.

He stepped out into the night and slammed the door behind him.

It was the third of April, 1971. A Saturday.

It was still only an hour and forty minutes old and nothing in particular had happened.

2

At a quarter to two the morphine stopped working.

He'd had the last injection just before ten, which meant the narcosis lasted less than four hours.

The pain came back sporadically, first on the left side of his diaphragm and then a few minutes later on the right as well. Then it radiated out towards his back and passed fitfully through his body, quick, cruel and biting, as if starving vultures had torn their way into his vitals.

He lay on his back in the tall, narrow bed and stared at the white plaster ceiling, where the dim glow of the night light and the reflections from outside produced an angular static pattern of shadows that were indecipherable and as cold and repellent as the room itself.

The ceiling wasn't flat but arched in two shallow curves and seemed distant. It was in fact high, over twelve feet, and old-fashioned like everything else in the building. The bed stood in the middle of the stone floor and there were only two other pieces of furniture: the night table and a straight-backed wooden chair.

The curtains were not completely drawn, and the window was ajar. Air filtered chilly and fresh through the two-inch crack from the spring-winter night outside, but he nevertheless felt a suffocating

5

disgust at the rotting odour from the flowers on the night table and from his own sick body.

He had not slept but lain wakeful and silent and thought about this very fact – that the painkiller would soon wear off.

It was about an hour since he'd heard the night nurse pass the double doors to the corridor in her wooden shoes. Since then he'd heard nothing but the sound of his own breathing and maybe of his blood, pulsing heavily and unevenly through his body. But these were not distinct sounds; they were more like figments of his imagination, fitting companions to his dread of the agony that would soon begin and to his mindless fear of dying.

He had always been a hard man, unwilling to tolerate mistakes or weakness in others and never prepared to admit that he himself might someday falter, either physically or mentally.

Now he was afraid and in pain. He felt betrayed and taken by surprise. His senses had sharpened during his weeks in the hospital. He had become unnaturally sensitive to all forms of pain and shuddered even at the prospect of an injection or the needle in the fold of his arm when the nurses took the daily blood tests. On top of that he was afraid of the dark and couldn't stand to be alone and had learned to hear noises he'd never heard before.

The examinations – which ironically enough the doctors referred to as the 'investigation' – wore him out and made him feel worse. And the sicker he felt, the more intense his fear of death became, until it circumscribed his entire conscious life and left him utterly naked, in a state of spiritual exposure and almost obscene egoism.

Something rustled outside the window. An animal of course, padding through the withered rose bed. A field mouse or a hedgehog, maybe a cat. But didn't hedgehogs hibernate?

It must be an animal, he thought, and then no longer in control of his actions, he raised his left hand towards the electric call-button that hung in comfortable reach, wound once around the bedpost.

6

But when his fingers brushed the cold metal of the bed frame, his hand trembled in an involuntary spasm and the switch slid away and fell to the floor with a little rattling bang.

The sound made him pull himself together.

If he'd gotten his hand on the switch and pushed the white button, a red light would have gone on out in the corridor above his door and soon the night nurse would have come trotting from her room in her clattering wooden clogs.

Since he wasn't only afraid but also vain, he was almost glad he hadn't managed to ring.

The night nurse would have come into the room and turned on the overhead light and stared at him questioningly as he lay there in his wretchedness and misery.

He lay still for a while and felt the pain recede and then approach again in sudden waves, as if it were a runaway train driven by an insane engineer.

He suddenly became aware of a new urgency. He needed to urinate.

There was a bottle within reach, stuck down in the yellow plastic wastebasket behind the night table. But he didn't want to use it. He was allowed to get up if he wanted to. One of the doctors had even said it would be good for him to move around a little.

So he thought he'd get up and open the double doors and walk to the toilet, which was right on the other side of the corridor. It was a distraction, a practical task, something that could force his mind into new combinations for a time.

He folded aside the blanket and the sheet, heaved himself into a sitting position and sat for several seconds on the edge of the bed with his feet dangling while he pulled at the white nightgown and heard the plastic mattress cover rustling underneath him.

Then he carefully eased himself down until he felt the cold stone floor beneath the damp soles of his feet. He tried to straighten up and, in spite of the broad bandages that pulled at his groin and tightened around his thighs, he succeeded. He was still wearing plastic foam pressure-dressings from the aortography the day before.

His slippers lay beside the table and he stuck his feet into them and walked cautiously and gropingly towards the door. He opened the first door in and the second out and walked straight across the shadowy corridor and into the lavatory.

He went to the toilet and rinsed off his hands in cold water and started back, then stopped in the corridor to listen. The muffled sound of the night nurse's radio could be heard a long way off. He was in pain again and his fear came back and he thought after all he could go in and ask for a couple of painkillers. They wouldn't have any particular effect, but anyway she'd have to unlock the medicine cabinet and take out the bottle and then give him some juice, and that way at least someone would have to fuss over him for a little while.

The distance to the office was about sixty feet and he took his time. Shuffled along slowly with the sweaty nightshirt slapping against his calves.

The light was on in the duty room but there was no one there. Only the transistor radio, which stood serenading itself between two half-emptied coffee cups.

The night nurse and the orderly were busy someplace else of course.

The room began to swim and he had to support himself against the door. It felt a little better after a minute or two, and he walked slowly back towards his room through the darkened corridor.

The doors were the way he'd left them, slightly ajar. He closed them carefully, took the few steps to the bed, stepped out of his slippers, lay down on his back and pulled the blanket up to his chin with a shiver. Lay still with wide-open eyes and felt the express train rushing through his body.

Something was different. The pattern on the ceiling had changed in some slight way.

He was aware of it almost at once.

But what was it that had made the pattern of shadows and reflections change?

His gaze ran over the bare walls, then he turned his head to the right and looked towards the window.

The window had been open when he left the room, he was certain of that.

Now it was closed.

Terror overwhelmed him immediately and he lifted his hand to the call button. But it wasn't in its place. He'd forgotten to pick up the cord and the switch from the floor.

He held his fingers tightly around the iron pipe where the buzzer ought to have been and stared at the window.

The gap between the long curtains was still about two inches wide, but they weren't hanging quite the way they had been, and the window was closed.

Could someone from the staff have been in the room?

It didn't seem likely.

He felt the sweat bursting from his pores, and his nightshirt cold and clammy against his sensitive skin.

Completely at the mercy of his fear and unable to tear his eyes from the window, he began to sit up in bed.

The curtains hung absolutely motionless, yet he was certain someone was standing behind them.

Who, he thought.

Who?

And then with a last flash of common sense: This must be a hallucination.

Now he stood beside the bed, ill and unsteady, his bare feet on the stone floor. Took two uncertain steps towards the window. Came to a stop, slightly bent, his lips twitching.

The man in the window alcove threw aside the curtains with his right hand as he simultaneously drew the bayonet with his left.

Reflections glittered on the long broad blade.

The man in the lumber jacket and the chequered tweed cap

9

took two quick steps forward and stopped, legs apart, tall, straight, with the weapon at shoulder height.

The sick man recognized him at once and started to open his mouth to bellow.

The heavy handle of the bayonet hit him across the mouth and he felt his lips being torn to shreds and his dental plate breaking.

And that was the last thing he felt.

The rest of it went too fast. Time rushed away from him.

The first blow caught him on the right side of his diaphragm just below his ribs, and the bayonet sank in to its hilt.

The sick man was still on his feet, his head thrown back, when the man in the lumber jacket raised the weapon for the third time and sliced open his throat, from the left ear to the right.

A bubbling, slightly hissing noise came from the open windpipe.

Nothing more.

3

It was Friday evening and Stockholm's cafés should have been full of happy people enjoying themselves after the drudgery of the week. Such, however, was not the case, and it wasn't hard to work out why. In the course of the preceding five years, restaurant prices had as good as doubled, and very few ordinary wage-earners could afford to treat themselves to even one night out a month. The restaurant owners complained and talked crisis, but the ones who had not turned their establishments into pubs or discotheques to attract the easy-spending young managed to keep their heads above water by means of the increasing number of businessmen with credit cards and expense accounts who preferred to conduct their transactions across a laden table.

The Golden Peace in the Old City was no exception. It was late, to be sure – Friday had turned into Saturday – but during the last hour there had been only two guests in the ground-floor dining room. A man and a woman. They'd eaten steak tartare and were now drinking coffee and *punsch* as they talked in low voices across the table in the alcove.

Two waitresses sat folding napkins at a little table opposite the entrance. The younger, who was red-haired and looked tired, stood up and threw a glance at the clock above the bar. She

11

yawned, picked up a napkin and walked over to the guests in the alcove.

'Will there be anything else before the bar closes?' she said, using the napkin to sweep some crumbs of tobacco from the table-cloth. 'Would you care for some more hot coffee, Inspector?'

Martin Beck noticed to his own surprise that he was flattered at her knowing who he was. He was normally irritated by any reminder that as chief of the National Murder Squad he was a more or less public personage, but it was a long time now since he'd had his picture in the papers or appeared on television, and he took the waitress's recognition only as an indication that the Peace was beginning to regard him as a regular customer. Rightly so, for that matter. He'd been living not far away for two years now, and when he now and again went out to eat he gave his custom mostly to the Peace. Having a companion, as he did this evening, was less usual.

The girl across from him was his daughter, Ingrid. She was nineteen years old, and if you overlooked the fact that she was very blonde and he very dark, they were strikingly similar.

'Do you want more coffee?' asked Martin Beck.

Ingrid shook her head and the waitress withdrew to prepare the bill. Martin Beck lifted the little bottle of *punsch* from its ice bucket and poured what remained into the two glasses. Ingrid sipped at hers.

'We ought to do this more often,' she said.

'Drink *punsch*?'

'Mmm, it is good. No, I mean get together. Next time I'll invite you to dinner. At my place on Klostervägen. You haven't seen it yet.'

Ingrid had moved away from home three months before her parents separated. Martin Beck sometimes wondered if he ever would have had the strength to break out of his stagnant marriage to Inga if Ingrid hadn't encouraged him. She hadn't been happy at home and moved in with a friend even before she was out of school. Now she was studying sociology at the university and had just recently found a one-room apartment in Stocksund. For the time being she was still subletting, but she had prospects of eventually getting the lease on her own.

'Mama and Rolf were out to visit the day before yesterday,' she said. 'I was hoping you'd come too, but I couldn't get hold of you.'

'No, I was in Örebro for a couple of days. How are they?'

'Fine. Mama had a whole trunkload of stuff with her. Towels and napkins and that blue coffee service and I don't know what all. Oh, and we talked about Rolf's birthday. Mama wants us to come out and have dinner with them. If you can.'

Rolf was three years younger than Ingrid. They were as different as a brother and sister can be, but they'd always got along well.

The redhead came with the bill. Martin Beck paid and emptied his glass. He looked at his wristwatch. It was a couple of minutes to one.

'Shall we go?' said Ingrid, quickly downing the last few drops of her *punsch*.

They strolled north on Österlänggatan. The stars were out and the air was quite chilly. A couple of drunken teenagers came walking out of Drakens Gränd, shouting and hollering until the walls of the old buildings echoed with the din.

Ingrid put her hand under her father's arm and matched her stride to his. She was long-legged and slim, almost skinny, Martin Beck thought, but she herself was always saying she'd have to go on a diet.

'Do you want to come up?' he asked on the hill up towards Köpmantorget.

'Yes, but only to call a taxi. It's late, and you have to sleep.'

Martin Beck yawned.

'As a matter of fact I am rather tired,' he said.

A man was squatting by the base of the statue of St George and the Dragon. He seemed to be sleeping, his forehead resting against his knees.

As Ingrid and Martin Beck passed, he lifted his head and said something inarticulate in a high thick voice, then stretched his legs out in front of him and fell asleep again with his chin on his chest.

'Shouldn't he be sleeping it off at Nicolai?' said Ingrid. 'It's a bit cold to be sitting outside.'

'He'll probably wind up there eventually,' Martin Beck said. 'If there's room. But it's a long time since it was my job to take care of drunks.'

They walked on into Köpmangatan in silence.

Martin Beck was thinking about the summer twenty-two years ago when he'd walked a beat in the Nicolai precinct. Stockholm was a different city then. The Old City had been an idyllic little town. More drunkenness and poverty and misery, of course, before they'd cleared out the slums and restored the buildings and raised the rents so the old tenants could no longer afford to stay. Living here had become fashionable, and he himself was now one of the privileged few.

They rode to the top floor in the lift, which had been installed when the building was renovated and was one of the few in the Old City. The flat was completely modernized and consisted of a hall, a small kitchen, a bathroom and two rooms whose windows opened on to a large open courtyard on the east. The rooms were snug and asymmetrical, with deep bay windows and low ceilings. The first of the two rooms was furnished with comfortable easy chairs and low tables and had a fireplace. The inner room contained a broad bed framed by deep built-in shelves and cupboards and, by the window, a huge desk with drawers beneath.

Without taking off her coat, Ingrid went in and sat down at the desk, lifted the receiver and dialled for a taxi.

'Won't you stay for a minute?' Martin called from the kitchen.

'No, I have to go home and get to bed. I'm dead tired. So are you, for that matter.'

Martin Beck made no objection. All of a sudden he didn't feel a bit sleepy, but all evening long he'd been yawning, and at the cinema – they'd been to see Truffaut's *The 400 Blows* – he'd several times been on the verge of dozing off.

Ingrid finally got hold of a taxi, came out to the kitchen and kissed Martin Beck on the cheek.

'Thanks for a good time. I'll see you at Rolf's birthday if not before. Sleep well.'

Martin Beck followed her out to the lift and whispered good night before closing the doors and going back into his flat.

He poured the beer he'd taken from the refrigerator into a big glass, walked in and set it on the desk. Then he went to the hi-fi by the fireplace, looked through his records and put one of Bach's Brandenburg Concertos on the turntable. The building was well insulated and he knew he could turn the volume quite high without bothering the neighbours. He sat down at the desk and drank the beer, which was fresh and cold and washed away the sweet sticky taste of *punsch.* He pinched together the paper mouthpiece of a Florida, put the cigarette between his teeth and lit a match. Then he rested his chin in his hands and stared out through the window.

The spring sky arched deep blue and starry above the moonlit roof on the other side of the courtyard. Martin Beck listened to the music and let his thoughts wander freely. He felt utterly relaxed and content.

When he'd turned the record, he walked over to the shelf above the bed and lifted down a half-completed model of the clipper ship *Flying Cloud.* He worked on masts and yards for almost an hour before putting the model back on its shelf.

While getting undressed, he admired his two completed models with a certain pride – the *Cutty Sark* and the training ship *Danmark.* Soon he'd have only the rigging left to do on the *Flying Cloud,* the most difficult and the most trying part.

He walked naked out to the kitchen and put the ashtray and the beer glass on the counter beside the sink. Then he turned out all the lights except the one above his pillow, closed the bedroom door to a crack and went to bed. He wound the clock, which said two thirty-five, and checked to see that the alarm button was pushed in. He had, he hoped, a free day in front of him and could sleep as long as he liked.

Kurt Bergengren's *Archipelago Steamboats* lay on the bedside table and he browsed through it, looking at pictures he'd studied carefully before and reading a passage here and a caption there with a strong feeling of nostalgia. The book was large and heavy and not particularly well suited for reading in bed, and his arms were soon tired from holding it. He put it aside and reached out to turn off the reading light.

Then the telephone rang.

4

Einar Rönn really was dead tired.

He'd been at work for over seventeen hours at a single stretch. Right at the moment, he was standing in the Criminal Division orderly room in the police building on Kungsholmsgatan, looking at a sobbing male adult who had laid hands on one of his fellow men.

For that matter maybe 'male adult' was saying too much, since the prisoner was by and large only a child. An eighteen-year-old boy with shoulder-length blond hair, bright red Levi's and a brown suede jacket with a fringe and the word LOVE painted on the back. The letters were surrounded by ornamental flowers in flourishes of pink and violet and baby blue. There were also flowers and words on the legs of his boots; to be precise, the words PEACE and MAGGIE. Long fringes of soft wavy human hair were ingeniously sewn to the jacket's arms.

It was enough to make you wonder if someone hadn't been scalped.

Rönn felt like sobbing himself. Partly from exhaustion, but mostly, as was so often the case these days, because he felt sorrier for the criminal than for the victim.

The young man with the pretty hair had tried to kill a drug

pusher. The attempt had not been particularly successful, yet successful enough that the police regarded him as a prime suspect for attempted murder in the second degree.

Rönn had been hunting him since five o'clock that afternoon, which meant he'd been forced to track down and search through no fewer than eighteen drug hangouts in different parts of his beautiful city, each one filthier and more repulsive than the one before.

All because some bastard who sold hash mixed with opium to school kids on Mariatorget had got a bump on the head. All right, caused by an iron pipe and motivated by the fact that the agent of the blow was broke. But after all. Rönn thought.

Plus: nine hours' overtime, which for that matter would be ten before he got home to his apartment in Vällingby.

But you had to take the bad with the good. In this case the good would be the salary.

Rönn was from Lapland, born in Arjeplog and married to a Lappish girl. He didn't particularly like Vällingby, but he liked the name of the street he lived on: Lapland Street.

He looked on while one of his younger colleagues, on night duty, wrote out a receipt for the transfer of the prisoner and delivered up the hair fetish to two guards, who in their turn shoved the prisoner into a lift for forwarding to the booking section three flights up.

A transfer receipt is a piece of paper bearing the name of the prisoner and binding on no one, on the back of which the duty officer writes appropriate remarks. For example: *Very wild, threw himself again and again against the wall and was injured.* Or: *Uncontrollable, ran into a door and was injured.* Maybe just: *Fell down and hurt himself.*

And so on.

The door from the yard opened and two constables ushered in an older man with a bushy grey beard. Just as they crossed the threshold one of the constables drove his fist into the prisoner's abdomen. The man doubled up and gave out a stifled cry, something like the howl of a dog. The two on-duty detectives shuffled their papers undisturbed.

Rönn threw a tired look at the constables but said nothing.

Then he yawned and looked at his watch.

Seventeen minutes after two.

The telephone rang. One of the detectives answered.

'Yes, this is Criminal, Gustavsson here.'

Rönn put on his fur hat and moved towards the door. He had his hand on the knob when the man named Gustavsson stopped him.

'What? Wait a second. Hey, Rönn?'

'Yeah?'

'Here's something for you.'

'What now?'

'Something at Mount Sabbath. Somebody's been shot or something. The guy on the phone sounds pretty confused.'

Rönn sighed and turned around. Gustavsson took his hand off the receiver.

'One of the boys from Violent Crime is here right now. One of the big wheels. Okay?'

A short pause.

'Yes, yes, I can hear you. It's awful, yes. Now, exactly where are you?'

Gustavsson was a thinnish man in his thirties with a tough and impassive air. He listened, then put his hand over the receiver again.

'He's at the main entrance to the central building at Mount Sabbath. Obviously needs help. Are you going?'

'Okay,' Rönn said. 'I suppose I will.'

'Do you need a ride? This radio car seems to be free.'

Rönn looked a little woefully at the two constables and shook his head. They were big and strong and armed with pistols and batons in leather holsters. Their prisoner lay like a whimpering bundle at their feet.

19

They themselves stared jealously and foolishly at Rönn, the hope of promotion in their shallow blue eyes.

'No, I'll take my own car,' he said, and left.

Einar Rönn was no big wheel, and right at the moment he didn't feel even like a cog. There were some people who thought he was a very able policeman, and others who said he was typically mediocre. Be that as it may, he had, after years of faithful service, become a deputy inspector on the Violent Crime Squad. A real sleuth, to use the language of the tabloids. That he was peaceable and middle-aged, red-nosed and slightly corpulent from sitting still too much – on those points everyone agreed.

It took him four minutes and twelve seconds to drive to the indicated address.

Mount Sabbath Hospital is spread out over a large, hilly, roughly triangular tract with its base in the north along Vasa Park, its sides along Dalagatan on the east and Torsgatan on the west, and its tip cut off abruptly by the approach to the new bridge over Barnhus Bay. A large brick building belonging to the gasworks pushes in from Torsgatan, putting a notch in one corner.

The hospital gets its name from an innkeeper, Vallentin Sabbath, who, at the beginning of the eighteenth century, owned two taverns in the Old City – the Rostock and the Lion. He bought land here and raised carp in ponds that have since dried out or been filled in, and for three years he operated a restaurant on the property before departing this life in 1720.

About ten years later a mineral springs, or spa, was opened on the premises. The two-hundred-year-old mineral springs hotel, which in the course of the years has seen service both as a hospital and a poorhouse, now crouches in the shadow of an eight-storey geriatric centre.

The original hospital was built a little more than a hundred years ago on the rocky outcropping along Dalagatan and consisted of a number of pavilions connected by long, covered passages.

Some of the old pavilions are still in use, but a number of them have quite recently been torn down and replaced by new ones, and the system of passages is now underground.

At the far end of the grounds stand a number of older buildings that house the old people's home. There is a little chapel here, and in the middle of a garden of lawns and hedges and gravel walks there is a yellow summerhouse with white trim and a spire on its rounded roof. An avenue of trees leads from the chapel to an old gatehouse down by the street. Behind the chapel the grounds rise higher only to come to a sudden stop high above Torsgatan, which curves between the cliff and the Bonnier Building across the way. This is the quietest and least frequented part of the hospital area. The main entrance is on Dalagatan where it was a hundred years ago, and next to it is the new central hospital building.

5

Rönn felt almost ghostlike in the blue light flashing from the roof of the patrol car. But it would soon get worse.

'What's happened?' he said.

'Don't know for sure. Something ugly.' The constable looked very young. His face was open and sympathetic, but his glance wandered and he seemed to be having trouble standing still. He was holding on to the car door with his left hand and fingering the butt of his pistol a little hesitantly with his right. Ten seconds earlier he'd made a sound that could only have been a sigh of relief.

The boy's scared, Rönn thought. He made his voice reassuring.

'Well, we'll see. Where is it?'

'It's a bit tricky to get there. I'll drive in front.'

Rönn nodded and went back to his own car. Started the engine and followed the blue flashes in a wide swing around the central hospital and into the grounds. In the course of thirty seconds the patrol car made three right turns, two left turns, then braked and stopped outside a long low building with yellow plaster walls and a black mansard roof. It looked ancient. Above the weathered wooden door a single flickering bulb in an old-fashioned milkglass globe was fighting what was pretty much a losing battle against the darkness. The constable climbed out and assumed his former stance, fingers on car door and pistol butt as a kind of shield against the night and what it might be presumed to conceal.

'In there,' he said, glancing guardedly at the double wooden door.

Rönn stifled a yawn and nodded.

'Shall I call for more men?'

'Well, we'll see,' Rönn repeated good-naturedly.

He was already on the steps pushing open the right-hand half of the door, which creaked mournfully on un-oiled hinges. Another couple of steps and another door and he found himself in a sparsely lit corridor. It was broad and high-ceilinged and stretched the entire length of the building.

On one side were private rooms and wards, the other was apparently reserved for lavatories and linen closets and examination rooms. On the wall was an old black pay phone of the kind that only cost ten öre to use. Rönn stared at an oval white enamel plate with the laconic inscription ENEMA and then went on to study the four people he could see from where he stood.

Two of them were uniformed policemen. One of these was stocky and solid and stood with feet apart and his arms at his sides and his eyes straight ahead. In his left hand he was holding an open notebook with a black cover. His colleague was leaning against the wall, head down, his gaze directed into an enamelled cast-iron washbasin with an old-fashioned brass tap. Of all the young men Rönn had encountered during his nine hours of overtime, this one looked to be easily the youngest. In his leather jacket and shoulder belt and apparently indispensable weaponry, he looked like a parody of a policeman. An older grey-haired woman with glasses sat collapsed in a wicker chair, staring apathetically at her white wooden clogs. She was wearing a white smock and had an ugly case of varicose veins on her pale calves. The quartet was completed by a man in his thirties. He had curly black hair and was biting his knuckles in irritation. He too was wearing a white coat and wooden-soled shoes.

The air in the corridor was unpleasant and smelled of disinfectant, vomit, or medicine, or maybe all three at once. Rönn sneezed suddenly and unexpectedly and, a little late, grabbed his nose between thumb and forefinger.

The only one to react was the policeman with the notebook. Without saying anything, he pointed to a tall door with light yellow crackled paint and a typewritten white card in a metal frame. The door was not quite closed. Rönn plucked it open without touching the handle. Inside there was another door. That one too was ajar, but opened inwards.

Rönn pushed it with his foot, looked into the room and gave a start. He let go of his reddish nose and took another look, this one more systematic.

'My, my,' he said to himself.

Then he took a step backwards, let the outer door swing back to its former position, put on his glasses and examined the nameplate.

'Jesus,' he said.

The policeman had put away the black notebook and had taken out his badge instead, which he now stood fingering as if it had been a rosary or an amulet.

Police badges were soon to be eliminated, Rönn remembered, irrationally. And with that, the long battle as to whether badges should be worn on the chest as forthright identification or hidden away in a pocket somewhere had come to a disappointing as well as surprising conclusion. They were simply done away with, replaced by ordinary ID cards, and policemen could safely go on hiding behind the anonymity of the uniform.

'What's your name?' he said out loud.

'Andersson.'

'What time did you get here?'

The policeman looked at his wristwatch.

24

'At two sixteen. Nine minutes ago. We were in the area. At Odenplan.'

Rönn took off his glasses and glanced at the uniformed boy, who was light green in the face and vomiting helplessly into the sink. The older constable followed his look.

'He's just a cadet,' he said under his breath. 'It's his first time out.'

'Better give him a hand,' said Rönn. 'And send out a call for five or six men from the Fifth.'

'The emergency bus from Precinct Five, yes sir,' Andersson said, looking as if he were about to salute or snap to attention or some other inane thing.

'Just a moment,' Rönn said. 'Have you seen anything suspicious around here?'

He hadn't put it too well perhaps, and the constable stared bewilderedly at the door to the sickroom.

'Well, ah . . .' he said evasively.

'Do you know who that is? The man in there?'

'Chief Inspector Nyman, isn't it?'

'Yes, it is.'

'Though you can't hardly tell by looking.'

'No,' Rönn said. 'Not hardly.'

Andersson went out.

Rönn wiped the sweat from his forehead and considered what he ought to do.

For ten seconds. Then he walked over to the pay phone and dialled Martin Beck's home number.

'Hi. It's Rönn. I'm at Mount Sabbath. Come on over.'

'Okay,' said Martin Beck.

'Quick.'

'Okay.'

Rönn hung up the receiver and went back to the others. Waited. Gave his handkerchief to the cadet, who self-consciously wiped his mouth.

'I'm sorry,' he said.

'It can happen to anyone.'

'I couldn't help it. Is it always like this?'

'No,' Rönn said. 'I wouldn't say that. I've been a policeman for twenty-one years and to be honest I've never seen anything like this before.'

Then he turned to the man with the curly black hair.

'Is there a psychiatric ward here?'

'*Nix verstehen*,' the doctor said.

Rönn put on his glasses and examined the plastic name badge on the doctor's white coat. Sure enough, there was his name.

DR ÜZK ÜKÖCÖTÜPZE.

'Oh,' he said to himself.

Put away his glasses and waited.

6

The room was fifteen feet long, ten feet wide, and almost twelve feet high. The colours were very drab – ceiling a dirty white and the plastered walls an indefinite greyish yellow. Grey-white marble tiles on the floor. Light grey window-frames and door. In front of the window hung heavy pale-yellow damask curtains and, behind them, thin white cotton nets. The iron bed was white, likewise the sheets and pillowcase. The night table was grey and the wooden chair light brown. The paint on the furniture was worn, and on the rough walls it was crackled with age. The plaster on the ceiling was flaking and in several places there were light brown spots where moisture had seeped through. Everything was old but very clean. On the table was a nickel silver vase with seven pale red roses. Plus a pair of glasses and a glasses case, a transparent plastic beaker containing two small white tablets, a little white transistor radio, a half-eaten apple, and a tumbler half full of some bright yellow liquid. On the shelf below lay a pile of magazines, four letters, a tablet of lined paper, a shiny Waterman pen with ballpoint cartridges in four different colours, and some loose change – to be exact, eight ten-öre pieces, two twenty-five-öre pieces, and six one-krona coins. The table had two drawers. In the upper one were three used handkerchiefs, a bar of soap in a plastic box, toothpaste, toothbrush, a small bottle of after-shave, a box of cough drops, and a leather case with a nail clipper, file and scissors. The other contained a wallet, an electric razor, a small folder of postage stamps, two pipes, a tobacco pouch and a blank picture postcard of the Stockholm city hall. There were some clothes hanging over the back of the straight chair – a grey cotton coat, trousers of the same colour and material, and a knee-length white shirt. Underwear and socks lay on the seat, and next to the bed stood a pair of slippers. A beige bathrobe hung on the clothes hook by the door.

There was only one completely dissident colour in the room. And that was a shocking red.

The dead man lay partly on his side between the bed and the window. The throat had been cut with such force that the head had been thrown back at an angle of almost ninety degrees and lay with its left cheek against the floor. The tongue had forced its way out through the gaping incision and the victim's broken false teeth stuck out between the mutilated lips.

As he fell backwards a thick stream of blood had pumped out through the carotid artery. This explained the crimson streak across the bed and the splashes of blood on the flower vase and night table.

On the other hand it was the wound in the midriff that had soaked the victim's shirt and provided the enormous pool of blood around the body. A superficial inspection of this wound indicated that someone, with a single blow, had cut through the liver, bile ducts, stomach, spleen and pancreas. Not to mention the aorta.

Virtually all the blood in the body had welled out in the course of a few seconds. The skin was bluish white and seemed almost transparent, where, that is, it could be seen at all, for example on the forehead and parts of the shins and feet.

The lesion on the torso was about ten inches long and wide open; the lacerated organs had pressed out between the sliced edges of the peritoneum.

The man had virtually been cut in two.

Even for people whose job it was to linger at the scenes of macabre and bloody crimes, this was strong stuff.

But Martin Beck's expression hadn't changed since he entered the room. To an outside observer it would have seemed almost as if everything were part of the routine – going to the Peace with his daughter, eating, drinking, getting undressed, pottering with a ship model, going to bed with a book. And then suddenly rushing off to inspect a slaughtered chief inspector of police. The worst part was that he felt that way himself. He never allowed himself to be taken aback, except by his own emotional coolness.

It was now three ten in the morning and he sat on his haunches beside the bed and surveyed the body, coldly and appraisingly.

'Yes, it's Nyman,' he said.

'Yes, I suppose it is.'

Rönn stood poking among the objects on the table. All at once he yawned and put his hand guiltily to his mouth.

Martin Beck threw him a quick glance.

'Have you got some sort of timetable?'

'Yes,' Rönn said.

He pulled out a small notebook where he'd made some indus-trious jottings in a tiny, stingy hand. Put on his glasses and rattled it off in a monotone.

'An assistant nurse opened those doors at ten minutes after two. Hadn't heard or seen anything unusual. Making a routine check on the patients. Nyman was dead then. She dialled 90-000 at two eleven. The officers in the radio car got the alarm at two twelve. They were at Odenplan and made it here in between three and four minutes. They reported to Criminal at two seventeen. I got here at two twenty-two. Called you at two twenty-nine. You got here at sixteen minutes to three.'

Rönn looked at his watch.

'It's now eight minutes to three. When I arrived he'd been dead at the most half an hour.'

'Is that what the doctor said?'

'No, that's my own conclusion, so to speak. The warmth of the body, coagulation –'

He stopped, as if it had been presumptuous to mention his own observations.

Martin Beck rubbed the bridge of his nose thoughtfully with the thumb and forefinger of his right hand.

'So then everything happened very fast,' he said.

Rönn didn't answer. He seemed to be thinking about something else.

'Well,' he said after a while, 'you understand why it was I called you. Not because – '

He stopped, seeming somehow distracted.

'Not because?'

'Not because Nyman was a chief inspector, but because . . . well, because of this.'

Rönn gestured vaguely towards the body.

'He was butchered.'

He paused for a second and then came up with a new conclusion.

'I mean, whoever did this must be raving mad.'

Martin Beck nodded.

'Yes,' he said. 'It looks that way.'

7

Martin Beck was beginning to feel ill at ease. The sensation was vague and hard to trace, somewhat like the sneaking fatigue when you're falling asleep over a book and go on reading without turning any pages.

He'd have to make an effort to gather his wits and get a grip on these slippery apprehensions.

Closely related to this lurking sensation of impotence, there was another feeling he couldn't seem to get rid of.

A sense of danger.

That something was about to happen. Something that had to be warded off at any price. But he didn't know what, and still less how.

He'd had such feelings before, if only at long intervals. His colleagues tended to laugh off this phenomenon and call it intuition.

Police work is built on realism, routine, stubbornness and system. It's true that a lot of difficult cases are cleared up by coincidence, but it's equally true that coincidence is an elastic concept that mustn't be confused with luck or accident. In a criminal investigation, it's a question of weaving the net of coincidence as fine as possible. And experience and industry play a larger role there than brilliant inspiration. A good memory and ordinary common sense are more valuable qualities than intellectual brilliance.

Intuition has no place in practical police work.

Intuition is not even a quality, any more than astrology and phrenology are sciences.

And still it was there, however reluctant he was to admit it, and there had been times when it seemed to have put him on the right track.

And yet his ambivalence might also depend on simpler, more tangible and immediate things.

On Rönn, for example.

Martin Beck expected a great deal of the people he worked with. The blame for that fell on Lennart Kollberg, for many years his right-hand man, first when he was a city detective in Stockholm and then later at the old National Criminal Division in Västberga. Kollberg had always been his surest complement, the man who played the best shots, asked the right leading questions and gave the proper cues.

But Kollberg wasn't available. He was at home asleep, presumably, and there was no acceptable reason for waking him. It would be against the rules, and an insult to Rönn what's more.

Martin Beck expected Rönn to do something or at least say something that showed he too sensed the danger. That he would come up with some assertion or supposition that Martin Beck could refute or pursue.

But Rönn said nothing.

Instead he did his job calmly and capably. The investigation was for the moment his, and he was doing everything that could reasonably be expected.

The area outside the window had been cordoned off with ropes and sawhorses, patrol cars had been driven up and headlights lit. Spotlights swept the terrain and small white patches of light from police flashlights wandered jerkily across the ground like frightened sand crabs across a beach in unorganized flight from approaching intruders.

Rönn had gone through what there was on and in the night table without finding anything but ordinary personal belongings and a few trivial letters of the insensitively hearty type that healthy people write to individuals who are suspected of being seriously ill. Civilian personnel from the Fifth Precinct had gone through the adjoining rooms and wards without finding anything of note.

If Martin Beck wanted to know anything in particular, he would have to ask, and furthermore would have to formulate his question clearly, in phrases that could not be misunderstood.

The truth of the matter was simply that they worked together badly. Both of them had discovered this years before, and they therefore generally avoided situations where they had only one another to fall back on.

Martin Beck's opinion of Rönn was none too high, a circumstance the latter was well aware of and which gave him an inferiority complex. Martin Beck, for his part, recognized as his own failing a difficulty in establishing contact and thus became inhibited himself.

Rönn had produced the beloved old murder kit, secured a number of fingerprints, and had plastic covers placed over several pieces of evidence in the room and on the ground outside, thereby ensuring that details that might prove valuable later on would not be effaced by natural causes or destroyed by carelessness. These pieces of evidence were mostly footprints.

Martin Beck had a cold, as usual at this time of year. He snuffled and blew his nose and coughed and hacked and Rönn didn't react. He did not, as a matter of fact, even say 'Bless you.' This small civility was apparently not a part of his upbringing, nor of his vocabulary. And if he thought anything, he kept it to himself.

There was no tacit communication between them and Martin Beck felt himself called upon to break the silence.

'Doesn't this whole ward seem a little old-fashioned?' he asked.

'Yes,' Rönn said. 'It's supposed to be vacated the day after tomorrow and modernized or turned into something else. The patients are going to be moved to new wards in the central building.'

Martin Beck's thoughts moved promptly off in new directions.

'I wonder what he used,' he said a while later, mostly to himself. 'Maybe a machete or a samurai sword.'

'Neither one,' said Rönn, who had just come into the room. 'We've found the weapon. It's lying outside, about twelve feet from the window.'

They went outside and looked.

In the cold white light of a spot lay a broad-bladed cutting tool.

'A bayonet,' said Martin Beck.

'Yes. Exactly. For a Mauser carbine.'

The six-millimetre carbine had been a common military weapon, used mostly by the artillery and cavalry. Martin Beck had one himself when he did his national service. The weapon had probably gone out of use by now and been struck from the quartermaster's rolls.

The blade was entirely covered with clotted blood.

'Can you get fingerprints from that grooved handle?'

Rönn shrugged his shoulders.

Every word had to be dragged from him, if not by force then by verbal pressure.

'You're letting it lie there until it gets light?'

'Yes,' Rönn said. 'Seems like a good idea.'

'I'd very much like to talk to Nyman's family as soon as possible. Do you think we could get his wife out of bed at this hour?'

'Yes, I suppose so,' said Rönn without conviction.

34

'We have to start somewhere. Are you coming along?'

Rönn mumbled something.

'What'd you say?' said Martin Beck and blew his nose.

'Got to get a photographer out here,' Rönn said. 'Yeah.'

But he didn't sound at all as if he cared.

8

Rönn walked out to the car and got into the driver's seat to wait for Martin Beck, who'd taken upon himself the unpleasant task of calling the widow.

'How much did you tell her?' he asked when Martin Beck had climbed in beside him.

'Only that he's dead. He was apparently seriously ill, so maybe it didn't come as such a surprise. But of course now she's wondering what we've got to do with it.'

'How did she sound? Shocked?'

'Yes, of course. She was going to jump in a taxi and come straight over to the hospital. There's a doctor talking to her now. I hope he manages to convince her to wait at home.'

'Yes. If she saw him now she'd really get a shock. It's bad enough having to tell her about it.'

Rönn drove north on Dalagatan towards Odengatan. Outside the Eastman Institute stood a black Volkswagen. Rönn nodded towards it.

'Not bad enough he parks in a no-parking zone, he's halfway up on the pavement too. Lucky for him we're not from Traffic.'

'On top of which he must have been drunk to park like that,' said Martin Beck.

'Or she,' Rönn said. 'It must be a woman. Women and cars . . .'

'Typical stereotyped thinking,' said Martin Beck. 'If my daughter could hear you now you'd be in for a real lecture.'

The car swung right on Odengatan and drove on past Gustav Vasa Church and Odenplan. At the taxi station there were two cabs with their FREE signs lit, and at the traffic lights outside the city library there was a yellow street-cleaning machine with a blinking orange light on its roof, waiting for the light to turn green.

Martin Beck and Rönn drove on in silence. They turned on to Sveavägen and passed the street-sweeper as it rumbled around the corner. At the School of Economics they took a left on to Kungstensgatan.

'Damn it to hell,' said Martin Beck suddenly with emphasis.

'Yeah,' said Rönn.

Then it was quiet again in the car. When they'd crossed Birger Jarlsgatan, Rönn slowed down and started hunting for the number. A door to a block of flats across from the Citizens School opened and a young man stuck out his head and looked in their direction. He held the door open while they parked the car and crossed the street.

When they reached the doorway they saw that the boy was younger than he'd looked from a distance. He was almost as tall as Martin Beck, but looked to be fifteen years old at the most.

'My name's Stefan,' he said. 'Mother's waiting upstairs.'

They followed him up the stairs to the second floor, where a door stood ajar. The boy showed them through the front hall and into the living room.

'I'll get Mother,' he mumbled and disappeared into the hall.

Martin Beck and Rönn remained standing in the middle of the room and looked around. It was very neat. One side was taken up by a suite of furniture that seemed to date from the 1940s and consisted of a sofa, three matching easy chairs in varnished blond wood and flowered cretonne upholstery, and an oval table of the same light wood. A white lace cloth lay on the table, and in the middle of the cloth was a large crystal vase of red tulips. The two windows looked out on the street, and behind the white lace curtains stood rows of well-tended potted plants. The wall at one end of the room was covered by a bookcase in gleaming mahogany, half filled with leather-bound books, half with souvenirs and knick-knacks. Small polished tables with pieces of silver and crystal stood here and there against the walls. A black piano with the lid closed over the keyboard completed the list of furniture. Framed portraits of the family stood lined up on the piano. Several still lifes and landscapes in wide ornate gold frames hung on the walls. A crystal chandelier burned in the middle of the room, and a wine-red Oriental rug lay beneath their feet.

Martin Beck took in the various details of the room as he listened to the footsteps approaching in the hall. Rönn had walked up to the bookcase and was suspiciously eyeing a brass reindeer-bell, one side of which was adorned with a brightly coloured picture of a mountain birch, a reindeer and a Lapp, plus the word ARJEPLOG in ornate red letters.

Mrs Nyman came into the room with her son. She was wearing a black wool dress, black shoes and stockings, and held a small white handkerchief clenched in one hand. She had been crying.

Martin Beck and Rönn introduced themselves. She didn't look as if she'd ever heard of them.

'But please sit down,' she said, and took a seat in one of the flowered chairs.

When the two policemen had seated themselves she looked at them with despair in her eyes.

'What is it that's actually happened?' she asked in a voice that was much too shrill.

Rönn took out his handkerchief and began to polish his florid nose, thoroughly and at length. But Martin Beck hadn't expected any help from that quarter.

'If you have anything to calm your nerves, Mrs Nyman – pills, I mean – I think it would be wise to take a couple now,' he said.

The boy, who had taken a seat on the piano stool, stood up.

'Papa has . . . There's a bottle of Restenil in the cabinet in the bathroom,' he said. 'Shall I get it?'

Martin Beck nodded and the boy went out to the bathroom and came back with the tablets and a glass of water. Martin Beck looked at the label, shook out two tablets into the lid of the bottle and handed them to Mrs Nyman, who obediently swallowed them with a gulp of water.

'Thank you,' she said. 'Now please tell me what it is you want. Stig is dead, and neither you nor I can do anything about that.'

She pressed the handkerchief to her mouth, and her voice was stifled when she spoke.

'Why wasn't I allowed to go to him? He's my husband after all. What have they done to him there at the hospital? That doctor . . . he sounded so odd . . .'

Her son went over and sat on the arm of her chair. He put his arm around her shoulders.

Martin Beck twisted in his chair so that he sat directly facing her, then he threw a glance at Rönn, sitting silently on the sofa.

'Mrs Nyman,' he said, 'your husband did not die of his illness. Someone entered his room and killed him.'

The woman stared at him and he could see in her eyes that several seconds passed before she understood the significance of what he'd said. She lowered the hand with the handkerchief and pressed it to her breast. She was very pale.

'Killed? Someone killed him? I don't understand . . .'

The son had gone white around the nostrils and his grip around his mother's shoulders tightened.

'Who?' he said.

'We don't know. A nurse found him on the floor of his room just after two o'clock. Someone had come in through the window and killed him with a bayonet. It must have happened in the course

39

of a few seconds, I don't think he had time to realize what was happening.'

Said Martin Beck. The giver of comfort.

'Everything indicates he was taken by surprise,' Rönn said. 'If he'd had time to react he would have tried to protect himself or ward off the blows, but there's no sign that he did.'

The woman now stared at Rönn.

'But why?' she said.

'We don't know,' Rönn said.

That was all he said.

'Mrs Nyman, maybe you can help us find out,' said Martin Beck. 'We don't want to cause you unnecessary pain, but we have to ask you a few questions. First of all, can you think of anyone who might have done it?'

The woman shook her head hopelessly.

'Do you know if your husband had ever received any threats? Or if there was anyone who thought he had reason to want to see him dead? Anyone who threatened him?'

She went on shaking her head.

'No,' she said. 'Why should anyone threaten him?'

'Anyone who hated him?'

'Why should anyone hate him?'

'Think carefully,' Martin Beck said. 'Wasn't there anyone who thought your husband had treated him badly? He was a policeman, after all, and making enemies is part of the job. Did he ever say someone was out to get him or had threatened him?'

The widow looked in confusion first at her son, then at Rönn, and then back at Martin Beck.

'Not that I can recall. And I'd certainly remember if he'd said anything like that.'

'Papa didn't talk much about his job,' Stefan said. 'You'd better ask at the station.'

'We'll ask there too,' said Martin Beck. 'How long had he been sick?'

'A long time, I don't remember exactly,' the boy said, and looked at his mother.

'Since June of last year,' she said. 'He got sick just before midsummer, an awful pain in his stomach, and he went to the doctor right after the holiday. The doctor thought it was an ulcer and had him go on sick leave. He's been on sick leave ever since, and he's been to several different doctors and they all say different things and prescribe different medicines. Then three weeks ago he went into Sabbath and they've been examining him and doing a lot of tests ever since, but they couldn't find out what it was.'

Talking seemed to distract her attention and help her repress the shock.

'Papa thought it was cancer,' the boy said. 'The doctors said it wasn't. But he was terribly sick all the time.'

'What did he do all this time? Hasn't he worked at all since last summer?'

'No,' Mrs Nyman said. 'He was really very ill. Had attacks of pain that lasted several days in a row when all he could do was lie in bed. He took a lot of pills, but they didn't help much. He went down to the station a few times last autumn to see how things were going, as he said, but he couldn't work.'

'Mrs Nyman, can't you remember anything he said or did that might have some connection with what's happened?' asked Martin Beck.

She shook her head and started sobbing dryly. Her eyes glided on past Martin Beck and she stared straight ahead at nothing.

'Do you have any brothers and sisters?' Rönn asked the boy.

'Yes, a sister, but she's married and lives in Malmö.'

Rönn glanced inquiringly at Martin Beck, who was rolling a cigarette thoughtfully back and forth between his fingers as he looked at the two people in front of him.

'We'll be going now,' he said to the boy. 'I'm sure you can take care of your mother, but I think the best thing would be if you could get a doctor to come over and give her something to make her sleep. Is there any doctor you can call at this time of night?'

The boy stood up and nodded.

'Doctor Blomberg,' he said. 'He usually comes when someone in the family's sick.'

He went out in the hall and they heard him dial a number and after a while someone seemed to answer.

The conversation was short and he came back and stood beside his mother. He looked more like an adult now than he had when they first saw him down in the doorway.

'He's coming,' the boy said. 'You don't need to wait. It won't take him long.'

They stood up and Rönn went over and put his hand on the woman's shoulder. She didn't move, and when they said good-bye she didn't respond.

The boy went with them to the door.

'We may have to come back,' said Martin Beck. 'We'll call you first to find out how your mother's doing.'

When they were out on the street he turned to Rönn.

'I suppose you knew Nyman?' he said.

'Not especially well,' said Rönn evasively.

9

The blue-white light of a flashbulb lit the dirty yellow façade of the hospital pavilion for an instant as Martin Beck and Rönn returned to the scene of the crime. An additional couple of cars had arrived and stood parked in the turnaround with their head-lights on.

'Apparently our photographer is here,' Rönn said.

The photographer came towards them as they got out of the car. He carried no camera bag but held his camera and flash in one hand, while his pockets bulged with rolls of film and flash-bulbs and lenses. Martin Beck recognized him from the scenes of previous crimes.

'Wrong,' he said to Rönn. 'It looks like the papers got here first.'

The photographer, who worked for one of the tabloids, greeted them and took a picture as they walked towards the door. A reporter from the same paper was standing at the foot of the stairs trying to talk to a uniformed officer.

'Good morning, Inspector,' he said when he caught sight of Martin Beck. 'I don't suppose I could follow you in?'

Martin Beck shook his head and walked up the steps with Rönn in his wake.

'But you'll give me a little interview at least?' the reporter said.

'Later,' said Martin Beck and held the door open for Rönn before closing it right on the nose of the reporter, who made a face.

The police photographer had also arrived and was standing outside the dead man's room with his camera bag. Further down the corridor was the doctor with the curious name and a plain-clothes detective from the Fifth. Rönn went into the sickroom with the photographer and put him to work. Martin Beck walked over to the two men in the hall.

'How's it going?' he said.

The same old question.

The plainclothes officer, whose name was Hansson, scratched the back of his neck.

'We've talked to most of the patients in this corridor, and none of them saw or heard anything. I was just trying to ask Doctor . . . uh . . . this doctor here, when we can talk to the other ones.'

'Have you questioned the people in the adjoining rooms?' Martin Beck asked.

'Yes,' Hansson said. 'And we've been in all the wards. No one heard anything, but then the walls are thick in a building this old.'

'We can wait on the others till breakfast,' said Martin Beck.

The doctor said nothing. He obviously didn't understand Swedish, and after a while he pointed towards the office and said, 'Have to go,' in English.

Hansson nodded, and the black curls hurried off in clattering wooden shoes.

'Did you know Nyman?' asked Martin Beck.

'Well, no, not really. I've never worked in his precinct, but of course we've met often enough. He's been around a long time. He was already an inspector when I started, twelve years ago.'

'Do you know anyone who knew him well?'

'You can always ask down at Klara,' Hansson said. 'That's where he was before he got sick.'

Martin Beck nodded and looked at the electric wall clock over the door to the bathroom. It said a quarter to five.

'I think I'll go on over there for a while,' he said. 'There's not much I can do here for the moment.'

'Go on,' said Hansson. 'I'll tell Rönn where you went.'

Martin Beck took a deep breath when he got outside. The chilly night air felt fresh and clean. The reporter and the photographer were nowhere to be seen, but the uniformed officer was still standing at the foot of the steps.

Martin Beck nodded to him and started walking towards the car park.

The centre of Stockholm had been subjected to sweeping and violent changes in the course of the last ten years. Entire districts had been levelled and new ones constructed. The structure of the city had been altered: streets had been broadened and motorways built. What was behind all this activity was hardly an ambition to create a humane social environment but rather a desire to achieve the fullest possible exploitation of valuable land. In the heart of the city it had not been enough to tear down ninety per cent of the buildings and completely obliterate the original street plan, violence had been visited on the natural topography itself.

Stockholm's inhabitants looked on with sorrow and bitterness as serviceable and irreplaceable old mansion blocks were razed to make way for sterile office buildings. Powerless, they let themselves be deported to distant suburbs while the pleasant, lively neighbourhoods where they had lived and worked were reduced to rubble. The inner city became a clamorous, all but impassable construction site from which the new city slowly and relentlessly arose with its broad, noisy traffic arteries, its shining façades of glass and light metal, its dead surfaces of flat concrete, its bleakness and its desolation.

In this frenzy of modernization, the city's police stations seemed to have been completely overlooked. All the station houses in the inner city were old-fashioned and the worse for wear, and in most cases, since the force had been enlarged over the years, crowded. In the Fourth Precinct, where Martin Beck was heading, this lack of space was one of the primary problems.

By the time he stepped out of the taxi in front of the Klara police station on Regeringsgatan, it had begun to get light. The sun would come up, there was still not a cloud in the sky, and it promised to be a pretty though rather chilly day.

He walked up the stone steps and pushed open the door. To the right was the switchboard, for the moment unmanned, and a counter behind which stood an older, grey-haired policeman. He had spread out the morning paper and was resting on his elbows as he read. When Martin Beck came in he straightened up and took off his glasses.

'Why it's Inspector Beck, up and about at this time of the morning,' he said. 'I was just looking to see if the morning papers had anything about Inspector Nyman. It sounds like a very nasty business.'

He put on his glasses again, licked his thumb and turned a page in the paper.

'It doesn't look as if they had time to get it in,' he went on.

'No,' said Martin Beck. 'I don't suppose they did.'

The Stockholm morning papers went to press early these days and had probably been ready for distribution even before Nyman was murdered.

He walked past the desk and into the duty room. It was empty. The morning papers lay on a table along with a couple of overflowing ashtrays and some coffee mugs. Through a window into one of the interrogation rooms he could see the officer in charge sitting talking to a young woman with long blonde hair. When he caught sight of Martin Beck he stood up, said something to the woman and came out of the glass cubicle. He closed the door behind him.

'Hi,' he said. 'Is it me you're looking for?'

Martin Beck sat down at the short end of the table, pulled an ashtray towards him and lit a cigarette.

'I'm not looking for anyone in particular,' he said. 'But have you got a minute?'

'Can you wait just a moment?' the other man said. 'I just want to get this woman sent over to Criminal.'

He disappeared and returned a few minutes later with a constable, picked up an envelope from the desk and handed it to him. The woman stood up, hung her purse on her shoulder and walked quickly towards the door.

'Come on, big boy,' she said without turning her head. 'Let's go for a ride.'

The constable looked at the officer, who shrugged his shoulders, amused. Then he put on his cap and followed her out.

'She seemed right at home,' said Martin Beck.

'Oh yeah, this isn't the first time. And certainly not the last.'

He sat down at the table and started cleaning his pipe into an ashtray.

'That was nasty, that business with Nyman,' he said. 'How did it happen, exactly?'

Martin Beck told him briefly what had happened.

'Ugh,' the officer said. 'Whoever did it must be a raving lunatic. But why Nyman?'

'You knew Nyman, didn't you?' Martin Beck asked him.

'Not very well. He wasn't the sort of person you knew well.'

'He was here on special assignment of course. When did he come here to the Fourth?'

'They gave him an office here three years ago. February '68.'

'What sort of a person was he?' Martin Beck asked.

The officer filled his pipe and lit it before answering.

'I don't really know how to describe him. You knew him too, I suppose? Ambitious, you could certainly call him; stubborn, not much of a sense of humour. Rather conservative in his views. The younger fellows were a little afraid of him, in spite of the fact they didn't really have anything to do with him. He could be a bit stern. But as I said, I didn't know him at all well.'

'Did he have any particular friends on the force?'

'Not here at any rate. I don't think he and our inspector got along very well. But otherwise I don't know.'

The man thought for a moment and then looked at Martin Beck oddly – appealingly and conspiratorially.

'Well . . .' he said.

'What?'

'I mean I expect he still had friends at headquarters, didn't he?'

Martin Beck didn't answer. Instead he put another question.

'What about enemies?'

'Don't know. He probably had enemies, but hardly here, and certainly not to the point that . . .'

'Do you know if he'd been threatened?'

'No, he didn't exactly confide in me. Although, for that matter . . .'

'Yes, what?'

'Well, for that matter, Nyman wasn't the kind of man who let himself be threatened.'

The telephone rang inside the glass cubicle and the officer went in and answered it. Martin Beck walked over and stood by the window with his hands in his pockets. The station was quiet. The only sounds to be heard were the voice of the man on the telephone and the dry coughing of the old policeman at the switchboard. Presumably things were not so quiet in the custody suite on the floor below.

Martin Beck suddenly realized how tired he was. His eyes ached from lack of sleep, and his throat from far too many cigarettes.

The phone call looked as if it was going to be a long one. Martin Beck yawned and leafed through the morning paper, read the headlines and an occasional picture caption but without really seeing what he read. Finally he folded up the paper, walked over and knocked on the window to the cubicle, and when the man on the phone looked up he made signs indicating he was about to leave. The officer waved and went on talking into the receiver.

Martin Beck lit another cigarette and thought distractedly that it must be his fiftieth since that first cigarette of the morning almost twenty-four hours ago.

10

If you really want to be sure of getting caught, the thing to do is kill a policeman.

This truth applies in most places and especially in Sweden. There are plenty of unsolved murders in Swedish criminal history, but not one of them involves the murder of a policeman.

When a member of their own troop meets with misfortune, the police seem to acquire many times their usual energy. All the complaints about lack of manpower and resources stop, and suddenly it's possible to mobilize several hundred men for an investigation that would normally have occupied no more than three or four.

A man who lays hands on a policeman always gets caught. Not because the general public takes a solid stand behind the forces of law and order – as it does, for example, in England or the socialist countries – but because the police chief's entire private army suddenly knows what it wants, and, what's more, wants it very badly.

Martin Beck stood on Regeringsgatan enjoying the chilly freshness of the early morning.

He wasn't armed, but in the inside right-hand pocket of his coat he was carrying a stencilled circular from National Police

Headquarters. It was a copy of a recent sociological study, and he'd found it on his desk the day before.

The police force took a very dim view of sociologists – particularly in recent years since they'd started focusing more and more on the activities and attitudes of policemen – and all their pronouncements were read with great suspicion by the men at the top. Perhaps the brass realized that in the long run it would prove untenable simply to insist that everyone involved in sociology was actually a communist or some other subversive.

Sociologists were capable of anything, as Superintendent Malm had recently pointed out in one of his many moments of indignation. Martin Beck, among others, was supposed to look on Malm as his superior.

Maybe Malm was right. Sociologists got all kinds of ideas. For example, they came up with the fact that you no longer needed better than a D average to get into the Police Academy, and that the average IQ of uniformed officers in Stockholm had dropped to 93.

'It's a lie!' Malm had shouted. 'And what's more it isn't true! And on top of that it isn't any lower than in New York!'

He'd just returned from a study tour in the States.

The report in Martin Beck's pocket revealed a number of interesting new facts. It proved that police work wasn't a bit more dangerous than any other profession. On the contrary, most other jobs involved much greater risks. Construction workers and lumberjacks lived considerably more hazardous lives, not to mention dockers or taxi drivers or housewives.

But hadn't it always been generally accepted that a policeman's lot was riskier and tougher and less well paid than any other? The answer was painfully simple. Yes, but only because no other professional group suffered from such role fixation or dramatized its daily life to the same degree as did the police.

It was all supported by figures. The number of injured policemen was negligible when compared with the number of people annually mistreated by the police. And so forth.

And it didn't apply only to Stockholm. In New York, for example, an average of seven policemen were killed every year, whereas taxi drivers perished at the rate of two a month, house-wives one a week, and among the unemployed the rate was one a day.

To these odious sociologists nothing was sacred. There was a Swedish team that had even managed to torpedo the myth of the English bobby and reduce it to its proper proportions, namely, to the fact that the English police are not armed and therefore don't provoke violence to the same degree as certain others. Even in Denmark responsible authorities had managed to grasp this fact, and only in exceptional situations were policemen permitted to sign out weapons.

But such was not the case in Stockholm.

Martin Beck had suddenly started thinking about this study as he stood looking at Nyman's body.

And now it came to mind again. He realized that the conclusions that document drew were correct, and paradoxically enough he sensed some sort of connection between those conclusions and the murder that occupied him at the moment.

It's not dangerous to be a policeman, and in fact it's the policemen who are dangerous, and a little while ago he'd been looking down at the butchered body of a policeman.

To his surprise, the corners of his mouth started to quiver, and for a moment it felt as if he were going to sit down on the steps leading from Regeringsgatan down to Kungsgatan and burst into laughter at the whole situation.

But with the same curious logic it suddenly occurred to him that he'd better go home and get his pistol.

It was over a year since he'd even looked at it.

An empty cab came up the street from Stureplan.

Martin Beck stuck out his hand and got it to stop.

It was a yellow Volvo with a black stripe along the sides. This was a relatively recent innovation and a relaxation of the old rule that all taxicabs in Stockholm had to be black. He climbed into the front seat next to the driver.

'Köpmangatan eight,' he said.

And as he said it he recognized the driver. He was one of those policemen who eke out their incomes by driving a cab during their off-duty hours. That he recognized the man was pure coincidence. Several days earlier, outside the Central Station, he'd watched two unusually maladroit constables drive an initially peaceable young drunk into a belligerent rage and then lose control of themselves. The man behind the wheel was one of them.

He was about twenty-five years old and extremely garrulous.

He was probably talkative from birth, and since his regular job permitted him only an occasionally angry grunt, he made up for it here in his cab.

One of the Sanitation Department's combination sweep-and-spray lorries temporarily blocked their path. The moonlighting constable fretfully studied a hoarding advertising Richard Attenborough's *10 Rillington Place.*

'Ten Rollington Palace, hunh?' he said in some sort of dialect. 'And people want to see that kind of crap. Murder and misery and crazy people. If you ask me it's a damned shame.'

Martin Beck nodded. The man, who obviously didn't recognize him, took the nod as encouragement and talked volubly on.

'But you know it's these foreigners that make all the trouble.'

Martin Beck said nothing.

'But I will say one thing, you're making a big mistake if you lump all foreigners together in one bag. The guy who drives this cab with me, he's Portuguese, for example.'

'Oh?'

'Yeah, and you couldn't find a better man. He works his arse off, doesn't lie around on his behind. And can he drive! And do you know why?'

Martin Beck shook his head.

'Yeah, well, he drove a tank in Africa for four years. You know,

Portugal's fighting a war of liberation down there, place called Angola. They're fighting like hell for their freedom down there, the Portuguese, but you never hear anything about it here in Sweden. This guy, the guy I'm talking about, he shot hundreds of commies those four years. And on him it really shows what a good thing the army is, and discipline and all that. He does exactly what you tell him, and he rakes in more money than anyone else I know. And if he gets some drunk Finn bastard in the car, well, he sees to it he gets a hundred per cent tip. They've got it coming, all those scroungers on welfare.'

Just then, fortunately, the car stopped outside the building where Martin Beck lived. He told the driver to wait, let himself into the building and rode up to his flat.

The pistol was a 7.65 mm Walther and lay in its place in a locked drawer of his desk. The clips were also where they belonged, in another locked drawer in the other room. He slipped one of them into the pistol and put the other in his right-hand coat pocket. But he had to hunt for five minutes before he could find his shoulder holster, which was lying in a pile of old ties and T-shirts on a shelf in the wardrobe.

Back down on the street, the effusive constable stood leaning against his yellow taxi, happily humming to himself. He held the door politely, climbed in behind the wheel and had already opened his mouth to resume his text when Martin Beck interrupted.

'Kungsholmsgatan thirty-seven, please,' he said.

'But that's the . . .'

'Right, Criminal Division. Drive along Skeppsbron, please.'

The driver immediately turned red in the face and didn't utter a sound the whole way there.

And that was welcome, Martin Beck thought. In spite of everything, he loved this city, and right at this place and at this time of day it was perhaps at its most beautiful. The morning sun was shining across Strömmen, and the surface of the water was smooth and calm and didn't reveal the terrible pollution that was unfortunately a fact. In his youth – in fact a lot more recently than that – you could go swimming here.

Down along the city quay lay an old cargo steamer with a tall straight stack and a black spar on the mainmast. You rarely saw them any more these days. An early Djurgård ferry was cutting through the water with a crisp little wave along its bows. He noticed that the smokestack was completely black and the name on the side was covered with white paint. But he recognized it anyway. The *Djurgård* 5.

'Do you want a receipt?' asked the driver in a stifled voice outside the doors to the police building.

'Yes, please.'

Martin Beck went up to the offices of the Violent Crime Division, studied some documents, made a few phone calls and did a little writing.

At the end of an hour he'd managed to put together a brief and very superficial summary of a human life. It began like this:

Stig Oscar Emil Nyman.

Born 6th November, 1911, in Säffle.

Parents: Oscar Abraham Nyman, logging foreman, and Karin Maria Nyman, née Rutgersson.

Schooling: Two years' elementary school in Säffle, two years' grade school in Säffle, five years secondary school in Amål.

Joined professional infantry 1928, lance corporal 1930, corporal 1931, sergeant 1933, Noncommissioned Officer's School.

And then Stig Oscar Emil Nyman had become a policeman. First as a deputy sheriff in Värmland, then as a regular police constable in Stockholm. During the depression in the thirties. His military experience was counted in his favour and led to quick promotions.

At the beginning of the Second World War he resumed his military career, was promoted and given a number of obscure special assignments. During the latter part of the war he was transferred to Karlsborg, but in 1946 he went into the reserve and one year later reappeared on the personnel roster of the Stockholm police, this time as a sergeant.

When Martin Beck went through the inspector's course in 1949, Nyman was already a deputy chief inspector and was given his first precinct command a few years later.

As a chief inspector, Nyman had at different times been chief of several precincts in the inner city. From time to time he'd been back at the old police headquarters on Agnegatan, again on assignments of a special nature.

He had spent the greater part of his life in uniform, but in spite of that was one of the men who had long been in the good graces of the highest police command.

Only circumstances had kept him from advancing even further and becoming chief for the regular metropolitan police in its entirety.

What circumstances?

Martin Beck knew the answer to that question.

At the end of the fifties, the Stockholm police department had undergone a substantial shake-up. There had been an infusion of fresh leadership and fresh air. Military thinking ceased to be so popular, and reactionary ideas were no longer necessarily an asset. The changes at headquarters spread to a certain extent out into the precincts, automatic promotion became less routine, and certain phenomena, among them the Prussian spit-and-polish of the regular police, died in the wake of the move towards greater democracy. Nyman was one of many who had watched his bridges burn before him.

It seemed to Martin Beck that the first half of the sixties had been an auspicious period in the history of the Stockholm police. Everything had seemed to be improving, common sense had been about to conquer rigidity and cliquishness, the recruiting base had been broadened, and even relations with the public had seemed to be getting better. But nationalization in 1965 had broken the positive trend. Since then, all the good prospects had been betrayed and all the good intentions laid to rest.

For Nyman, however, it came too late. It was now almost seven years since he'd had his last precinct command.

During that time he'd worked mostly on things like civil defence. But no one had been able to take away his reputation as an expert in maintaining order, and he had been eagerly consulted as a specialist in connection with the frequent large demonstrations towards the end of the sixties.

Martin Beck scratched the back of his neck and read through the last few lines of his inconsequential notes.

Married 1945, two children from the marriage, daughter Annelotte born 1949 and son Stefan born 1956.

Early retirement due to illness 1970.

He picked up his ballpoint pen and wrote:

Died in Stockholm, 3rd April, 1971.

Read through the whole thing one more time. Looked at the clock. Ten minutes to seven.

He wondered how things were going for Rönn.

11

The city woke up and yawned and stretched.

As did Gunvald Larsson. Woke up, yawned and stretched. Then he put a large hairy hand on the electric alarm clock, threw off the blanket and swung his long shaggy legs out of bed.

He put on his bathrobe and slippers and walked over to the window to check the weather. Dry, fair, thirty-seven degrees. The suburb he lived in was called Bollmora and consisted of some high-rise blocks of flats in the woods.

Then he looked in the mirror and saw a very large blond man, still six feet three and a half inches tall, but weighing in these days at sixteen and a half stone. He got a little heavier with every year, and it was no longer pure muscle that bulged beneath the white silk robe. But he was in good shape and felt stronger than ever, which was saying a good deal. For several seconds he stared into his own porcelain-blue eyes under a wrinkled brow. Then he combed his blond hair back with his fingers, pulled open his lips and examined his large strong teeth.

He got the morning paper from the letter box and went out to the kitchen to make breakfast. There he made tea – Twining's Irish Breakfast – and toast and boiled two eggs. He got out the butter, some Cheddar cheese and Scottish marmalade, three different kinds.

He leafed through the paper as he ate.

Sweden had done badly in the international ice hockey championships, and the managers, trainers and players were now emphasizing their lack of sportsmanship by hurling accusations at each other in public. There was also a fight going on within Swedish television – the monopoly's central management was apparently doing everything it could to maintain a tight hold on the news services of the different channels.

Censorship, thought Gunvald Larsson. With laminated plastic gloves. Typical of this meddlesome capitalist society.

The biggest piece of news was that the readers were being given the opportunity to christen three bear cubs at Skansen. The results of a military study showing forty-year-old reservists to be in better physical condition than eighteen-year-old recruits were noted with resignation in a less prominent place. And on the culture page, where there was no risk of its being seen by unauthorized readers, there was an article on Rhodesia.

He read it while he drank his tea and ate his eggs and six pieces of toast.

Gunvald Larsson had never been in Rhodesia, but many times in South Africa, Sierra Leone, Angola and Mozambique. He'd been a seaman then, and had already known his own mind.

He finished his meal, washed the dishes and threw the paper in the rubbish. Since it was Saturday, he changed the sheets before making the bed. Then with great care he selected the clothes he would wear that day and laid them neatly on the bed. Removed his robe and pyjamas and took a shower.

His bachelor flat bore witness to good taste and a feeling for quality. Furniture, rugs, curtains, everything, from his white leather Italian slippers to his pivoting Nordmende colour TV, was first class.

Gunvald Larsson was an inspector with the Violent Crime Division in Stockholm, and higher up the ladder he would never go. As a matter of fact it was odd he hadn't been fired already. His colleagues thought him peculiar, and they almost all disliked him. He himself detested not only the men he worked with but also his own family and the upper-class background he came from. His own brothers and sisters regarded him with profound distaste. Partly as a result of his dissident views, but mostly because he was a policeman.

While showering, he wondered if he would die that day.

It was not a foreboding. He'd wondered the same thing every morning since he was eight years old and brushed his teeth before dragging himself reluctantly off to Broms School on Sturegatan.

Lennart Kollberg lay in his bed dreaming. It was not a pleasant dream. He'd had it before, and when he woke from it he'd be dripping with sweat and he'd say to Gun, 'Put your arms around me, I had such an awful nightmare.'

And Gun, who'd been his wife for five years, would put her arms around him and right away he'd forget everything else.

In the dream, his daughter Bodil is standing in the open window five storeys above the street. He tries to run over to her, but his legs are paralysed and she starts to fall, slowly, as if in slow motion, and she screams and stretches her arms out towards him and he fights to reach her, but his muscles won't obey him and she falls and falls, screaming all the time.

He woke up. The scream in the nightmare became the drilling buzz of the alarm clock, and when he looked up he saw Bodil sitting astride his shins.

She was reading *The Cat Trip*. She was only three and a half and she couldn't read, but Gun and he had read the story to her so many times they all knew it by heart, and he could hear Bodil whispering it to herself.

'A little old man with a big blue nose, all dressed up in calico clothes.'

He turned off the alarm clock and she immediately stopped whispering and said 'Hi!' in a clear high voice.

Kollberg turned his head and looked at Gun. She was still asleep, with the quilt pulled up to her nose, and her dark ruffled hair was a tiny bit damp at the temples. He put his finger to his lips.

'Shh,' he whispered. 'Don't wake Mummy. And don't sit on my legs, it hurts. Come up here and lie down.'

He made room for her to creep down under the quilt between him and Gun. She gave him the book and arranged herself with her head in his armpit.

'Read it,' she ordered.

He put the book aside.

'No, not now,' he said. 'Did you get the newspaper?'

She scrambled across his midriff and picked up the newspaper, which was on the floor beside the bed. He groaned, lifted her up and put her back in the bed beside him again. Then he opened the paper and started to read. He made it all the way to the foreign news on page twelve before Bodil interrupted.

'Papa?'

'Mmm.'

'Josha did a big poo.'

'Mmm.'

'He took off his nappy and put it on the wall. All over the wall.'

Kollberg put down the paper and groaned again, got out of bed and went into the children's room. Joshua, who would soon be one, was standing up in his cot and when he saw his father he let go of the railing and sat down on the pillow with a little bounce. Bodil had not exaggerated his adornment of the wall.

Kollberg picked him up under one arm, carried him into the bathroom and rinsed him off with the shower hose. Then he wrapped him in a towel and went in and put him down beside Gun, who was still asleep. He rinsed out the bedclothes and the pyjamas, cleaned the cot and the wallpaper and got out a clean nappy and a fresh pair of plastic pants. Bodil scampered along beside him through it all. She was very pleased that for once his irritation was directed at Joshua instead of at herself, and she clucked and fussed officiously at her brother's bad behaviour. When he'd finished cleaning up it was after seven thirty and there wasn't any point in going back to bed.

His mood improved as soon as he walked into the bedroom. Gun was awake, playing with Joshua. She had drawn up her knees and was holding him under the arms and letting him play roller coaster down her legs. Gun was an attractive and sensuous woman with both intelligence and a sense of humour. Kollberg had always imagined he would marry a woman like Gun, and though there had been quite a few women in his life, he'd been forty-one years old and had almost given up hope. She was fourteen years younger than he, and well worth waiting for. Their relationship had, from the very beginning, been uncomplicated, intimate and straight-forward.

She smiled at him and held up their son, who gurgled with delight.

'Hi,' she said. 'Did you already give him his bath?'

Kollberg described his labours.

'Poor dear. Come lie down for a while,' she said, throwing a glance at the clock. 'You've got time.'

Actually he didn't, but he was easy to convince. He lay down next to her with his arm under her neck, but after a while he got up again, carried Joshua in and put him down on his mattress, which was virtually dry, dressed him in a nappy and a terrycloth romper suit, threw some toys in the cot and went back to Gun. Bodil was sitting on the rug in the living room, playing with her barn.

After a while she came in and looked at them.

'Play horsey,' she said delightedly. 'Daddy's the horsey.'

She tried to climb up on his back but he got rid of her and closed the door. Then the children didn't bother them for a long time, and when they'd made love he all but fell asleep in his wife's arms.

When Kollberg walked across the street to his car the clock on the Skärmarbrink metro station said eight twenty-three. Before getting in, he turned and waved to Gun and Bodil, who were standing in the kitchen window.

He didn't have to drive into town to get to Västberga Avenue but could take the route through Årsta and Enskede and avoid the worst of the traffic.

As he drove, Lennart Kollberg whistled an Irish folksong very loudly and very much out of tune.

The sun was shining, there was spring in the air, and crocuses and Star-of-Bethlehem were blooming in the gardens he passed. He was in a good mood. If he was lucky, he'd have a short day and would be able to go home fairly early in the afternoon. Gun was going to go in to Arvid Nordquist's and buy something good, and they'd have dinner after the children were in bed. After five years of marriage their idea of a really pleasant evening was to be at home, alone, help each other make a good dinner and then sit for a long time and eat and drink and talk.

Kollberg was very fond of good food and drink, and as a result had put on a little fat over the years, a little 'substance' as he preferred to call it. Anyone who thought this fleshiness prejudicial to his agility, however, was making a serious error. He could be unexpectedly quick and lithe, and he was still in command of all the technique and all the tricks he'd once learned in the paratroops.

He stopped whistling and started thinking about a problem that had occupied him a lot these last few years. He liked his job less and less, and would really prefer to resign from the force. The problem was not easy to solve and had been complicated by the fact that a year earlier he'd been promoted to deputy chief inspector, with an appropriate raise in salary. It wasn't easy for a forty-six-year-old deputy chief inspector of police to find a different and equally well-paying job. Gun kept telling him to forget the money – the children were getting older and by and by she'd be able to go back to work. In addition to which, she'd been studying and had learned another

63

couple of languages during the four years she'd been a housewife and would certainly draw a considerably higher salary now than she had before. Before Bodil was born, she'd been an executive secretary, and she could get a well-paid position whenever she wanted. But Kollberg didn't want her to feel she had to go back to work before she really wanted to.

On top of that he had a hard time picturing himself as a homemaker.

He was by nature somewhat lazy, but needed a certain amount of activity and change around him.

As he drove his car into the garage at Södra police station he remembered that Martin Beck had the day off.

First of all that means I'll have to stay here all day, Kollberg thought, and secondly that I won't have anyone sensible to talk to. His spirits immediately sank.

In order to cheer himself up, he started whistling again while he waited for the lift.

12

Kollberg hadn't even had time to take off his overcoat when the telephone rang.

'Yes, Kollberg here . . . what?'

He stood by his littered desk and stared absently out of the window. The transition from the pleasures of private life to the ugliness of the job wasn't as easy for him as it was for some, for example Martin Beck.

'What's it about? . . . You don't? Well, okay, tell them I'm coming.'

Down to the car again, and this time no way to avoid the traffic.

He arrived at Kungsholmsgatan at a quarter to nine and parked in the yard. Just as Kollberg was getting out of his car, Gunvald Larsson got into his and drove away.

They nodded to each other but didn't speak. He ran into Rönn in the corridor.

'So you're here too,' Rönn said.

'Yes, what's up?'

'Somebody sliced up Stig Nyman.'

'Sliced up?'

'Yeah, with a bayonet,' said Rönn mournfully. 'At Mount Sabbath.'

'I just saw Larsson. Is that where he was headed?'

Rönn nodded.

'Where's Martin?'

'He's in Melander's office.'

Kollberg looked at him more closely.

'You look just about done in,' he said.

'I am,' said Rönn.

'Why don't you go home and go to bed?'

Rönn gave him a doleful look and walked on down the corridor. He was holding some papers in his hand and presumably had work to do.

Kollberg rapped once on the door and walked in. Martin Beck didn't even look up from his notes.

'Hi,' he said.

'What's all this Rönn was talking about?'

'Here. Take a look.'

He handed him two typewritten sheets of paper. Kollberg sat down on the edge of the desk and read.

'Well,' said Martin Beck. 'What do you think?'

'I think Rönn writes a god-awful report,' said Kollberg.

But he said it quietly and seriously, and five seconds later he went on.

'This sounds unpleasant.'

'Right,' said Martin Beck. 'I think so too.'

'What'd it look like?'

'Worse than you can imagine.'

Kollberg shook his head. There was nothing wrong with his imagination.

'We'd better get our hands on this guy pretty damned quick.'

'Right again,' said Martin Beck.

'What do we have to go on?'

'Something. We've got a few prints. Footprints, maybe some fingerprints. No one saw anything or heard anything.'

'Not good,' Kollberg said. 'That can take time. And this guy's dangerous.'

Martin Beck nodded.

Rönn came into the room after a discreet knock on the door.

'Negative so far,' he said. 'The fingerprints, I mean.'

'The fingerprints aren't worth a damn,' Kollberg said.

'I've got a pretty good cast too,' Rönn said. 'Of a boot or a heavy work shoe.' He was looking surprised.

'That's not worth a damn either,' Kollberg said. 'I mean, don't get me wrong. That can all be essential later on, as evidence. But right now it's a question of getting our hands on whoever slaughtered Nyman. We can tie him to the crime later on.'

'That sounds illogical,' Rönn said.

'Okay, but don't worry about it now. We've still got another couple of important details.'

'Yes, the murder weapon,' said Martin Beck thoughtfully. 'An old carbine bayonet.'

'And the motive,' said Kollberg.

'The motive?' Rönn said.

'Of course,' said Kollberg. 'Revenge. It's the only conceivable motive.'

'But if it's revenge . . .'

Rönn said, and left the sentence hanging.

'Then it's possible whoever stabbed Nyman is planning to take revenge on other people too,' Kollberg said. 'And therefore . . .'

'We have to find him fast,' said Martin Beck.

'Exactly,' said Kollberg. 'Now, what's your reasoning been?'

Rönn looked unhappily at Martin Beck, who in his turn looked out of the window.

Kollberg looked at them both admonishingly.

'Wait a minute,' he said. 'Have you asked the question, Who was Nyman?'

'Who he was?'

Rönn seemed confused and Martin Beck said nothing.

'Right. Who was Nyman? Or, more to the point, *what* was Nyman?'

'A policeman,' said Martin Beck finally.

'That's not a very complete answer,' Kollberg said. 'Come now, you both knew him. What was Nyman?'

'A chief inspector,' mumbled Rönn.

Then he blinked wearily.

'I have to make a couple of phone calls,' he said evasively.

'Well?' said Kollberg, when Rönn had closed the door behind him. 'What was Nyman?'

Martin Beck looked him in the eye and said, reluctantly, 'He was a bad policeman.'

'Wrong,' said Kollberg. 'Now listen. Nyman was one *hell* of a bad policeman. He was a barbaric son of a bitch of the very worst sort.'

'You said it, I didn't,' said Martin Beck.

'Yes. But you'll have to admit I'm right.'

'I didn't know him very well.'

'Don't try to sneak out of it. You knew him well enough to know that much. I realize Einar doesn't want to admit it, out of misdirected loyalty. But dammit, *you've* got to play with your cards on the table.'

'All right,' said Martin Beck. 'The things I've heard about him aren't exactly positive. But I never really worked with him.'

'Your choice of words isn't very apt,' Kollberg said. 'It wasn't possible to work *with* Nyman. All you could do was take orders from him and do as you were told. Of course you could give him orders too, if you happened to be in that position. And then have them sabotaged, or simply not carried out at all.'

'You sound like an expert on Stig Nyman,' said Martin Beck, a little acidly.

'Yes, I know some things about him the rest of you don't know. But I'll get to that later. First of all, let's get it straight that he was a bastard and a damned lousy policeman. Even today he'd be a disgrace to the force. For my part I'm ashamed to have been a policeman in the same city with him. And at the same time.'

'In that case there are a lot of people who ought to be ashamed.'

'Exactly. But there aren't so many who have the sense to be.'

'And every policeman in London ought to be ashamed about Challenor.'

'Wrong again,' said Kollberg. 'Challenor and some of his underlings were finally brought to trial, even if they did manage to do a lot of damage beforehand. And that showed that in the long run there was some limit to what the system would tolerate in the police.'

Martin Beck massaged his temple thoughtfully.

'But Nyman's name has never been discredited. And why not?'

Kollberg had to answer his own question.

'Because everyone knows it's pointless to report a policeman. The general public has no legal rights vis-à-vis the police. And if you can't win a case against a beat constable, then how in the world could you win a case against a chief inspector?'

'You're exaggerating.'

'Not much, Martin. Not much, and you know it as well as I do. It's just that our damned solidarity has become some kind of second nature. We're impregnated with esprit de corps.'

'It's important to keep up a good front in this job,' said Martin Beck. 'It always has been.'

'And pretty soon it'll be the only thing left.'

Kollberg caught his breath before he went on.

'Okay. The police stick together. That's axiomatic. But stick together against whom?'

'The day someone answers that question . . .'

Martin Beck left the sentence hanging.

'Neither you nor I,' said Kollberg with finality, 'will live to see that day.'

'What's all this got to do with Nyman?'

'Everything.'

'In what way?'

'Nyman's dead and doesn't need to be defended any more.

Whoever killed him is probably insane, a danger to himself and other people.'

'And you mean we can find him in Nyman's past.'

'Yes. He ought to be there. The comparison you just made wasn't so bad.'

'Which comparison?'

'With Challenor.'

'I don't know the truth about Challenor,' said Martin Beck with a certain chill. 'But maybe you do?'

'No, nobody does. But I do know a lot of people were mistreated and still more were sentenced to long prison terms because policemen perjured themselves in court. Without any reaction either from their subordinates or their superiors.'

'Their superiors out of false loyalty,' said Martin Beck. 'And their subordinates out of fear of losing their jobs.'

'Worse than that. Some of those subordinates simply thought that was the way it was supposed to be. They'd never learned any other way.'

Martin Beck stood up and walked towards the window.

'Tell me what it is you know about Nyman that other people don't know,' he said.

'Nyman was also in a position to give orders directly to a lot of young policemen, by and large pretty much as he pleased.'

'That's a long time ago now,' said Martin Beck.

'Not so long ago, but a lot of people on the force today learned most of what they know from him. Do you realize what that means? Over the years he managed to corrupt scores of young policemen. Who consequently had a warped attitude towards their jobs right from the beginning. And a lot of them out and out admired him, and hoped they could be like him some day. Just as hard and high-handed. Do you understand?'

'Yes,' said Martin Beck wearily. 'I see what you mean. You don't have to spell it out again and again.'

He turned and looked at Kollberg.

'But that doesn't mean I believe it. Did you know Nyman?'

'Yes.'

'Did you ever work under him?'

'Yes.'

Martin Beck raised his eyebrows.

'And when was that, pray tell?' he said suspiciously.

'The abominable man from Säffle,' said Kollberg to himself.

'What was that?'

'The abominable man from Säffle. That's what we called him.'

'Where?'

'In the army. During the war. A lot of what I know I learned from Stig Nyman.'

'For example?'

'That's a good question,' said Kollberg absently.

Martin Beck looked at him searchingly.

'Like what, Lennart?' he asked quietly.

'Like how to cut off a pig's penis without its squealing. Like how to cut the legs off the same pig also without its squealing. Like how to gouge its eyes out. And finally how to cut it to pieces and flay it, still without a sound.'

He shivered.

'Do you know how?' he said.

Martin Beck shook his head.

'It's easy. You start by cutting out its tongue.'

Kollberg looked out through the window, up towards the cold blue sky above the roofs on the other side of the street.

'Oh, he taught me a great deal. How to cut a sheep's throat with piano wire before it has a chance to bleat. How to handle a full-grown wildcat you're locked up in a closet with. The way to bellow when you charge a cow and stick a bayonet in its belly. And what happens if you don't bellow properly. Fill your pack with bricks and climb the ladder on the training tower. Fifty times up and fifty times down. You weren't allowed to kill the wildcat, by the way, it had to be used again. Know what you did?'

71

'No.'

'You nailed it to the wall with your sheath knife. Through its skin.'

'You were a paratrooper, weren't you?'

'Yes. And Nyman was my instructor in hand-to-hand combat. Among other things. He taught me how it feels to lie buried in the guts of freshly slaughtered animals, and he taught me to eat my own vomit when I'd thrown up inside a gas mask, and my own shit to avoid leaving a track.'

'What was his rank?'

'He was a sergeant. A lot of the things he taught couldn't be learned in the classroom. For example how to break an arm or a leg or crush a larynx or press eyes out with your thumbs. You can only learn that by doing it, on something that's alive. Sheep and pigs were convenient. We also tested different kinds of ammunition on live animals, particularly pigs, and by God there wasn't any crap about anaesthetizing them first like they do these days.'

'Was that normal training?'

'I don't know. For that matter, what do you mean? Can you ever call that sort of thing *normal*?'

'Maybe not.'

'But even if you suppose that for some ridiculous reason all of that was necessary, it wasn't necessary to do it with joy and pride.'

'No. But Nyman did, you mean?'

'I'll say. And he taught his craft to a lot of recruits. To brag about brutality, to enjoy cruelty. Some people have a gift for it.'

'In other words he was a sadist.'

'In the highest degree. He called it "hardness" himself. He was naturally hard. And for a real man, the only thing that mattered was being hard. Physically and mentally. He always encouraged bullying. Said it was part of a soldier's education.'

'That doesn't necessarily make him a sadist.'

'He exposed himself in a lot of ways. He was a tremendous disciplinarian. Maintaining discipline is one thing, but dealing out your own punishments is another. Nyman nailed someone or several people every day, for trifles. A lost button, that sort of thing. And the men he caught always had to choose.'

'Between what?'

'A report or a beating. A report meant three days in the brig and a black mark on your military record. So most people chose the beating.'

'What did that involve?'

'I took the bait just once. I was late back to camp one Saturday night. Climbed over the fence. Nyman caught me, of course. And I chose the beating. What it involved in my case was that I stood at attention with a bar of soap in my mouth while he broke two of my ribs with his fists. Then he treated me to a cup of coffee and a piece of cake and told me he thought I could probably get to be really hard, a real soldier.'

'And then?'

'As soon as the war was over I saw to it that I got drummed out of the army, quickly and neatly. Then I came here and became a cop. And one of the first people I saw was Nyman. He was already a sergeant.'

'And you mean to say he went on using the same methods as a policeman?'

'Maybe not the same. He could hardly get away with that. But he's probably committed hundreds of outrages of one kind and another. Towards his subordinates and towards arrestees. I've heard various stories over the years.'

'He must have been reported now and then,' said Martin Beck thoughtfully.

'I'm sure. But because of our esprit de corps I'm also sure that none of those reports are still around. They all wound up in wastepaper baskets, naturally – most of them no doubt dismissed out of hand. So we won't find out anything around here.'

Martin Beck suddenly had a thought.

'But the Justice Department Ombudsman,' he said. 'Some of

the people who really were mistreated must have lodged complaints with the J.O.'

'To no avail,' Kollberg said. 'A man like Nyman always sees to it that there are policemen ready to take an oath that he hadn't done anything. Young fellows, whose jobs would be hell if they refused. And the kind of men who are already so indoctrinated they reckon they're only doing what loyalty demands. No one outside the force can get at a chief inspector.'

'True enough,' said Martin Beck. 'But the J.O. doesn't throw away his reports, even when they don't lead to any action. They're filed away, and they're still there.'

'That's an idea,' said Kollberg slowly. 'Not a bad idea at all. You have your moments.'

He thought about it for a while.

'Best of all would be if we had a civilian review board that recorded every case of police misconduct. Unfortunately, there is no such thing in this country. But maybe the J.O. can give us something.'

'And the murder weapon,' Martin Beck said. 'A carbine bayonet must come from the army. Not everybody has a chance to get his hands on one of those. I'll put Rönn on that detail.'

'Yes, do. And then take Rönn with you and go to the J.O.'s archive.'

'What are you planning to do?'

'Actually I'm thinking of going over and having a look at Nyman,' Kollberg said. 'Larsson's there, of course, but I don't care. I'm doing it mostly for my own sake, want to see how I react. Maybe I'll get sick, but at least no one can make me eat my vomit.'

Martin Beck no longer looked quite so tired. He straightened up.

'Lennart?'

'Yeah?'

'What was it you called him? The abominable man from Säffle?'

'That's right. He came from Säffle, and he never stopped telling us about it. Men from Säffle were really hard, he'd say. Real men.

And like I said, he was certainly abominable. One of the most sadistic men I've ever met.'

Martin looked at him for a long time.

'Maybe you're right,' he said.

'There's a chance. Good luck. I hope you find something.'

Again Martin Beck had an indefinable sense of danger.

'I think this is going to be a rough day.'

'Yes,' said Kollberg. 'It's got all the makings. Do you feel a little cured of your loyalty?'

'I think so.'

'Remember, Nyman doesn't need any gratuitous loyalty any more. Which reminds me, by the way, that he had an unswervingly faithful sidekick all these years. Guy named Hult. He ought to be a captain by now, if he's still around. Somebody ought to talk to him.'

Martin Beck nodded.

Rönn scratched at the door and came in. He was unsteady on his feet and looked all done in from exhaustion. His eyes were red and sticky from the lack of sleep.

'What do we do now?' he said.

'We've got a lot of work in front of us. Can you make it?'

'Well yes, I suppose I can,' Rönn said, and stifled a yawn.

13

Martin Beck had no trouble gathering biographical data on the man Kollberg described as Nyman's faithful sidekick. His name was Harald Hult, and he'd been a policeman all of his adult life. His career was easily followed in the department's own archives.

He'd started out, at nineteen, as a deputy constable in Falun and was now a captain. As far as Martin Beck could see, Hult and Nyman had first served together in 1936 and 1937 when they'd been constables in the same Stockholm precinct. In the middle of the forties they'd been reunited in another inner-city precinct. The somewhat younger Nyman was by then a lieutenant, while Hult was still only a constable.

During the fifties and sixties, Hult began little by little to advance and on several occasions served under Nyman. Presumably, Nyman had been allowed to choose the assistants he needed for his special assignments, and Hult had quite clearly been one of his favourites. If Nyman was the kind of man Kollberg said he was, and there was no reason to doubt it, then any man who'd been his 'unswervingly faithful sidekick' ought to be a very interesting psychological phenomenon.

Martin Beck started to be curious about Harald Hult and decided to take Kollberg's advice and look him up. He called and made sure the man was at home before taking a taxi to the specified address on Reimersholme.

Hult lived on the northern tip of the island, in one of the blocks of flats facing the Långholm Channel. The building stood on a high point of land, and on the other side of the street, which stopped abruptly in front of the last block in the row, the ground sloped steeply down to the water.

The area looked pretty much the way it had at the end of the thirties when it was built, and owing to its location there was no through traffic. Reimersholme was a fairly small island, with only one bridge in and out, and the buildings were few and far between. A third of its area was occupied by the old alcohol plant and various other old factories and warehouses. There were generous gardens and grounds between the blocks of flats, and the shore along Långholm Bay had been left in peace, so that the natural vegetation – alder and aspen and weeping willow – grew rank and lush right down to the water.

Captain Harald Hult lived alone in a two-room flat on the second floor. It was clean and neat and somehow so tidy it seemed desolate. Almost, thought Martin Beck, as if it were unoccupied.

Hult himself looked to be about sixty, a large, heavy man with a strong chin and expressionless grey eyes.

They sat down by a low, varnished table near the window. The tabletop was bare, and nothing stood on the windowsill. There was, in fact, a general lack of ordinary personal possessions. There didn't seem to be any paper in the flat, for example, not even so much as a newspaper, and the only books he could discover were the three parts of the telephone directory, standing neatly on a little shelf in the front hall.

Martin Beck unbuttoned his jacket and loosened his tie a bit. Then he took out his pack of Floridas and a box of matches and started looking around for an ashtray.

Hult followed his glance.

'I don't smoke,' he said. 'I don't think I've ever owned an ashtray.'

He got a white saucer from the kitchen cabinet.

'Can I get you something . . .?' he asked before sitting down again. 'I've already had my coffee, but I can make some more.'

Martin Beck shook his head. He noticed that Hult was a trifle uncertain about how to address him, whether or not he ought to say 'sir' to the head of the National Murder Squad. That showed he was a man of the old school, where rank and discipline had been taken for granted. Although Hult had the day off, he was wearing his uniform trousers, a light blue shirt and a tie.

'Haven't you got the day off?' Martin Beck asked.

'I wear my uniform most of the time,' Hult said tonelessly. 'I prefer it.'

'Nice place you've got,' said Martin Beck, glancing out of the window at the view.

'Yes,' Hult said. 'I suppose so. Though it's pretty lonely.'

He put his large, meaty hands on the table in front of him as if they were a pair of clubs, and stared at them.

'I'm a widower. My wife died three years ago. Cancer. Since then it's been a bit dull.'

Hult didn't smoke and didn't drink. He certainly never read a book and probably not the papers either. Martin Beck could picture him sitting passively in front of the TV while the darkness gathered outside.

'What's it all about?'

'Stig Nyman is dead.'

There was virtually no reaction at all. The man threw a vacant look at his visitor.

'Oh?'

'I suppose you knew already.'

'No. But it's hardly unexpected. Stig was sick. His body failed him.'

He looked back at his clublike fists, as if wondering how long it would be before his own body betrayed him.

'Did you know Stig?' he asked after a moment.

'Not very well,' Martin Beck said. 'About as well as I know you.'

'That's not very well. We've only met a couple of times, sir, you and I.'

And then he dropped the 'sir' and went on in a more familiar tone.

'I've always been in the regular police. Never had much chance to hang around with you people at Criminal.'

'On the other hand you knew Nyman pretty well, didn't you?'

'Yes. We worked together for years.'

'And what did you think of him?'

'He was a very good man.'

'I've heard the opposite.'

'Who from?'

'Different places.'

'In that case it's wrong. Stig Nyman was a very good man. That's all I can tell you.'

'Oh,' said Martin Beck. 'I'm sure you can fill out the picture a bit.'

'No. In what way?'

'You know perfectly well, for example, that a lot of people criticized him. That there were people who didn't like him.'

'No, I don't know anything about that.'

'Really? I know, for example, that Nyman had his own particular methods.'

'He was good,' Hult repeated monotonously. 'Very competent. A real man, and the best boss you could imagine.'

'But he took rather strong measures now and then?'

'Who says so? Someone who's trying to run him down now that he's dead, of course. If anyone says anything like that, then it's a lie.'

'But he was inclined to be pretty hard, wasn't he?'

'Never more than the situation required. Anything else is slander.'

'But you knew there were quite a lot of complaints about Nyman?'

'No, I didn't know.'

'Let's put it this way – I know you knew. You worked directly under him.'

'Just lies, to blacken the name of a fine and capable policeman.'

'There are people who think Nyman wasn't a fine policeman at all.'

'In that case they don't know what they're talking about.'

'But you do.'

'Yes, I do. Stig Nyman was the best commander I ever had.'

'There are people who say that you're not a particularly good policeman either.'

'Maybe not. I've never had a bad mark on my record, but maybe not anyway. Trying to run down Stig Nyman is another story completely. And if anyone does it in my presence, I'll . . .'

'You'll what?'

'I'll shut their mouths.'

'How?'

'That's my business. I'm an old hand. I know this job. I learned it from the bottom up.'

'From Stig Nyman?'

Hult looked back at his hands.

'Yes. I suppose you could say that. He taught me a lot.'

'How to commit perjury, for example? How to copy each other's reports so everything'll jibe, even if every word's a lie? How to rough people up in their cells? Where the best places are to park in peace and quiet if you want to give some poor bastard a little extra going over on the way from the precinct to Criminal?'

'I've never heard of that kind of thing.'

'No?'

'No.'

'Not even *heard* of it?'

'No. In any case not in connection with Nyman.'

'And you've never helped cut down strikers? Back in the days when the police carried sabres? And on Nyman's orders?'

'No.'

'Or ride down student protesters? Or club unarmed schoolchildren at demonstrations? Still according to Nyman's instructions?'

Hult didn't move, just looked calmly at Martin Beck.

'No, I've never done any of that.'

'How long have you been a policeman?'

'For forty years.'

'And how long have you known Nyman?'

'Since the middle of the thirties.'

Martin Beck shrugged his shoulders.

'It seems odd,' he said dispassionately, 'that you know nothing at all about any of the things I've mentioned. Stig Nyman was supposed to be an expert on maintaining order.'

'Not only supposed to be. He was the best.'

'And among other things he wrote studies on how the police should conduct themselves in demonstrations, strikes and riots. Studies where he recommended just such things as shock attacks with drawn sabres. Later on, when the sabres had disappeared, with batons. He also suggested that motorcycle police should drive into crowds to break them up.'

'I've never seen anything like that.'

'No. That tactic was forbidden. They decided there was too much risk that the policemen would fall off their machines and injure themselves.'

'I don't know anything about it.'

'No, so you said. Nyman also had views on how to use tear gas and water cannons. Views he expressed officially and in his capacity as expert.'

'All I know is that Stig Nyman never used more force than necessity required.'

'Personally?'

'And he didn't let his subordinates do so either.'

'In other words he was always right? Always stuck to the regulations, I mean.'

'Yes.'

'And no one had cause to complain?'

'No.'

'And still it did happen that people reported Nyman for misconduct,' Martin Beck pointed out.

'Then their reports were fabrications.'

Martin Beck stood up and paced a few steps back and forth.

'There's one thing I haven't told you,' he said. 'But I'll tell you now.'

'There's something I'd like to say too,' Hult said.

'What is it?'

The man sat motionless, but his eyes sought out the window.

'I don't have very much to do when I'm off work,' he said. 'Like I said before, it's been a bit dull since Maja died. I sit here by the window a lot and count the cars that go by. There aren't an awful lot on a street like this. So I mostly sit and think.'

He stopped talking and Martin Beck waited.

'I don't have much to think about,' he said, 'except the way my own life's been. Forty years in uniform in this city. How many times have people puked on me? How many times have people spat at me and stuck their tongues out at me and called me a pig or a swine or a murderer? How many suicides have I cleaned up? How many hours of unpaid overtime have I put in? All my life I've worked like a dog in order to try to maintain a little law and order, so respectable people could live in peace, so decent women wouldn't get raped, so every single shop window wouldn't get broken and every damn thing in sight get stolen. I've handled bodies so rotten that big white maggots fell out of my cuffs at night when I got home and sat down to eat. I've changed the nappies on babies whose mothers had the DTs. I've looked for lost kittens and I've stepped into knife fights. The whole time it's only been getting worse and worse – more and more violence and blood and more and more people running us down. They always say us policemen are supposed to protect society, sometimes against working men and sometimes against students, sometimes against Nazis and sometimes against Communists. And now there's hardly anything left to protect any more. But you put up with it, because the morale on the force has been good. And if there'd been more men like Stig Nyman, then things wouldn't be the way they are today. So anyone who wants to hear a lot of old women's gossip about his mates, he doesn't need to come to me.'

He lifted his hands an inch or so from the table and let them fall back again with a heavy smack.

'Yes, well, that turned out to be a real speech,' he said. 'Nice to get it said. You've been a beat officer yourself, haven't you?'

Martin Beck nodded.

'When?'

'Over twenty years ago. After the war.'

'Yes,' Hult said. 'Those were the days.'

The apology was apparently over. Martin Beck cleared his throat.

'Now for what I wanted to say. Nyman didn't die of his illness. He was murdered. We think whoever killed him was after revenge. It's possible the man in question may have other people on his list.'

Hult stood up and went out in the hall. He took down the jacket to his uniform and put it on. Then he tightened the shoulder belt and adjusted his holster.

'When I came here, it was to ask a particular question,' said

Martin Beck. 'Who could have hated Stig Nyman enough to want to kill him?'

'No one. Now I have to go.'

'Where to?'

'To work,' Hult said, and held open the door.

14

Einar Rönn sat with his elbows on the tabletop and his head in his hands and read. He was so tired that letters and words and whole lines kept flowing together or sagging or hopping out of place, upward sometimes and sometimes down, just the way they often did on his ageing Remington whenever he tried really hard to type something perfectly with no mistakes. He yawned and blinked and cleaned his glasses and started over from the beginning.

The text before him was handwritten on a piece of brown paper bag from a state alcohol shop, and despite the misspellings and the writer's shaky hand, it gave the impression of having been written with patience and industry.

To His Honour The Justise Department Ombusman in Stockholm

On the second of February this year I got drunk I had got my pay and boght a fith of vodka. I remember I was sitting singing down by the Djurgård ferry and then a police car came up and three Policemen just yung kids I am old enough to be there father althogh I would want my children to be Human Beings not Pigs like that if I had any got out and

85

took away my bottel which there was some left in and dragged me to a grey VW bus and there was another Policeman with strips on his slieve and he grabbed me by the hair and when the others had threw me in the vehicle he hit my face several times against the floor and it started bleeding thogh I felt nothing at the time. Then I sat in a cell with bars and then came a big man and observed me thrugh the door he laffed at my misery and told another Policeman to unlock the door and then he took of his coat which there was a broad strip on the sleive and rolled up his shirt-sleives and then he came in to the cell and shouted that I should stand at attension and that I had called the Police Nastards which maybe I had and I do not know wether he thot I ment Bastards or Nazis and I was sober then and he punched me in my stomuch and another place I wont right and I fell down and then he kicked me in the abdomen and other places and afterwards he left and first he sed now I knew what happened to people who fooled with the Police. The subsequent morning, I was released and then I asked who the Policeman was with the strip who kicked and shouted and punched but they said I better forget about that and I better go befor they changed there mind and give me a real working over. But a nother one who's name was Vilford and was from the city of Gothenburg said that the one who kicked and shouted and hit me was named Chief Inspector Nyman and I would be well advised to keep my mouth shut. I have thought about this for several days and thought I am a ordanary common worker and I did not do anything bad except sing and be under the infiuance of Alcohol but I want to have my Rights because persons who kick and beat a poor drunk man who has always worked all his life shold not be a Policeman because he is not a proper person. I swear that this is true.

Respectfully
John Bertilsson, labourer

It was a friend of mine at my work who is called the
Professor who said I shold write this and I could get justise
in this way which is now common.

OFFICIAL REMARKS: *The officer named in the complaint is Chief*
Inspector Stig Oscar Nyman. He knows nothing of the case.
Emergency Squad commander, Lieutenant Harald Hult, certifies
the apprehension of the complainant Bertilsson, who is a noto-
rious troublemaker and alcoholic. No violence was employed in
the apprehension of Bertilsson nor later in the detention cell.
Chief Inspector Nyman was not even on duty at the time. Three
constables then on duty testify that no violence was employed
against Bertilsson. This man shows alcoholic brain damage and
is often delinquent. He is in the habit of bursting out with
unfounded accusations against the officers who are forced to take
action against him.

A red stamp completed the document: NO ACTION.

Rönn sighed gloomily and wrote down the complainant's name
in his notebook. The woman who'd been stuck with this extra
Saturday overtime slammed the file drawers demonstratively.

So far she'd found seven complaints that had to do with Nyman
in one way or another.

One was now out of the way, and six remained. Rönn took
them in order.

The next letter was correctly addressed and neatly typed on
heavy linen paper. The body of the letter ran as follows:

On the afternoon of Saturday the 14th of this month, I was
on the pavement outside the entrance to number 75
Pontonjärgatan together with my five-year-old daughter.
*   We were waiting for my wife, who was visiting an invalid*
in the building. To pass the time, we were playing tag on the
pavement. There was no one on the street as far as I can

remember. It was, as I said, a Saturday afternoon and the shops were closed. Consequently I have no witnesses to what occurred.

I had tagged my daughter, lifted her up in the air and had just put her down on the pavement when I discovered that a police car had stopped at the kerb. Two officers got out of the car and came up to me. One of them immediately grabbed my arm and said, 'What are you doing to the kid, you son of a bitch?' (To be fair, I should add that I was casually dressed in khaki trousers, windcheater and a cap, all of it clean and fairly new to be sure, but I may nevertheless have looked shabby to the officer in question.) I was too astonished to say anything right away. The other officer took my daughter by the hand and told her to go find her mother. I explained that I was her father. One of the officers then twisted my arm behind my back, which was extremely painful, and shoved me into the back seat of the police car. On the way to the station, one of them hit me with his fist in the chest, side and stomach, all the time calling me names like 'child molester' and 'dirty old bastard' and so forth.

Once at the station, they locked me in a cell. A while later the door opened and Chief Inspector Stig Nyman (I didn't know who it was at the time, but found out later) came into the cell.

'Are you the guy who chases little girls? I'll take that out of you,' he said, and hit me so hard in the stomach that I doubled up. As soon as I'd caught my breath I told him I was the girl's father and he kneed me in the groin. He continued to beat me until someone came and told him my wife and daughter were there. As soon as the Chief Inspector understood that I had been telling the truth, he told me to go, without apologizing or in any way attempting to explain his behaviour.

I wish hereby to draw your attention to the events

*described and to request that Chief Inspector Nyman and
the two officers be held to account for this mistreatment of a
completely innocent citizen.*

Sture Magnusson, engineer

OFFICIAL REMARKS: *Chief Inspector Nyman has no recollection
of the complainant. Constables Strom and Rosenkvist claim to
have apprehended the complainant on the grounds that he
acted oddly and threatened the child. They applied no more
force than was required to move Magnusson into and out of
the car. None of the five officers who were in the precinct station
at the time admits to having witnessed any mistreatment of
the complainant. Nor did any of them notice that Chief
Inspector Nyman entered the detention cell and believe they
can say he did not. No action.*

Rönn put the paper to one side, made a note in his notebook
and went on to the next complaint.

The Justice Department Ombudsman Stockholm

*Last Friday, 18th October, I attended a party at the home of
a good friend on Östermalmsgatan. At about ten p.m.
another friend of mine and I called a taxi and left the party
to go to my flat. We were standing in the entrance, waiting
for the taxi, when two policemen came walking down the
other side of the street. They crossed the street and came up
to us and asked us if we lived in the building. We answered
that we did not. 'Then move along, don't hang around here,'
they said. We said that we were waiting for a taxi and stayed
where we were. The policemen then grabbed hold of us rather
brusquely and pushed us out of the entrance and told us to
keep moving. But we wanted the taxi we'd ordered, and said
so. The two officers first tried to force us to move on by*

pushing us in front of them, and when we protested, one of them took out his baton and started to hit my friend with it. I tried to protect my friend and so I too received several blows. Both of them now had their batons out and were pummelling us as hard as they could. I kept hoping the taxi would come so we would be able to get away, but it didn't come and finally my friend yelled, 'They'll beat us to death, we'd better get out of here.' We then ran up to Karlavägen where we took a bus to my flat. We were both of us black and blue and my right wrist started to swell when we got home. It was badly bruised and discoloured. We decided to report the incident at the police station where we supposed the two officers had come from and took a taxi there. The two policemen were nowhere to be seen, but we were able to speak to a chief inspector whose name was Nyman. We were told to wait until the officers came in, which they did at one o'clock. Then all four of us, the two policemen and the two of us, were called into Inspector Nyman's office and we repeated our story of what had happened. Nyman asked the policemen if it was true and they denied it. The Chief Inspector naturally believed them and told us we had better watch out for trying to blacken the names of honest hard-working policemen, and that it would go hard with us if we did it again. Then he told us to get out.

I now wonder if Chief Inspector Nyman acted properly. What I have described is absolutely true, as my friend can testify. We were not drunk. On Monday I showed my hand to our doctor at work and he wrote the enclosed certification. We never found out the names of the two constables, but we would recognize them.

    Respectfully, Olof Johansson

Rönn didn't understand all the terms in the doctor's report, but it appeared that the hand and wrist were swollen from an exudation of fluid, that the swelling would have to be punctured if it didn't go down by itself, and that the patient, who was a typographer, should refrain from working until one or the other had occurred.

Then he read through the official comment.

Chief Inspector Stig O. Nyman recalls the incident. He claims he had no reason to doubt the testimony of Constables Bergman and Sjögren, as they had always shown themselves to be honest and conscientious. Constables Bergman and Sjögren deny that they used their batons against the complainant and his companion, who, the officers claim, were defiant and unruly. They gave the impression of being inebriated, and Constable Sjögren claims to have noticed a strong smell of alcohol from at least one of the men. No action.

The woman had stopped slamming file drawers and came over to Rönn.

'I can't find any more from that year involving this Inspector Nyman. So unless I go further back . . .'

'No, that's okay, just bring me the ones you find,' said Rönn cryptically.

'Will you be much longer?'

'I'll be done in a minute, just want to look through these,' he said, and the woman's steps moved away behind him.

He took off his glasses and polished them before he went on reading.

The undersigned is a widow, employed, and the sole support of one child. The child is four years old and stays at a day-care centre while I am at work. My nerves and health have been bad ever since my husband was killed in a car accident one year ago.

Last Monday I went to work as usual after leaving my

91

daughter at the day-care centre. Something happened at my place of work during the afternoon which I won't go into here, but it left me very upset. The staff doctor, who is aware of the state of my nerves, gave me a hypo and sent me home in a taxi. When I got home it didn't seem to me the sedative was having any effect, so I took two tranquillizers. I then went to get my daughter from the day-care centre. When I'd gone two blocks, a police car stopped and two policemen got out and shoved me into the back seat. I was feeling a little drowsy from the medicine and it's possible I staggered a little on the street, because I gathered from the policemen's scornful way of treating me that they thought I was drunk. I tried to explain to them what the situation was and that I had to pick up my child, but they only made fun of me.

At the police station I was taken to the chief who wouldn't listen to me either but ordered them to put me in a cell 'to sleep it off'.

There was a buzzer in the cell and I rang it again and again but no one came. I shouted and yelled that someone had to take care of my child, but no one paid any attention. The day-care centre closes at six o'clock and the staff people naturally get uneasy if you haven't picked up your child by then. It was five thirty when I was locked up.

I tried to attract someone's attention in order to be allowed to call the day-care centre and see to it that my child was taken care of. I was very upset about this.

I wasn't let out until ten o'clock that night, and by that time I was beside myself with worry and desperation. I have not yet recovered and am now on sick leave.

The woman who wrote the letter had included her own address and those of the day-care centre, her place of work, her doctor, and the police station to which she'd been taken.

The comment on the back of the letter read as follows:

The designated beat officers are Hans Lennart Svensson and Göran Broström. They say they acted in good faith, as the woman appeared to be highly inebriated. Chief Inspector Stig Oscar Nyman claims the woman was so far gone she could not make herself understood. No action.

Rönn put the letter down and sighed. He remembered reading in an interview with the National Chief of Police that of 742 complaints about police misconduct received by the Ombudsman over a period of three years, only one had been delivered to the public prosecutor for legal action.

A man might well wonder what that went to prove, Rönn thought.

That the National Chief of Police publicized the fact only demonstrated what Rönn already knew about that gentleman's intellectual gifts.

The next document was brief, pencilled in block letters on a lined sheet from a spiral notebook.

Dear J.O.,

Last Friday I got drunk and there's nothing funny about that since I've got drunk before and when the police take me in I sleep it off in the stasion. I'm a peaceful man and don't make no trouble. So now last Friday they took me in and I thought I'd get to bed down in a cell like usual, but I was sadly mistaken because a policeman I seen there before came into the cell and started to give me a beating. I was surprised because I hadn't done nothing and this policeman he cursed and raised hell, I'm sure he's the chief at the stasion, and beat me and shouted so now I want to report this police chief so he won't do it again. He is a big tall man and has a gold stripe on his jacket.
    Respectfully Joel Johansson

OFFICIAL REMARKS: *The complainant is known for countless drinking offences, not only in the precinct in question. The policeman referred to would appear to be Inspector Stig Nyman. He claims he has never seen the complainant, whose name is however familiar to him. Inspector Nyman dismisses the suggestion that he or anyone else mistreated the complainant in his cell. No action.*

Rönn made a note in his notebook and hoped he'd be able to decipher his own handwriting. Before getting down to the two remaining complaints, he took off his glasses and rubbed his aching eyes. Then he blinked several times and read on.

My husband was born in Hungary and does not write Swedish well, so I, his wife, am writing this instead. My husband has suffered from epilepsy for many years and is now retired due to his illness. Because of his illness he sometimes has attacks and then he falls down, although he usually knows in advance when they are coming so he can stay at home, but sometimes he can't tell in advance and then it can happen anywhere. He gets medicine from his doctor, and after all these years we've been married I know how to take care of him. I want to say that there is one thing my husband never does and never has done and that is to drink. He would rather die than taste strong drink.

Now my husband and I would like to report something that happened to him last Sunday when he was coming home from the metro. He had been out to see a football match. Then when he was sitting on the metro he could tell he was going to have an attack and he hurried up to get home quick and as he was walking along he fell down and the next thing he knew he was lying on a bed in a prison. By now he was better but he needed his medicine and wanted to get home to me, his wife. He had to stay there for several hours before the police let him go because all the time they thought he was drunk which he absolutely was not since he never drinks a drop. When they let him out they made him go in to see the Inspector himself and he tells him that he is sick and not drunk, but the Inspector didn't want to understand at all and says my husband is lying and he'd better stay sober in the future and that he has had enough of drunken foreigners which my husband is of course. But he can't help it he speaks Swedish so badly. Then my husband told the Inspector that he never drinks and whether the Inspector misunderstood or whatever anyway he got mad and knocked my husband down on the floor and then picked him up and threw him out of the room. Then my husband got to come home, and of course I was terribly worried all evening and called all the hospitals but how was I to imagine the police would take a sick man and throw him into jail and then beat him up as if he was the worst criminal.

Now my daughter tells me, we have a daughter though she is married, that we can report this to Your Honour. When my husband got home it was past midnight although the game was over at seven o'clock.

Respectfully Ester Nagy

OFFICIAL REMARKS: *The chief inspector named in the complaint, Stig Oscar Nyman, says he remembers the man, who was treated well and sent home as quickly as possible. Constables Lars Ivar Ivarsson and Sten Holmgren, who brought Nagy in, claim that Nagy gave the impression of being dazed by alcohol or narcotics. No action.*

The final petition appeared also to be the most interesting, in that it had been written by a policeman.

The Office of the Parliamentary Ombudsman
Västra Trödgårdsgatan 4
Box 16327
Stockholm 16

Sir,

I hereby respectfully request that the Justice Department Ombudsman take up for review and reconsideration my petitions of 1st September, 1961, and 31st December, 1962, regarding official misconduct by Chief Inspector of Police Stig Oscar Nyman and Police Sergeant Harald Hult.
      Respectfully,
      Åke Reinhold Eriksson, Constable

'Oh, him,' said Rönn to himself. He went on to study the remarks, which for once were longer than the petition itself.

In view of the meticulousness with which the indicated petitions were previously investigated, and considering the length of time that has passed since the presumed occurrence of the events and incidents set forth therein, as well as with regard to the large number of petitions submitted by the suppliant over the past few years, I do not find that cause for reconsideration exists, particularly inasmuch as the new facts and fresh proofs that might corroborate the petitioner's previous assertions and affirmations have not to my knowledge been manifested, and do therefore determine that the suppliant's petition be left without action or proceeding.

Rönn shook his head and wondered if he had read that correctly. Probably not. In any case the signature was illegible, and, what's more, he knew something about the case of Constable Eriksson.

More than ever now, the writing had a tendency to flow together and distort, and when the woman put a new bundle of documents by his right elbow, he made a gesture as if to ward them off.

'Shall I go further back in time?' she asked pertly. 'Do you want what there is on this man Hult too? And on yourself?'

'I'd rather not,' Rönn said meekly. 'I'll just take the names on these latest ones, and then we can go. Both of us.'

He blinked and scribbled some more in his notebook.

'I can get out Ullholm's petitions too,' the woman said sarcastically. 'If you really want.'

Ullholm was an inspector in Solna, notorious for a greater degree of cantankerousness and a greater number of written complaints to every imaginable authority than anyone else on the force.

Rönn drooped over the table and shook his head dejectedly.

15

On his way to Mount Sabbath, Lennart Kollberg suddenly remembered that he hadn't paid the application fee for a correspondence chess tournament he wanted to enter. The deadline was Monday, so he stopped the car by Vasa Park and went into the post office across from Tennstopet.

When he'd filled in the money order, he stepped obediently into line and waited his turn.

In front of him was a man in a goatskin coat and a fur hat. As always when Kollberg stood in line, he found himself behind a person with about two dozen complicated errands. The man was holding a thick packet of postal orders and notices and correspondence in his hand.

Kollberg shrugged his massive shoulders, sighed and waited. A small piece of paper suddenly loosened from the man's sheaf of papers and fluttered to the floor. A stamp. Kollberg bent down and picked it up. Then touched the man on the shoulder.

'You dropped this.'

The man turned his head and looked at Kollberg with brown eyes that registered surprise, recognition and antipathy, in that order.

'You dropped this,' Kollberg repeated.

'It's too damned much,' the man said slowly, 'when you can't even drop a postage stamp without the police come sticking their filthy noses in.'

Kollberg held out the stamp.

'Keep it,' the man said, and turned away.

Shortly afterwards he finished his postal chores and walked away without so much as a glance at Kollberg.

The episode bewildered him. It was probably some kind of a joke, but on the other hand the man hadn't seemed the least bit jocular. Since Kollberg was a poor physiognomist and often failed to place faces he ought to have recognized, there was nothing remarkable in the fact that the other man had recognized him while Kollberg, for his part, hadn't the vaguest idea who it was he'd spoken to.

He sent off his application fee.

Then he looked suspiciously at the stamp. It was rather pretty, with a picture of a bird. It belonged to a series of newly released stamps which, if he understood the thing correctly, guaranteed that letters bearing them would be conveyed with special sluggishness. The kind of subtlety so typical of the post office.

No, he thought, the post office really functioned pretty well and a person shouldn't grumble, not now that it had apparently recovered from the after-effects of the post code system introduced a few years before.

Still lost in thought about the peculiarities of life, he drove on to the hospital.

The crime scene was still carefully cordoned off and nothing in particular had been altered in Nyman's room.

Gunvald Larsson was there, of course.

Kollberg and Gunvald Larsson did not have any particular fondness for one another. The people with a fondness for Gunvald Larsson could, for that matter, be counted on the index finger of one hand, and as easily named – Rönn.

The thought that they would be forced to work together was

extremely uninviting to both Kollberg and Gunvald Larsson. At the moment there didn't seem to be any great risk – it was merely that circumstances had brought them together in the same room.

The circumstances were Nyman, whose appearance was so disagreeable that Kollberg felt called upon to deliver himself of an 'Ugh!'

Gunvald Larsson grimaced in reluctant agreement.

'Did you know him?' he said.

Kollberg nodded.

'So did I. He was one of the most glorious assholes ever to grace this department. But I never had to work with him much, thank God.'

Gunvald Larsson had never really served in the regular police, only belonged to it *pro forma* for a time. Before becoming a policeman he'd been a ship's officer, first in the navy and then in the merchant marine. So unlike Kollberg and Martin Beck, he had not come up the so-called hard way.

'How's the investigation going here?'

'I don't think we'll get anything beyond what's already obvious,' said Gunvald Larsson. 'Some mad bastard came in through that window and butchered him. In cold blood.'

Kollberg nodded.

'But that bayonet interests me,' Gunvald Larsson muttered, more or less to himself. 'And whoever used it knew what he was doing. Familiar with weapons. And who does that apply to?'

'Exactly,' Kollberg said. 'An army man for example, maybe a butcher.'

'A policeman,' Gunvald Larsson said.

Of all the men in the department, he was probably the least susceptible to camaraderie and false loyalty.

And that didn't make him particularly popular.

'Come on, Larsson, now you're exaggerating,' Kollberg said.

'Could be. Are you going to be working on this?'

Kollberg nodded.

'And you?' he said.

'Looks that way.'

They stared at each other without the slightest enthusiasm.

'Maybe we won't have to work together,' Kollberg said.

'We can always hope,' said Gunvald Larsson.

16

It was almost ten o'clock in the morning and Martin Beck was sweating in the sunshine as he walked down the quay along Söder Mälarstrand towards Slussen. The sun didn't in fact give out much heat, and the wind from Riddarfjärden was biting cold, but he'd been walking fast and his winter coat was warm.

Hult had offered to drive him to Kungsholmsgatan, but he had turned him down. He was afraid of falling asleep in the car and hoped a brisk walk would wake him up. He unbuttoned his coat and slowed his pace.

When he got to Slussen he went into a telephone booth, called headquarters and was told that Rönn hadn't yet returned. He didn't really have anything to do until Rönn came back, and that would be at least another hour, he thought. If he went straight home, he could be lying in bed in ten minutes. He was really awfully tired, and the thought of his bed was very tempting. If he set the alarm, he could get an hour's sleep.

Martin Beck walked determinedly across Slussplan and into Järntorgsgatan. When he came out into Järntorget he started walking slower. He could imagine how tired he would still be when the alarm went off in an hour, how tough it would be to get up, and how hard to get dressed and on his way to Kungsholm. On the other hand, it would be nice to get out of his clothes for a while and wash or maybe take a shower.

He came to a stop in the middle of the square, as if paralysed by his own indecision. He could blame it on exhaustion, of course, but it irritated him nonetheless.

He changed course and headed towards Skeppsbron. He didn't know what he was going to do when he got there, but when he caught sight of a taxi he made a quick decision. He would go somewhere and have a sauna.

The driver looked to be about Methuselah's age – doddering, toothless and obviously deaf. Martin Beck, who'd climbed into the front seat, hoped that he at least still had his sight. The man was presumably an old taxi owner who hadn't driven his own cab for many years. He took wrong turns incessantly and on one occasion wound up on the left side of the street as if he'd forgotten about the introduction of right-hand traffic. He muttered darkly to himself and his dry old body was periodically shaken by a hacking cough. When he finally brought the car to a halt in front of the Central Baths, Martin Beck gave him much too large a tip in his relief at having arrived in one piece. He looked at the old man's violently shaking hands and decided not to ask for a receipt.

Martin Beck hesitated for a moment at the ticket window. He usually bathed downstairs where there was a swimming pool, but the thought of a swim didn't appeal to him right now. Instead he bought a ticket to the Turkish section one flight up.

To be on the safe side, he asked the bath attendant who gave him his towels to wake him at eleven o'clock. Then he went into the hottest room and sat there until the sweat ran streaming from his pores. He showered and took a quick dip in the ice-cold water in the tiny pool. Towelled himself dry, wrapped himself in an enormous bath sheet and lay down on the bunk in his cubicle.

He closed his eyes.

He tried to think of something soothing, but his thoughts kept coming back to Harald Hult, sitting there in his desolate impersonal flat, alone and with nothing to do, wearing his uniform on his day off. A man whose life was filled with one thing – being a policeman. Take that away from him and there'd be nothing left.

Martin Beck wondered what would happen to Hult when he retired. Maybe he would just sit quietly by the window with his hands on the table until he withered away.

Did he even own civilian clothes? Probably not.

His eyes burned and stung beneath their lids, and Martin Beck opened them and stared up at the ceiling. He was too tired to sleep. He put his arm over his face and concentrated on trying to relax. But his muscles stayed taut.

From the massage room came rapid cracking noises and the sound of a bucket of water being dumped on a marble bench. Heavy, rattling snores came from someone in a cubicle nearby.

In his mind's eye, Martin Beck suddenly saw a picture of Nyman's mutilated body. He thought about what Kollberg had told him. About how Nyman had taught him to kill.

Martin Beck had never killed a human being.

He tried to imagine what it would feel like. Not shooting someone – he didn't think that would be hard, maybe because the force it takes to pull a trigger is out of all proportion to the force of the bullet that does the killing. Killing with firearms didn't require any great physical effort, and the distance to the victim ought to make the act feel less immediate. But killing someone directly, with your hands, with a piece of rope, or a knife, or a bayonet, that was another matter. He thought of the body on the marble floor of the hospital, the gaping wound in the throat, the blood, the entrails welling out of the belly, and he knew he'd never be able to kill that way.

During his many years as a policeman, Martin Beck had often asked himself if he was a coward, and the older he got the more certain he was of the answer. Yes, he was a coward. But the question didn't bother him the way it had when he was young.

He didn't know for sure if he was afraid of dying. It was his profession to pry into the way that other people died, and that had blunted his own fear. He rarely thought about his own death.

When the attendant knocked on the wall of the cubicle and announced that it was eleven o'clock, Martin Beck hadn't slept a wink.

17

He looked at Rönn and felt profoundly guilty. To be sure, they had had about equal amounts of sleep during the last thirty hours, that is to say none at all, but by comparison with his colleague, Martin Beck had passed the time quite pleasantly, in fact to some extent luxuriously.

The whites of Rönn's eyes were by now as red as his nose, while his cheeks and forehead were unwholesomely pale, and the bags beneath his eyes were heavy and dark blue. Yawning uncontrollably, he fumbled his electric razor out of the drawer in his desk.

The tired heroes, thought Martin Beck.

True, he was forty-eight and the elder of the two, but Rönn was forty-three, and the time when they could skip a night's sleep and go unpunished lay irrevocably, and several years, behind them.

On top of it all, Rönn still stubbornly refused to offer information of his own accord, and Martin Beck had to force himself to ask a question.

'Well, what did you find?'

Rönn pointed unhappily at his notebook, as if it had been a dead cat or some other repulsive, shameful thing.

'There,' he said thickly. 'About twenty names. I only read through the complaints from Nyman's last year as a precinct captain. Then I wrote down the names and addresses of the people who reported him for a couple of years before that. If I'd gone through everything it would have taken all day.'

Martin Beck nodded.

'Yes,' Rönn went on. 'And all day tomorrow too and maybe the next day . . . and the next.'

'I wouldn't guess there's any point in digging any deeper than that,' said Martin Beck. 'I expect even what you've got there is pretty old.'

'Yes, I suppose it is,' Rönn said.

He picked up his electric razor and left the room at a listless pace, dragging the cord behind him.

Martin Beck sat down at Rönn's desk and with knitted eyebrows began to decipher Rönn's cramped and scraggly notations, which always gave him trouble and would probably continue to give him trouble through all eternity.

Afterwards he transferred the names, addresses and nature of the complaints to a lined stenographer's tablet.

John Bertilsson, unskilled labourer, Gotgatan 20, brutality.

And so forth.

When Rönn came back from the men's room, the list was finished. It included twenty-two names.

Rönn's ablutions had not managed to affect his appearance, which was if possible even more wretched than before, but hopefully he felt a little less shabby. To expect him to feel less exhausted would have been an unreasonable demand.

Maybe some kind of encouragement would be in order. A 'pep talk', that's what they called it these days.

'Okay, Einar, I know both of us ought to go home and go to bed. But if we stick with it for a while longer maybe we can come up with something conclusive. It's worth the effort, isn't it?'

'Yes, I suppose it is,' said Rönn sceptically.

'For example, if you'll take the first ten names and I take the rest, we can pretty quickly locate most of these people and cross them off the list, if nothing else. Okay?'

'Sure. If you say so.'

His voice didn't carry an ounce of conviction, let alone clichés like resolve and fighting spirit.

Rönn blinked his eyes and shivered uncontrollably, but he sat down very nicely at his desk and pulled the telephone towards him.

In his own mind, Martin Beck had to admit that the whole thing seemed pointless.

In the course of his active career, Nyman had of course maltreated hundreds of people. Only a few of them had lodged written complaints and Rönn's brief investigation had uncovered only a few of those.

But many years of experience had taught him that most of his work was in fact pointless, and that even the things that provided results in the long run almost always looked pointless to begin with.

Martin Beck went into the room next door and started to phone, but after only three calls he got sidetracked and ended up sitting passively with his hand on the receiver. He hadn't succeeded in locating any of the people on the list and was now thinking about something entirely different.

After a while he took out his own notebook, shuffled through it and dialled Nyman's home phone. It was the boy who answered.

'Nyman.'

The voice sounded earnestly grown-up.

'This is Inspector Beck. We met last night.'

'Yes?'

'How's your mother now?'

'Oh, pretty good. She's much better. Doctor Blomberg was here and then she got a couple of hours sleep. Now she seems pretty much okay and . . .'

The voice trailed off.

'Yes?'

'. . . and I mean it wasn't entirely unexpected,' said the boy uncertainly. 'I mean that Papa's gone. He was awfully sick. For such a long time too.'

'Do you think your mother can come to the phone?'

'Yes, I'm sure she can. She's out in the kitchen. Wait a moment, I'll go and get her.'

'Thank you,' said Martin Beck.

He heard steps moving away from the phone.

What kind of a husband and father had a man like Nyman been? It had seemed like a happy home. There was nothing to say he couldn't have been a loving and lovable family man.

His son, in any case, had been very close to tears.

'Yes, hello? This is Anna Nyman.'

'Inspector Beck. Just one thing I wanted to ask.'

'Yes?'

'How many people knew your husband was in the hospital?'

'There weren't very many,' she said slowly.

'But he'd been sick for some time, hadn't he?'

'Yes, that's true. But Stig didn't really want people to find out about it. Although . . .'

'Yes?'

'Some people knew, of course.'

'Who? Can you say?'

'The family, first of all.'

'Which means?'

'The children and I, of course. And Stig has, had, two younger brothers, one in Gothenburg and one in Boden.'

Martin Beck nodded to himself. The letters in the hospital room had indeed been written by Nyman's brothers.

'Anyone else?'

'I'm an only child myself. And my parents are dead, so I don't have any close relatives alive. Except for an uncle, but he lives in America and I've never met him.'

'What about your friends?'

'We don't have so many. Didn't have, I mean. Gunnar Blomberg who was here last night, we saw a lot of him, and then he was Stig's doctor too. He knew of course.'

'I see.'

'And then there's Captain Palm and his wife, he was an old friend of my husband's from his regiment. We saw them a good deal.'

'Any others?'

'No. There really aren't. We had very few real friends. Only the ones I've named.'

She paused. Martin waited.

'Stig used to say . . .'

She left the sentence unfinished.

'Yes, what did he used to say?'

'That a policeman never really has many friends.'

That was God's own truth. Martin Beck himself had no friends. Except for his daughter, and Kollberg. And a woman named Åsa Torell. But she was also on the force.

And then maybe Per Månsson, a policeman in Malmö.

'And these people knew your husband had been admitted to Mount Sabbath?'

'Well, no, I wouldn't say that. The only person who knew exactly where he was was Doctor Blomberg. Of our friends, that is.'

'Who visited him?'

'Stefan and I. We went every day.'

'No one else?'

'No.'

'Not even Doctor Blomberg?'

'No. Stig didn't want anyone to come except me and our son. He didn't really even want Stefan to come.'

'Why not?'

'He didn't want anyone to see him. You understand . . .'

Martin Beck waited.

110

'Well,' she said finally. 'Stig had always been an unusually strong and vigorous man. Now towards the end he'd grown quite thin and weak and I suppose he was ashamed for people to see him.'

'Mmm,' said Martin Beck.

'Although Stefan didn't care about that. He worshipped his papa. They were very close.'

'What about your daughter?'

'Stig never cared for her the same way. Do you have children yourself?'

'Yes.'

'Both boys and girls?'

'Yes.'

'Then you know how it is. With fathers and sons, I mean.'

As a matter of fact he didn't know. And he thought about it for such a long time that she finally broke in.

'Are you still there, Inspector Beck?'

'Yes, of course. Yes. What about the neighbours?'

'The neighbours?'

'Yes, did they know your husband was in the hospital?'

'Of course not.'

'How did you explain the fact that he wasn't at home?'

'I didn't explain it at all. We don't see each other socially.'

'What about your son? Maybe he mentioned it to some of his friends?'

'Stefan? No, absolutely not. He knew what his father wanted. It would never occur to him to do anything Stig didn't like. Except that he went with me to visit him every evening. And deep down I think Stig liked that.'

Martin Beck made some notes on the shorthand pad in front of him and then summed it up.

'That means, then, that only you, Stefan, Doctor Blomberg and Inspector Nyman's two brothers knew exactly where your husband was – in which ward and in which room.'

'Yes.'

'Then that's about all. Just one more thing.'

'Yes, what?'

'Which of his colleagues did your husband see outside of work?'

'I don't understand.'

Martin Beck put down his pen and massaged the bridge of his nose between his thumb and forefinger. Had he really put the question that badly?

'What I mean is this – what people in the police department did you and your husband see socially?'

'Why, none at all.'

'What?'

'What do you mean?'

'Didn't your husband have any friends in the department? People he saw in his off-duty hours?'

'No. During the twenty-six years Stig and I were married, no policeman ever set foot in our home.'

'Do you really mean that?'

'Yes I do. You yourself and that man you had with you last night would be the only ones. But Stig was already dead by then.'

'But there must have been messengers, even if they were only subordinates who came to fetch him or leave things for him.'

'Yes, that's right. Orderlies.'

'Beg pardon?'

'That's what my husband used to call them, the men who came here. That happened every now and then. But they were never allowed inside the door. Stig was very particular about that.'

'Really?'

'Yes. Always. If a constable came to pick him up or leave something or something else, we never let him in. If it was I or one of the children who went to the door, we always asked whoever it was to wait and then closed the door until Stig could come.'

'Was that his idea?'

'Yes. He told us quite specifically that that's the way it would be. Once and for all.'

'But what of those colleagues he'd worked with for years and years? Was the same thing true of them?'

'Yes.'

'And you don't know any of them?'

'No. At least not more than their names.'

'But he used to talk about them, surely?'

'Very seldom.'

'His superiors then?'

'As I said, very seldom. You see, one of Stig's principles was that his job wasn't to interfere with his private life in any way.'

'But you know some of them by name, you said. Which ones?'

'Well, some of the higher officials. The National Chief of Police, and the Commissioner, naturally, and the Superintendent . . .'

'Of the regular metropolitan police?'

'Yes,' she said. 'Is there more than one superintendent?'

Rönn came into the room with some papers. Martin Beck stared at him blankly. Then he gathered his wits and went on with the conversation.

'But he must have mentioned the names of some of the people he worked with directly.'

'Yes, one at least. I know he had a subordinate he set great store by. A man named Hult. Stig mentioned him now and then. They'd worked together for a long time even before we met.'

'So you know Hult?'

'No. As far as I know I've never even seen him.'

'No?'

'No. But I've talked to him on the telephone.'

'Is that all?'

'Yes.'

'Can you wait a moment, Mrs Nyman?'

'Yes, of course.'

Martin Beck put the receiver down on the table in front of him. Thought hard while he rubbed his hairline with the tips of his fingers. Rönn yawned.

He put the receiver back to his ear.

'Mrs Nyman?'

'Yes.'

'Do you know Captain Hult's first name?'

'Yes, it just happens I do. Palmon Harald Hult. On the other hand, I didn't know his rank.'

'It just happens, you say?'

'Yes, just by chance. I have the name written down right here in front of me. On the telephone pad. Palmon Harald Hult.'

'Who wrote it there?'

'I did.'

Martin Beck didn't say anything.

'Mr Hult phoned last evening and asked for my husband. He was very upset when he heard Stig was sick.'

'And you gave him the address of the hospital?'

'Yes. He wanted to send flowers. And as I said, I knew who he was. He was the only person I'd think of giving the address to, except . . .'

'Yes?'

'Well, the National Chief or the Commissioner or the Superintendent, of course . . .'

'I understand. And so you gave Hult the address?'

'Yes.'

She paused.

'What do you mean?' she said then, with dawning confusion.

'Nothing,' Martin Beck said soothingly. 'I'm sure it doesn't mean a thing.'

'But you seem so . . .'

'It's just that we have to check out everything, Mrs Nyman. You've been very helpful. Thank you.'

'Thank you,' she said bewilderedly.

'Thank you,' Martin Beck repeated, and hung up.

Rönn was leaning against the doorjamb.

'I think I've checked as far as I can for now,' he said. 'Two of

114

them are dead. And no one knows a thing about this damned Eriksson.'

'Uh-hunh,' said Martin Beck absently, and printed a name on the shorthand pad.

PALMON HARALD HULT.

18

If Hult was at work, then he ought to be at his desk. He was getting on in years and no longer did anything but paperwork, at least officially.

But the man who answered at Maria police station seemed utterly uncomprehending.

'Hult? No, he's not here. He always has Saturdays and Sundays off.'

'Hasn't he been in at all today?'

'No.'

'Are you sure?'

'Yeah. Anyway I haven't seen him.'

'Would you mind asking the others?'

'What others?'

'I hope we're not so understaffed there's only one man in the whole Second Precinct,' said Martin Beck, a little irritated. 'You're not at the station all alone, are you?'

'No, of course not,' the man said, somewhat dampened. 'Wait a minute. I'll ask.'

Martin Beck heard the clatter of the receiver on the table and the sound of footsteps clumping off.

And a distant voice.

'Hey, everybody,' it shouted, 'has anyone seen Hult today? That snob Beck from the Murder Squad's on the phone and . . .'

The rest of it was lost in noise and other voices.

Martin Beck waited, throwing a weary glance at Rönn, who looked even more wearily at his wristwatch.

Why did the man at Maria think he was a snob? Presumably because he didn't call people by their first names. Martin Beck had a hard time using first names to constables who were hardly dry behind the ears, and he couldn't get used to their calling him 'Martin'.

And yet he was certainly no stickler for formality.

How had a man like Nyman reacted in such situations?

There was a clattering in the receiver.

'Yes, about Hult . . .'

'Yes?'

'As a matter of fact he was here for a while. About an hour and a half ago. But apparently he left again almost right away.'

'Where to?'

'Nobody knows.'

Martin Beck let this generalization pass without objection.

'Thanks,' he said.

Just to be sure, he dialled Hult's home phone, but as he'd expected there was no answer, and he hung up after the fifth ring.

'Who are you looking for?' Rönn asked.

'Hult.'

'Oh.'

You couldn't say Rönn was especially observant, thought Martin Beck irritably.

'Einar?' he said.

'Yeah?'

'Hult called Nyman's wife last night and got the address of the hospital.'

'Oh?'

'We might ask ourselves why.'

'He probably wanted to send flowers or something,' said Rönn disinterestedly. 'Hult and Nyman were friends, after all.'

'Apparently there weren't very many people who knew Nyman was at Mount Sabbath.'

'So that's why Hult had to call up and ask,' Rönn said.

'Curious coincidence.'

This was not a question, and Rönn quite correctly neglected to answer it. Instead he changed the subject.

'Oh yes, I told you I couldn't get hold of this man Eriksson.'

'Which man Eriksson?'

'Åke Eriksson. That constable who was always writing complaints.'

Martin Beck nodded. He remembered the name, although it must have been a long time since it was mentioned much. But it wasn't a name he wanted to remember, and on top of that he was busy thinking about Hult.

He had talked to Hult less than two hours ago. How had he behaved? News of Nyman's murder hadn't produced any reaction at all at first. And then Hult had gone to work, as he'd put it.

Martin Beck hadn't found anything odd in all of that. Hult was a thick-skinned old policeman and fairly slow-witted, anything but impulsive. That he voluntarily lent a hand when a colleague had been killed seemed perfectly natural. In certain situations, Martin Beck would have behaved exactly the same way.

What did seem odd was the telephone call. Why hadn't he said he'd been in touch with Nyman's wife as recently as the evening before? And if his only reason was to send a greeting, why had he called at night?

If, on the other hand, he'd wanted to know Nyman's exact whereabouts for some reason other than sending flowers.

Martin Beck forced himself to interrupt that line of thought.

Had Hult really called at night?

In that case, what time?

He needed more information.

Martin Beck sighed heavily, lifted the receiver and, for the third time, dialled Anna Nyman's number.

This time it was she herself who answered.

'Oh yes,' she said resignedly. 'Inspector Beck.'

'I'm sorry, but I have to ask you a few more questions about that telephone call.'

'Yes?'

'You said that Captain Hult called you last night?'

'Yes?'

'What time?'

'Fairly late, but I can't say exactly when.'

'Well about what time?'

'Well . . .'

'Had you already gone to bed?'

'Oh no . . . no, wait a moment.'

She put down the phone and Martin Beck drummed his fingers impatiently on the table. He could hear her talking to someone, probably her son, but he couldn't distinguish the words.

'Yes, hello?'

'Yes.'

'I was talking to Stefan. We were sitting watching television. First a film with Humphrey Bogart, but it was so unpleasant we switched to Channel Two. There was a variety show with Benny Hill and it had just started when the phone rang.'

'Splendid. How long had the programme been going?'

'Only a few minutes. Five at the most.'

'Thank you, Mrs Nyman. There's just one more thing.'

'Yes, what?'

'Can you remember exactly what Hult said?'

'No, not word for word. He just asked to speak to Stig and so I said –'

'Forgive me for interrupting. Did he say, "Can I talk to Stig?"'

'No, of course not. He was quite correct.'

'How so?'

'He apologized and asked if he might speak to Inspector Nyman.'

'Why did he apologize?'

'For calling so late, of course.'

'And what did you say?'

'I asked who was calling. Or to be exact, I said, "May I say who's calling?"'

'And what did Mr Hult say then?'

'"I'm a colleague of Inspector Nyman's." Something like that. And then he said his name.'

'And what did you say?'

'As I told you before, I recognized the name immediately and I knew he'd called before and that he was one of the few people Stig really thought well of.'

'Called before, you say. How often?'

'A few times over the years. When my husband was well and at home, he was almost always the one who answered the phone, so this Mr Hult may have called any number of times.'

'And what did you say then?'

'I told you all this before.'

'I'm sorry if I seem persistent,' said Martin Beck. 'But this could be important.'

'I said Stig was ill. And he seemed surprised and sorry and asked me if it was serious and . . .'

'And?'

'And I said I was afraid it was quite serious and that Stig was in the hospital. And then he asked if he might go visit him, and I said my husband would probably rather he didn't.'

'Did that seem to satisfy him?'

'Yes of course. Harald Hult knew Stig very well. From work.'

'But he said he was going to send flowers?'

Leading question, he thought to himself. Damn.

'Yes. And he wanted to write a note. So I said Stig was at Mount Sabbath and I gave him the room number and the ward. I remember Stig's saying a couple of times that Hult was dependable and correct.'

'And then?'

'He begged my pardon again. Thanked me and said good night.'

Martin Beck thanked her too, and in his haste very nearly said good night himself. Then he turned to Rönn.

'Did you watch TV last night?'

Rönn responded with an injured look.

'No, of course not. You were on duty. But can you find out what time the programme with Benny Hill started on Channel Two?'

'I suppose so,' Rönn said, and slouched out to the day room.

He came back with a newspaper in his hand, studied it for a long time.

'Nine twenty-five.'

'So Hult called at nine thirty in the evening. That's a bit late, unless he had some fairly pressing business.'

'Didn't he then?'

'He doesn't seem to have mentioned it, in any case. On the other hand he was careful to find out where Nyman was.'

'Sure. Because he was going to send flowers.'

Martin Beck looked at Rönn for a long time. He needed a chance to talk this thing through.

'Einar, can you listen for a while?'

'I suppose so.'

Martin Beck summarized everything he knew about Hult's actions during the preceding twenty-four hours, from the telephone call to the conversation on Reimersholme and the fact that, at the moment, the man couldn't be located.

'Do you think it was Hult who knifed Nyman?'

The question was unusually direct to have come from Rönn.

'Well, no, I wouldn't say that exactly.'

'I think it sounds a bit farfetched,' Rönn said. 'And pretty peculiar.'

'Hult's behaviour is pretty peculiar too, to put it mildly.'

Rönn didn't respond.

'In any case, I want to get hold of Hult and ask him some questions about this telephone call,' said Martin Beck energetically.

The firmness in his tone made no great impression on Rönn, who yawned widely.

'Send out a call on the radio then,' he said. 'He can't be far away.'

Martin Beck looked at him in surprise.

'Yes, that's really a pretty constructive suggestion.'

'What do you mean "constructive"?' Rönn said, as if he'd been accused of something unsavoury.

Martin Beck picked up the phone again and started giving instructions to the effect that Captain Harald Hult should be requested to contact the Violent Crime Squad on Kungsholmsgatan as soon as he could be located.

Finished with that, he sat at his desk with his head in his hands.

There was something that didn't fit. And still that feeling of danger. From whom? Hult? Or was there something else he'd overlooked?

'Though there is one thing,' Rönn said.

'What?'

'Well, if I called your wife and asked for you –'

He interrupted himself.

'No, that wouldn't happen,' he muttered. 'You're divorced.'

'What were you going to say?'

'Nothing,' said Rönn unhappily. 'I wasn't thinking. I don't want to mess in your private life.'

'But what were you going to say?'

Rönn thought out a better way of putting it.

'Well, if you were married and I called and got your wife and asked to speak to you and she asked me who I was, well . . .'

'Well what?'

'Well, I wouldn't say, "This is Einar Valentino Rönn."'

'Who in the world is that?'

'Me. That's my name. After some movie star. My mother was a little weird sometimes.'

Martin Beck perked up immediately.

'So you mean . . .?'

'I mean it seems sort of odd and unlikely that Hult calls up Nyman's wife and says this is Palmon Harald Hult.'

'How did you know what his name was?'

'You've got it printed on Melander's tablet there. And what's more . . .'

'What's more what?'

'What's more, I've got it in my own papers. On Åke Eriksson's J.O. petition.'

Martin Beck's gaze slowly cleared.

'Good, Einar,' he said. 'Very good.'

Rönn yawned.

'Who's on duty here?' Martin Beck asked suddenly.

'Gunvald. But he's not here. He's hopeless about things like that.'

'There must be somebody else.'

'Yes. Strömgren.'

'And where's Melander?'

'Home, I suppose. He's got Saturdays off these days.'

'I think maybe we'll take a closer look at friend Eriksson,' said Martin Beck. 'The trouble is, I don't remember any details.'

'Me neither,' Rönn said. 'But Melander remembers. He remembers everything.'

'Tell Strömgren to pull out everything he can find on Åke Eriksson. And call Melander and ask him to come down here. Right away.'

'That may not be so easy. He's an assistant chief inspector now. He doesn't like to give up his free time.'

'Use my name,' said Martin Beck.

'Yes, I suppose I will,' Rönn said, and left the room with dragging steps.

Two minutes later he was back.

'Strömgren's looking,' he said.

123

'And Melander?'

'He's on his way, but . . .'

'But what?'

'He didn't sound happy about it.'

Well, that would be asking the impossible.

Martin Beck waited. First of all for Hult to turn up.

And then for the chance to talk to Fredrik Melander.

Fredrik Melander was one of the Violent Crime Squad's few priceless resources. He was the man with the legendary memory. An awful bore, but a detective with unusual qualities. The whole of modern technology seemed paltry by comparison, for in the course of a few minutes Melander could sort out everything of importance he'd ever heard, seen or read about some particular person or some particular subject and then present it clearly and lucidly in narrative form.

There wasn't a computer in the world that could do the same.

On the other hand, he wasn't much with a pen. Martin Beck studied some notes on Melander's pad. They were written in a cramped, distinctive hand that was guaranteed to be illegible.

19

Rönn leaned against the doorjamb and giggled. Martin Beck looked at him wonderingly.

'What are you laughing at?'

'Well, it just struck me that you're looking for a policeman and I'm looking for a policeman and it may be the same man.'

'The same man?'

'No, I suppose that couldn't be,' Rönn said. 'Åke Eriksson is Åke Eriksson and Palmon Harald Hult is Palmon Harald Hult.'

Martin Beck wondered if maybe he shouldn't send Rönn home. There was some question as to whether Rönn's presence was even legal, since according to a new law that had gone into effect at the beginning of the year, no policeman was allowed to serve more than a hundred and fifty hours of overtime per year, nor more than fifty in any given quarter. Theoretically, this could mean that a policeman drew his salary but was at the same time forbidden to work. There was one exception – situations of extreme urgency.

Was this one of those? Conceivably.

Or maybe he ought to put Rönn under arrest. The quarter was only four days old, and Rönn had already used up his overtime quota. It would undeniably be a first in the history of detection.

Otherwise the work was going along normally.

To the extent that Strömgren had searched out a mass of old papers and periodically came in with more.

Martin Beck regarded them with growing distaste.

He kept thinking of more questions he ought to ask Anna Nyman.

But with his hand on the phone, he hesitated. Wasn't it a little much to call her again so soon? Couldn't he get Rönn to do it? In that case he'd have to call her anyway and apologize not only for himself but also for Rönn.

In the face of that dismal prospect he recovered his courage, lifted the receiver and dialled the number to the bereaved household for the fourth time.

'Nymans'. Hello?'

The widow's voice sounded more spirited every time he heard it. Everything was on its way back to normal. One more demonstration of that resilience for which the human race was so well known. He pulled himself together.

'Hello, this is Beck again.'

'But it's only ten minutes since I talked to you . . .'

'I know. I'm sorry. I suppose it's painful for you to talk about this . . . incident.'

Couldn't he really have found a better word?

'I'm beginning to get used to it,' she said with a certain chill. 'What would you like now, Chief Inspector?'

In any case she certainly knew her ranks.

'Well, I'd like to go back to that phone call.'

'From Captain Hult?'

'Yes, right. You said that wasn't the first time you'd spoken to him.'

'No.'

'Did you recognize his voice?'

'Of course not.'

'Why "of course"?'

'Because then I wouldn't have had to ask who it was.'

Mother! Well that's the way it goes. He should have let Rönn make the call after all.

'Didn't you think of that, Inspector?' she asked.

'No, as a matter of fact I didn't.'

Most people would have blushed or hemmed and hawed. Not Martin Beck. He went on undaunted.

'So it could have been anyone at all?'

'Doesn't it seem odd that just anyone at all would call up and say his name was Palmon Harald Hult?'

'I mean it could have been someone other than Hult.'

'Who?'

Good question, he thought.

'Could you tell if it was an older or a younger man?'

'No.'

'Can you describe the voice at all?'

'Well . . . it was distinct. Maybe a little gruff.'

Yes, that was an excellent description of Hult's voice. Gruff and distinct. But there were a lot of policemen who talked that way, particularly the ones with a military background. And not only policemen of course.

'Wouldn't it be easier to ask Captain Hult?' the woman said.

Martin Beck declined to comment. Instead he headed into deeper water.

'Being a policeman almost always involves making a few enemies.'

'Yes, you said so before. The second time we talked. Are you aware, Inspector, that this is our fifth conversation in less than twelve hours?'

'I'm sorry. You said you didn't know your husband had any enemies.'

'That's right.'

'But of course you knew he had certain professional problems.'

127

It sounded as if she had laughed.

'Now I really don't understand what you mean.'

Yes, she had actually laughed.

'What I mean,' said Martin Beck mercilessly, 'is that many people seemed to think your husband was a bad policeman and outright derelict in his duty.'

That hit home. Gravity was restored.

'Are you joking, Inspector?'

'No,' he said, a little more gently. 'I'm not joking. Your husband incurred a lot of complaints.'

'For what?'

'Brutality.'

She drew a sharp breath.

'That's utterly absurd,' she said. 'You must be confusing him with someone else.'

'I don't believe so.'

'But Stig was the gentlest person I ever met. For example, we've always had a dog. Dogs, I mean. Four of them, one after the other. Stig loved them, and he was endlessly patient, even before they were housebroken. He'd work with them for weeks without losing his temper.'

'Really?'

'And he never so much as lifted his hand to the children, especially when they were little.'

Martin Beck had often raised his hand to his children, especially when they were little.

'So he never said anything about his troubles on the job.'

'No. I've already told you he practically never mentioned his job. What's more, I don't believe that talk for a moment. There simply must be some mistake.'

'But he must have had certain opinions? In general, I mean?'

'Yes, he thought society was suffering a moral breakdown. Because of the government.'

Well, that was a view you could hardly blame him for. The trouble

128

was that Stig Nyman belonged to a little minority that would undoubtedly make everything even worse if they got the chance.

'Was there anything else?' Mrs Nyman asked. 'I really have a great deal to do.'

'No, not right now anyway. I'm very sorry I've had to trouble you.'

'It's quite all right.'

She didn't sound convinced.

'The only thing might be if we have to ask you to identify the voice.'

'Captain Hult's?'

'Yes, do you think you'd recognize it now?'

'Very likely. Good-bye.'

'Good-bye.'

Martin Beck pushed away the telephone. Strömgren came in with still more papers. Rönn stood by the window looking out, his glasses pushed down to the tip of his nose.

'Yes indeed,' he said tranquilly.

Another quarter heard from.

'What branch of the service was Hult in?'

'The cavalry,' Rönn said.

A bully's paradise.

'And Eriksson?'

'He was in the artillery.'

There was silence for fifteen seconds.

'Is it the bayonet you're thinking of?' Rönn said at last.

'Yes.'

'Yes, I thought so.'

'What do you mean?'

'It's just that anyone can buy one of those things for five kronor. From army surplus.'

Martin Beck said nothing.

He'd never been awfully impressed with Rönn, but it had never occurred to him that the feeling might be mutual.

There was a tapping on the door.

Melander.

Probably the only man in the world who would tap on his own door.

20

Lennart Kollberg was uneasy about the time factor. He had a feeling something dramatic ought to happen, but so far nothing had interrupted the routine. The body was gone and the floor had been washed. The bloody bedclothes had been removed. The bed had been rolled away in one direction and the night table in another. All the personal belongings had been put in plastic bags, which had then been placed in a sack. This now lay in the corridor waiting for someone to collect it. The lab men were gone and not even a chalk outline on the floor recalled the existence of the late Stig Nyman. That method was old-fashioned and rarely used any more. The only ones who missed it seemed to be the newspaper photographers.

As a matter of fact the only thing left in the room was the visitor's chair, and Kollberg sat on that himself, and thought.

What does a person do after killing someone? He knew from experience that there were a lot of answers to that question.

Kollberg had killed a man himself one time. What had he done afterwards? He'd thought about it long and hard, for years in fact, and in the end he'd turned in his service revolver, with the licence and everything, and said he never wanted to carry arms again. That had all happened several years ago and he had a vague memory that the last time he'd carried a pistol was in Motala in the summer of 1964, during the notorious Roseanna case. But he still sometimes caught himself thinking of that unhappy occasion. Like when he looked at himself in the mirror. That person there has killed a man.

During his years on the force he'd stood face to face with more murderers than he cared to think about. And he was aware of the fact that a person's behaviour after committing a violent act has infinite variations. Some people throw up, some people eat a hearty meal, and some people kill themselves. Others panic and run, to no place in particular, just run, and still others quite simply go home and go to bed.

Trying to make guesses on that point was not only difficult, it was also professionally unsound, since it could lead the investigation down the wrong track.

Nevertheless, there was something about the circumstances surrounding Nyman's murder that made him ask himself what the man with the bayonet had done afterwards, and what he was doing right now.

What circumstances? In part the purely external violence, which must be an expression of an inner violence at least as great and thus destined to further expression.

But was it really that simple? Kollberg remembered the way he'd felt when Nyman was teaching him to be a paratrooper. At first he'd felt weak and sick and couldn't eat, but it wasn't long before he would climb out of his pile of steaming offal, throw off his protective clothes, shower and head straight for the canteen. And wolf down coffee and pastry. So even things like that could get to be routine.

Another circumstance that influenced Kollberg's thinking was the way Martin Beck had acted. Kollberg was a very sensitive man, not least of all in regard to his boss. He knew Martin Beck inside and out and had no trouble picking up the nuances in his behaviour. Today Martin Beck had seemed uneasy, maybe downright frightened, and that was a thing that happened rarely and never without cause.

So now he sat here with his question. What had the murderer done after the murder?

Gunvald Larsson, never reluctant to guess and take chances, had had an immediate answer.

'He probably went straight home and shot himself,' he'd said.

It was doubtless a possibility worth considering. And maybe it was as simple as that. Gunvald Larsson was often right, but it happened at least as often that he guessed wrong.

Kollberg was prepared to admit that that was only human, but absolutely nothing more. He had always considered Gunvald Larsson's qualifications as a policeman highly doubtful.

And it was the very same dubious individual who now interrupted Kollberg's speculations by marching into the room together with a corpulent bald-headed man in his sixties. The man looked frustrated, but most people did in the company of Gunvald Larsson.

'This is Lennart Kollberg,' Gunvald Larsson said.

Kollberg stood up and looked questioningly at the stranger, and Gunvald Larsson completed his laconic introduction.

'This is Nyman's medico.'

They shook hands.

'Kollberg.'

'Blomberg.'

And Gunvald Larsson started throwing out meaningless questions.

'What's your first name?'

'Gunnar.'

'How long have you been Nyman's doctor?'

'Over twenty years.'

'What was he suffering from?'

'Well, it may be a little involved for a layman . . .'

'Go right ahead.'

133

'It's actually pretty complicated even for a doctor.'

'Oh?'

'The fact is I've just come from looking at the X-rays. Seventy of them.'

'And?'

'The diagnosis is largely positive. Good news.'

'What?'

Gunvald Larsson was so taken aback he looked almost dangerous, and the doctor hurriedly went on.

'Well, I mean if he were still alive, of course. Very good news.'

'Which is to say?'

'That he could have been cured.'

Blomberg thought for a moment and then modified his statement.

'Well, at least restored to relative good health.'

'What was wrong with him?'

'As I said, we've now determined that. Stig had a medium-sized cyst on the jejunum.'

'On the what?'

'The small intestine. And a small tumour in the liver.'

'And what does that mean?'

'That he could have been restored to a state of relative good health, as I said. The cyst was operable. It could have been removed. It was not of a malignant nature.'

'What's "malignant"?'

'Cancer. It kills you.'

Gunvald Larsson seemed noticeably encouraged.

'That isn't so hard to understand,' he said.

'As you gentlemen may know, however, we cannot operate on the liver. But the tumour was very small, and Stig ought to have been able to live for several more years.'

Doctor Blomberg nodded in affirmation of himself.

'Stig is physically strong. His general condition is excellent.'

'What?'

'Was, I mean. Good blood pressure and a strong heart. Excellent general condition.'

Gunvald Larsson seemed to have had enough.

The physician made motions as if to go.

'One moment, Doctor,' Kollberg said.

'Yes?'

'You were Inspector Nyman's doctor for a long time and knew him well?'

'Yes, that's right.'

'What kind of a person was Nyman?'

'Yes, aside from his general condition,' said Gunvald Larsson.

'I'm not a psychiatrist,' said Blomberg and shook his head. 'I prefer to stick to internal medicine.'

But Kollberg wasn't ready to give up quite yet.

'Still, you must have had some opinion about him.'

'Stig Nyman was a complex human being, as we all are,' said the doctor cryptically.

'Is that all you have to say?'

'Yes.'

'Thank you.'

'Good-bye,' said Gunvald Larsson.

And there the interview ended.

When the physician had gone, Gunvald Larsson turned to one of his more irritating habits. He pulled systematically at each of his long fingers, one after the other, until the knuckles cracked. In several cases he had to pull two or three times. This was particularly true of his right index finger, which didn't crack until the eighth attempt.

Kollberg followed the procedure with resigned aversion.

'Larsson?' he said at last.

'Yes, what?'

'Why do you do that?'

'That's my business,' said Gunvald Larsson.

Kollberg went on trying to guess riddles.

'Larsson,' he said after a while, 'can you think yourself into the position of this man who killed Nyman, and the way he reasoned? Afterwards?'

'How do you know it was a man?'

'Very few women know how to handle that kind of a weapon, and still fewer wear a size twelve shoe. Well, can you? Think yourself into his situation?'

Gunvald Larsson looked at him with steady clear-blue eyes.

'No, I can't. How the hell could I?'

He lifted his head, brushed the blond hair out of his eyes, and listened.

'What the hell's all that noise?' he said.

Shouts and excited voices could be heard somewhere nearby. Kollberg and Gunvald Larsson immediately left the room and went outside. One of the police department's black-and-white VW minibuses stood by the foot of the steps, and about fifty feet further off there were five young constables and an older uniformed police officer in the process of pushing back a crowd of civilians.

The constables had linked hands and their commander was waving his rubber baton threateningly above his grey crew cut.

Among the crowd were some press photographers, a few female hospital orderlies in white coats, a taxi driver in his uniform, and a number of other people of various ages. The usual collection of thrill-seekers. Several of them were protesting loudly, and one of the younger ones picked up an object from the ground. An empty beer can. He threw it at the policemen and missed.

'Get 'em, boys,' the officer yelled. 'That'll be enough of that.'

More white batons came into sight.

'Hold it!' demanded Gunvald Larsson in a stentorian bellow.

All activity ceased.

Gunvald Larsson walked towards the crowd.

'What's this all about?'

'I'm clearing the area in front of the cordon,' said the older policeman.

The gold stripe on his sleeve indicated that he was a captain.

'But there's nothing here to cordon off, for Christ's sake,' said Gunvald Larsson angrily.

'No, Hult, that's true enough,' Kollberg said. 'And where did you get these fellows?'

'An emergency squad from the Fifth Precinct,' said the man, coming automatically to attention. 'They were here already and I assumed command.'

'Well stop this nonsense at once,' said Gunvald Larsson. 'Put a guard on the steps to keep unauthorized people out of the building itself. I doubt even that's really necessary. And send the rest of them back to the station. I'm sure they need them more back there.'

From inside the police bus came the sound of shortwave static and then a metallic voice.

'Captain Harald Hult is requested to contact central and report to Chief Inspector Beck.'

Hult still had his baton in his hand and looked sullenly at the two detectives.

'Well,' said Kollberg. 'Aren't you going to contact central? It sounds like someone's looking for you.'

'All in good time,' the man said. 'Anyway I'm here voluntarily.'

'I don't think we need any volunteers here,' said Kollberg.

He was wrong.

'What a lot of bullshit,' said Gunvald Larsson. 'But at least I've done my bit around here.'

He was also wrong.

Just as he took the first long stride towards his car, a shot rang out and a shrill, frantic voice started calling for help.

Gunvald Larsson stopped in bewilderment and looked at his watch. It was ten minutes after twelve.

Kollberg also responded at once.

Maybe this was what he'd been waiting for.

21

'As to Eriksson,' Melander said, putting down the bundle of papers, 'it's a long story. You must know some of it already.'

'Assume we don't know anything and tell it to us from the beginning,' said Martin Beck.

Melander leaned back in his chair and started to fill his pipe.

'Okay,' he said. 'From the beginning then. Åke Eriksson was born in Stockholm in 1935. He was an only child, and his father was a lathe operator. He left school in '54, did his national service the following year, and when he got out he applied to the police force. He started OCS night school and the Police Academy at the same time.'

He lit his pipe elaborately and blew small clouds of smoke across the tabletop. Rönn, who was sitting across from him, reproached him with an ostentatious cough. Melander took no notice and went on puffing.

'Okay,' he said, 'that's a short résumé of the earlier and comparatively less interesting half of Eriksson's life. In 1956 he started as a constable in Katarina precinct. There's not much to be said about the next few years. As far as I can understand, he was a pretty average policeman, neither awfully good nor awfully bad. There were no complaints about him, but on the other hand I can't recall that he distinguished himself in any way.'

'Was he in Katarina that whole time?' asked Martin Beck, who was standing by the door with one arm on the filing cabinet.

'No,' Melander said. 'He was stationed in probably three or four different precincts those first four years.'

He stopped and furrowed his brow. Then he took his pipe out of his mouth and pointed the stem at Martin Beck.

'Correction,' he said. 'I said he didn't distinguish himself in any way. That's wrong. He was an excellent shot, always placed very high in the matches.'

'Yes,' Rönn said. 'I remember that myself. He was good with a pistol.'

'He was excellent at long range, too,' Melander said. 'And all this time he went on with his voluntary officer's training. He used to spend his holidays at OCS camps.'

'You said he was in three or four different precincts those first years,' said Martin Beck. 'Was he ever in Stig Nyman's precinct?'

'He was for a while, yes. Autumn of '57 and all of '58. Then Nyman got a new precinct.'

'Do you know anything about the way Nyman treated Eriksson? He could be pretty rough on the ones he didn't like.'

'There's nothing to indicate he was harder on Eriksson than on the other young men. And Eriksson's complaints against Nyman don't have much to do with that period. But knowing something about Nyman's methods for "making men out of mama's boys", as he used to put it, I think we can assume that Åke Eriksson got his share.'

Melander had directed most of his remarks to Martin Beck. Now he looked at Rönn, who sat crumpled in the visitor's chair and looked as if he might fall asleep at any moment. Martin Beck followed his glance.

'A cup of coffee doesn't sound like such a bad idea, does it, Einar?' he said.

Rönn straightened up.

'No, I suppose not,' he mumbled. 'I'll get it.'

He shambled out of the room and Martin Beck watched him and wondered if he looked that miserable himself.

When Rönn had come back with the coffee and collapsed in his easy chair again, Martin Beck looked at Melander.

'Go on, Fredrik,' he said.

Melander put down his pipe and slurped his coffee thoughtfully.

'Jesus,' he said. 'That's awful.'

He pushed away the plastic mug and went back to his beloved pipe.

'Well, at the beginning of 1959, Åke Eriksson got married. The girl was five years younger than he, and her name was Marja. She was Finnish, but she'd lived in Sweden for several years and had a job as an assistant in a photographic studio. Her Swedish wasn't very good, which may have something to do with what happened later. They had a baby in December the same year they were married, and she then packed in her job and became a housewife. When the child was a year and a half old, that is, in the summer of '61, Marja Eriksson died under circumstances you can hardly have forgotten.'

Rönn nodded in sad assent. Or was it simply that he was about to doze off?

'No, but don't worry about that,' said Martin Beck. 'Tell us anyway.'

'Well,' said Melander, 'this may be where Stig Nyman comes into the story. And Harald Hult, who at that time was a sergeant in Nyman's precinct. Marja Eriksson died at their precinct station. In a drunk cell, the night between the twenty-sixth and twenty-seventh of June, 1961.'

'Were Nyman and Hult at the station that night?' asked Martin Beck.

'Nyman was there when they brought her in, but he went home

140

later on, at some hour that hasn't been determined exactly. Hult was out on patrol that night, but it's quite certain that he happened to be at the station when she was discovered dead.'

Melander straightened a paper clip and started to clean out his pipe into the ashtray.

'There was an investigation eventually, and the chain of events was reconstructed. What happened seems to have been the following. During the day on June twenty-sixth, Marja Eriksson and her daughter went to visit a friend of hers in Vaxholm. The photographer she'd worked for previously had asked her to help him with a two-week assignment, and Marja's girl friend was going to take care of the child. Late in the afternoon she went back into town again. Åke Eriksson finished work at seven that evening, and she wanted to be home ahead of him. It's worth noting that Eriksson was not assigned to Nyman's precinct at that time.'

Martin Beck's legs were starting to get tired. Since the only two chairs in the room were taken, he left the filing cabinet and walked over to the window and half sat against the sill. He nodded to Melander to go on.

'Marja Eriksson had diabetes and needed regular injections of insulin. There weren't many people who knew about that – the girl friend in Vaxholm, for example, did not. Marja Eriksson never used to be careless about her injections – for that matter she wasn't in a position where she could afford to be careless – but on that particular day, for some reason, she'd left her syringe at home.'

Both Martin Beck and Rönn now looked at Melander intently, as if they meant to weigh his version of the story very carefully.

'Two officers from Nyman's precinct discovered Marja Eriksson just after seven o'clock in the evening. She was sitting on a bench, and looked to be on her last legs. They tried to talk to her and became convinced that she was under the influence of drugs, or maybe just blind drunk. They dragged her to a taxi and drove her to the police station. They said themselves at the hearing that they didn't quite know what to do with her when they got her there, since she was virtually helpless. The taxi driver said later that she had said something in a foreign language, that is, Finnish, and it's possible there was some sort of a ruckus in the taxi. The two officers denied it, of course.'

Melander paused a long while as he fussed ceremoniously with his pipe.

'Now then, according to what these constables first said, Nyman had a look at her and told them to put her in a drunk cell for the time being. Nyman denied ever having seen the woman, and at a later hearing the constables changed their story and said they assumed Nyman must have been busy with something else when they brought her in. They themselves had been forced to leave again immediately on some urgent mission. According to the custody guard, it was the constables themselves who decided to lock her up. That is to say, everyone blamed everyone else. There wasn't a sound from her cell, and the guard thought she was asleep. There hadn't been any chance of getting a transport to Criminal for nearly three hours. When his relief came, the night guard unlocked the cell and found she was dead. Hult was at the station right then, and he called an ambulance but couldn't get them to take her to the hospital because she was already dead.'

'What time did she die?' asked Martin Beck.

'She appeared to have died about an hour earlier.'

Rönn straightened up in his chair. 'When you've got diabetes,' he said, 'I mean, don't people with diseases like that carry a card or something that says what it is that's wrong with them . . .?'

'Yes indeed,' Melander said. 'And Marja Eriksson had one, too – in her purse. But as you probably know, part of the whole problem was that she was never searched. They didn't have any female personnel at the precinct, so she would have been searched here at Criminal. If she'd ever arrived.'

Martin Beck nodded.

'Later, at the hearing, Nyman said he'd never seen either the woman or her purse, so the two constables and the guard had to take the whole responsibility. As far as I know, they got off with a warning.'

'How did Åke Eriksson react when he found out what had happened?' asked Martin Beck.

'He fell apart and had to go on sick leave for a couple of months. Lost all interest in everything, apparently. When his wife didn't come home, he finally discovered she hadn't taken her syringe. First he called around to all the hospitals and then took his car and went out looking for her, so it was quite some time before he found out she was dead. I don't think they told him the truth right away, but eventually he must have found out what had happened, because in September he sent in his first written complaint against Nyman and Hult. But by then the investigation was already closed.'

22

Melander's office grew quiet.

Melander had clasped his hands behind his neck and was staring at the ceiling, Martin Beck was leaning against the windowsill looking pensively and expectantly at Melander, and Rönn was just sitting.

Finally Martin Beck broke the silence.

'What happened to Eriksson after his wife's death? I mean, not the external events, but what happened to him psychologically?'

'Well, I'm no psychiatrist,' Melander said, 'and there's no expert opinion, because as far as I know he never went to a doctor after going back to work in September '61. Which he maybe should have done.'

'But he was different afterwards, wasn't he?'

'Yes,' Melander said. 'It's obvious he underwent some sort of personality change.'

He put his hand on the bundle of papers that Strömgren had gathered from various files.

'Have you read through this?' he asked.

Rönn shook his head.

'Only part of it,' said Martin Beck. 'That can wait. I think we can get a clear picture faster if you'll summarize it for us.'

He thought of adding a word of praise, but didn't, since he knew Melander was immune to flattery.

Melander nodded and put his pipe between his teeth.

'Okay,' he said. 'When Åke Eriksson went back to work again, he was uncommunicative and quiet and kept to himself as much as possible. The other officers on his watch tried to cheer him up, but without success. To begin with they were patient with him. They knew what had happened, after all, and they felt sorry for him. But since he never said a word unless it was absolutely necessary, and since he never listened to anyone else either, they all finally tried to avoid having to work with him. He'd been popular before, and they probably hoped he'd be his old self again when the worst of his grief was over. Instead he only got worse – touchy, sullen and downright priggish in his work. He started sending letters full of complaints and threats and accusations, and that went on periodically for years. We've all gotten one or more, I suppose.'

'Not me,' Rönn said.

'Maybe you haven't received any personally, but you've seen his letters to the Violent Crime Squad.'

'Yes,' Rönn said.

'He started out by reporting Nyman and Hult to the J.O. for breach of duty. He sent in that complaint several times. Then he started reporting everyone in sight for breach of duty, even the governor. He's reported me, and you too, Martin, hasn't he?'

'Oh yes,' said Martin Beck. 'For not opening an investigation into the murder of his wife. But that was a long time ago, and as a matter of fact I'd forgotten about him.'

'By about a year after his wife's death, he'd made himself so impossible that the chief in his precinct asked to have him transferred.'

'Do you know what he stated as cause?' Martin Beck asked.

'That inspector was a decent man and apparently he'd closed his eyes to a great deal in Eriksson's case. But in the end it just got to be too much, for the sake of the other men. He said that Eriksson spread disharmony around him, that he was difficult to work with, and that it would be better for Eriksson himself if he were transferred to a precinct where he might feel more at home. That's more or less the way he put it. Anyway, Eriksson was transferred to a new precinct in the summer of '62. He wasn't especially popular there either, and his new chief didn't back him up the way the other one had. The other constables complained about him and he picked up a few demerits.'

'What for?' asked Martin Beck. 'Was he violent?'

'No, not at all. He was never brutal or anything, rather overly nice, a lot of people thought. He behaved correctly towards everyone he came in contact with. No, apparently the trouble was his ridiculous pedantry. He'd spend hours on things that shouldn't really have taken more than fifteen minutes. He'd submerge himself in unimportant details, and occasionally he'd ignore specific instructions in order to do something completely different that he thought was more important. He overstepped his authority by getting involved in things other people had been assigned to deal with. He criticized both his colleagues and his superiors, in fact that's what all his complaints and reports were about – the way people on the force neglected their jobs, from the cadets in his own precinct all the way up to the Chief of Police. I don't doubt he made complaints about the Minister of the Interior, since he was the ultimate chief of police in those days.'

'Did he think he was perfect himself?' Rönn said. 'Maybe he had delusions of grandeur.'

'Like I said, I'm no psychiatrist,' Melander said. 'But it looks as if his wife's death was something he blamed on the whole police force, not just on Nyman and his crowd.'

Martin Beck walked back to the door and assumed his favourite position with one arm on the filing cabinet.

'You mean he quite simply rejects a police force where a thing like that can happen,' he said.

Melander nodded and sucked on his pipe, which had gone out.

'Yes, at least I can imagine that's roughly the way he reasoned.'

'Is anything known about his private life all this time?' asked Martin Beck.

'Not much. He was something of a lone wolf, after all, and didn't have any friends on the force. He gave up officer's training when he got married. He did a good deal of target shooting, but otherwise he didn't take part in any police athletics.'

'His personal relationships then? He had a daughter, who ought to be . . . how old now?'

'Eleven,' Rönn said.

'Yes,' said Melander. 'He took care of his daughter himself. They lived in the flat he and his wife found when they got married.'

Melander didn't have any children, but Rönn and Martin Beck pondered the practical difficulties of being a single parent and a policeman on top of it.

'Didn't he have someone to take care of the kid?' said Rönn incredulously. 'Like when he was at work, I mean?'

Rönn's son had just turned seven. During those seven years, especially holidays and weekends, he had often marvelled at the fact that at certain periods of its life a single child was capable of occupying the entire time and energy of two full-grown adults virtually twenty-four hours a day.

'Up until 1964 he had the little girl at a day-care centre, and since both of his parents were alive, they took care of her when he worked nights.'

'Then what?' Rönn said. 'After '64?'

'I suppose after that we don't know anything about him,' said Martin Beck, and looked questioningly at Melander.

'No,' Melander said. 'He was fired in August that year. No one missed him. Everyone who'd had anything to do with him just wanted to forget him as quickly as possible. For one reason or another.'

'Don't we even know what kind of job he got next?' asked Martin Beck.

'He applied for a job as a night watchman in October that same year, but I don't know if he got it. And then he vanishes from our picture.'

'When he was fired,' Rönn said, 'was it just a question of the straw that broke the camel's back?'

'How do you mean?'

'I mean did he have too many demerits, or did he do something in particular?'

'Well, the camel's back was ready to break all right, but the direct cause of his dismissal was a breach of discipline. On Friday the seventh of August, Åke Eriksson had the afternoon watch outside the American Embassy. That was 1964, before the big demonstrations against the war in Vietnam had started. As you'll recall, in those days there was only one man on routine watch outside the US Embassy. It wasn't a popular job, it was so dull just wandering back and forth out there.'

'But in those days you could still juggle your baton,' said Martin Beck.

'I remember one guy in particular,' Rönn said. 'He was fantastic. If Eriksson was as good as that, perhaps he got a job in a circus.'

Melander threw a tired glance at Rönn. Then he looked at his watch.

'I promised Saga to be home for lunch,' he said. 'So if I might continue . . .'

'I'm sorry. I just happened to think of that guy,' muttered Rönn, offended. 'Go on.'

'As I was saying, Eriksson was supposed to be watching the embassy, but he just simply said the hell with it. He went out there and relieved the man on the preceding watch. And then he just left. The fact was that a week or so earlier Eriksson had been called to a place on Fredrikshofsgatan where they'd found the caretaker dead in the cellar. He'd put a rope around a pipe in the furnace room and hanged himself, and there was no reason to doubt it was suicide. In a locked room in the basement they found a cache of stolen goods – cameras, radios, TVs, furniture, rugs, paintings, a whole load of stuff from burglaries committed earlier that year. The caretaker had been a fence, and within a few days they'd arrested the men who were using the cellar as a hiding place. Well, all Eriksson really had to do with it was that he'd gone out on the call, and once he and his partner had roped off the area and called in some people from down here, all they had to do was report the suicide and that was that. But Eriksson got the idea that the thing hadn't really been cleared up. As I remember, he thought, for one thing, that the caretaker had been murdered, and for another, he was hoping to catch some more members of the gang. So instead of going back to the embassy, which of course he never should have left, he spent the whole afternoon at Fredrikshofsgatan questioning the tenants and snooping around. On an ordinary day perhaps no one would even have noticed he wasn't on duty, but as luck would have it one of the first real demonstrations against the embassy took place that very afternoon. Two days before, on the fifth of August, the US had attacked North Vietnam and dropped bombs all up and down the coast, and so now several hundred people had gathered to protest the aggression. Since the demonstration was completely unexpected, the embassy's own security people were taken by surprise, and since on top of that our friend Eriksson was nowhere in sight, it was quite a while before the police arrived in any strength. The demonstration was peaceful, people were chanting slogans and standing around with their picket signs while a delegation went in to deliver a written protest to the ambassador. But as you know, the regular police weren't used to demonstrations and acted the way they always do at a riot, and there was one hell of an uproar. Crowds of people were hauled into the station and some of them had been treated pretty badly. All of this was blamed on Eriksson, and since he was guilty of a grave dereliction of duty he was immediately relieved of his duties and a couple of days later officially dismissed. Exit Åke Eriksson.'

Melander stood up.

'And exit Fredrik Melander,' he said. 'I'm not planning to miss my lunch. I sincerely hope you won't need me again today, but if you do you know where I am.'

He put away his tobacco pouch and pipe and got into his coat. Martin Beck walked over and sat down in his chair.

'Do you really think it's Eriksson who cut down Nyman?' said Melander from the door.

Rönn shrugged his shoulders and Martin Beck didn't answer.

'I think it seems unlikely,' Melander said. 'In that case he should have done it back then when his wife died. Revenge and hate can cool off quite a bit in ten years. You're on the wrong track. But good luck. So long.'

He left.

Rönn looked at Martin Beck.

'He's probably right.'

Martin Beck sat silently, shuffling at random through the papers on the table.

'I was thinking of something Melander said. About his parents. Maybe they still live where they lived ten years ago.'

He started shuffling more purposefully in the pile of documents. Rönn didn't say a word, but he looked at Martin Beck without enthusiasm. Martin Beck finally found what he was looking for.

'Here's the address. Gamla Södertäljevägen in Segeltorp.'

23

The car was a black Plymouth with white mudguards and two blue lights on the roof. As if that weren't enough, the four words POLICE, POLICE, POLICE, and POLICE were written on the hood, boot and both sides in large and extremely legible white letters.

Despite the 'B' on the licence plate, which meant it was registered outside Stockholm, the car was at the moment moving at a good speed across the city limits at Norrtull. Heading away from the road to Uppsala and, more importantly, away from the Solna police station.

The patrol car was new and well provided with modern equipment, but technical refinements could do nothing significant to improve its crew. This consisted of constables Karl Kristiansson and Kurt Kvant, two blond giants from Skåne whose nearly twelve years of adventure as radio policemen included several successful and a vast number of entirely unsuccessful actions.

At this particular moment they seemed once again well on their way to trouble.

To be specific, Kristiansson had found himself compelled to arrest the Rump some four minutes earlier. This misfortune could be blamed neither on bad luck nor overzealousness. On the contrary, it had been occasioned by an unusually flagrant and thoughtless provocation.

It had started with Kvant's pulling up and stopping in front of the newsstand at Haga Terminal. He had then taken out his wallet and lent Kristiansson ten kronor, whereupon the latter got out of the car.

Kristiansson was always broke, which was a result of the fact that he squandered all his money on the football pools. Only two people knew of this overwhelming mania. One of them was Kvant, since two men in a radio car are very much dependent on each other and can hardly keep secrets except the ones they have in common. The other was Kristiansson's wife, whose name was Kerstin and who suffered from the same addiction. In fact they had even begun to neglect their sex life, since all of their time together was spent filling in the pools coupons and working out incredibly complicated systems based on a combination of calculated odds and random selections supplied by their two young children, aided by a pair of dice manufactured specifically for this purpose.

At the newsstand, Kristiansson bought copies of *Sports News* and two other speciality newspapers, as well as a stick of liquorice for Kvant. He took the change in his right hand and stuffed it in his pocket. He held the papers in his left, and as he turned towards the car he was already devouring the first page of *All Right* with his eyes. His mind was completely occupied by the question of how Millwall, one of his key teams, would fare in its difficult match against Portsmouth, when he suddenly heard a wheedling voice behind him.

'You forgot this, Inspector.'

Kristiansson felt something brush the sleeve of his coat, and he automatically drew his right hand from his pocket and closed his fingers around something strikingly cold and slimy. He gave a start and looked up, to his horror, directly into the face of the Rump.

Then he looked at the object in his hand.

Karl Kristiansson was very much on duty, standing in a crowded public place. He was wearing a uniform with shiny buttons and a shoulder belt, plus a pistol and a baton in white holsters at his waist. In one hand he was holding a pickled pig's foot.

'To each his own! Hope you like it! Otherwise you can cram it!' howled the Rump and burst into roaring laughter.

The Rump was a vagabond beggar and pedlar. His name had been given him for obvious reasons, since the portion of anatomy in question was quite overwhelming and made his head, arms and legs look like immaterial afterthoughts. He was just under five feet tall, that is, more than a foot shorter than Kristiansson and Kvant.

What made the man so uninviting, however, was not his physical constitution but his clothing.

The Rump was wearing two long overcoats, three suit jackets, four pairs of trousers and five waistcoats. This means a good fifty pockets, and he was known among other things for carrying considerable amounts of cash, always in coin of the realm and never in denominations larger than ten öre.

Kristiansson and Kvant had apprehended the Rump exactly eleven times but had taken him into the station only twice. Namely, the first two times, and then only due to lack of judgement and experience.

On the first occasion he had had 1,230 one-öre pieces, 2,780 two-öre pieces, 2,037 five-öre pieces and one ten-öre in forty-three pockets. The search had taken three hours and twenty minutes, and at the subsequent trial he was indeed sentenced to pay a fine of ten kronor for insulting an officer of the law, and true enough the pig snout he had affixed to the radiator of the patrol car was confiscated by the crown, but on the other hand Kristiansson and Kvant had been forced to appear as witnesses, and that on their day off.

They weren't so lucky the second time. On that occasion, the Rump had had no less than three hundred and twenty kronor, ninety-three öre in sixty-two pockets. The search had taken all of seven hours, and to make their misery complete he was later found not guilty by an idiotic judge who utterly failed to appreciate the niceties of the *skånsk* idiom and could hear nothing disparaging or slanderous in the expressions *fubbick, mögbör, gåsapick* and *puggasole*. When Kvant, with great difficulty, managed to translate *mögbör* (to 'vehicle for the transport of fertilizer'), the judge had remarked sourly that it was Kristiansson and not the patrol car who was the plaintiff, and that the court considered it as good as impossible to insult a Plymouth sedan, particularly not by comparing it with some other practical conveyance.

The Rump, like Kristiansson and Kvant, emanated from the plains of southern Sweden and knew how to choose his words.

When in addition Kvant happened to call the defendant 'the Rump' instead of Carl Fredrik Gustaf Oscar Jönsson-Käck, the day was irretrievably lost. The judge threw the case out and admonished Kvant to avoid the use of doubtful and enigmatic dialectical invective in open court.

And now it was all about to begin again.

Kristiansson looked around surreptitiously and saw nothing but happily expectant or already openly cackling citizens.

To make matters worse, the Rump now extracted an additional pig's foot from one of his inner pockets.

'This here's from one of your relatives and pals who went to his reward the other day,' he shouted. 'His last wish was it should go to somebody who's as big a swine as he was. And that he'd see you soon where every fucking pig winds up. In the big lard bucket in hell.'

Kristiansson's perplexed blue eyes sought out Kvant, but he was looking the other way, thereby indicating that all of this had little or nothing to do with him.

'You look really good with hoofs, Inspector,' said the Rump. 'But it looks like you're missing your curly tail. Don't worry, we'll fix that up.'

He inserted his free hand into his wardrobe.

Cheerful faces were now visible on every side, and some

unidentifiable person on the edge of the crowd added his two cents' worth in a loud voice.

'Go for it,' he said. 'Give the bastard what's coming to him.'

The Rump was troubled by Kristiansson's obvious uncertainty.

'Fucking cop!' he screeched. 'Sow-hole! Hog-prick! Cunt-licker!'

An expectant rustle swelled in the crowd.

Kristiansson stuck out the pig's foot in order to grab hold of his antagonist. At the same time, he was searching desperately for a way out. He could already hear thousands of copper coins clanking in secret pockets.

'He's putting his paws on me,' howled the Rump.

With well-feigned anguish.

'On me, a poor invalid. The cock-sucker's laying hands on an honest pedlar, just because I showed him a little human kindness. Let me go, you fucking son of a bitch!'

When it came right down to it, Kristiansson was handicapped by the pig's foot and unable to carry out any specific act of violence, but the Rump facilitated matters by jerking open the door of the police car and leaping into the back seat before Kristiansson had time to make use of his somewhat inappropriate weapon.

Kvant didn't even turn his head.

'How the hell could you be such an idiot, Karl?' he said. 'Falling right into his hands like that? This is all your fault.'

He started the engine.

'Jesus,' said Kristiansson, not very constructively.

'Where does he want to go?' Kvant asked furiously.

'Solnavägen ninety-two,' squeaked the prisoner happily.

The Rump was by no means stupid. He asked to be taken to the precinct central station. He was looking forward with ill-concealed delight to getting his coins counted.

'We can't dump him anywhere in our precinct,' Kvant said. 'It's too risky.'

'Drive me to the station,' the Rump entreated them. 'Call them on the radio and tell them we're coming so they can put on the coffeepot. I can have a cup while you start counting.'

He shook himself to make his point.

And sure enough. An enormous number of copper coins rattled and clattered ominously from a profusion of secret hiding places beneath his clothes.

Searching the Rump was the job of whatever man or men had been foolish enough to bring him in. That was an unwritten but nevertheless inflexible rule.

'Ask him where he wants to go,' Kvant said.

'You just asked him that yourself,' said Kristiansson peevishly.

'I wasn't the one who picked him up,' Kvant retorted. 'I never even saw him till he got in the car.'

One of Kvant's specialities was seeing nothing and hearing nothing.

Kristiansson knew of only one way to touch the Rump's human frailty. He rattled the change in his pocket.

'How much?' the Rump asked greedily.

Kristiansson pulled out his change from the ten and looked at it. 'Six fifty at least.'

'That's bribery,' the prisoner complained.

The strictly legal aspects of this were a mystery to both Kristiansson and Kvant. Had *he* offered *them* money, it would have been a clear attempt to suborn a civil servant. But this was the other way around.

'Anyway, six fifty isn't enough. I need money for a bottle of dessert wine.'

Kvant took out his wallet and peeled off another ten. The Rump took it.

'Drop me at an alcohol shop,' he said.

'Not here in Solna,' said Kvant. 'That's too much of a risk, dammit.'

'Then take me to Sigtunagatan. They know me there, and I've got some mates in Vasa Park, down by the Gents.'

'We can't just drop him off right in front of the alcohol shop, for Christ's sake,' said Kristiansson anxiously.

They drove south past the post office and Tennstopet and on down Dalagatan.

'I'll take a swing into the park here,' Kvant said. 'Drive in a ways and let him out.'

'Hey, you never paid me for the pig's feet,' said the Rump.

They didn't hit him. Their physical superiority was much too obvious, and then too they weren't in the habit of hitting people, at least not without cause.

Moreover, neither of them was a particularly zealous policeman. Kvant almost always reported whatever he happened to see and hear, but he managed to see and hear exceedingly little. Kristiansson was more an out-and-out slacker who simply ignored everything that might cause complications or unnecessary trouble.

Kvant turned into the park alongside the Eastman Institute. The trees were bare and the park was sad and empty. As soon as he'd made the turn, he stopped.

'Get out here, Karl. I'll drive on in a ways and drop him off as quietly as I can. If you see anything that looks like trouble, blow your whistle, the usual signal.'

The car smelled, as always, of sweaty feet and old vomit, but even more strongly at the moment of cheap booze and body odour from the prisoner.

Kristiansson nodded and got out. He left his newspapers in the back seat but still held the pig's foot in his right hand.

The car disappeared behind him. He walked up towards the street and at first saw nothing that looked in the least like trouble. But he felt uneasy somehow, and waited impatiently for Kvant to come back with the car so they could retreat to the peace and security of their own precinct. He'd have to listen to Kvant bitch about his wife, her physical inadequacy and her fierce temper, until their watch was over. But he was used to that. For his part, he liked his own wife fine, particularly in regard to this business with the football pools, and he seldom mentioned her.

Kvant seemed to be taking his time. He probably didn't want to risk being seen, or else maybe the Rump had upped the price.

In front of the steps up to the Eastman Institute there was a sort of open space, with a round stone fountain or whatever it was in the middle. On the other side of this stood a black Volkswagen, parked so obviously in violation of the law that not even as lazy a policeman as Kristiansson could avoid reacting.

He wasn't exactly thinking of doing anything about it, but the minutes were dragging, so he started strolling slowly around the circular basin. He could at least pretend to be having a look at this car whose owner seemed to think he could park continental-style right in the middle of the capital of Sweden, Land of Prohibitions. Walking up and looking at a parked car doesn't place you under any obligation after all.

The decorative fountain was about twelve feet in diameter, and as Kristiansson got to the other side he thought he saw the sun dazzle for an instant in a window high up in the building across the street.

A fraction of a second later he heard a short, sharp report and at the same instant something hit him like a hammer in the right knee. The leg seemed to disappear beneath him. He staggered and fell backwards over the stone balustrade and down into the basin of the fountain, the bottom of which, at this time of year, was covered with spruce twigs, rotting leaves and litter.

He lay on his back and heard himself scream.

He was dimly aware of several more echoing explosions, but apparently none of them were aimed at him.

He still held the pig's foot in one hand and had not succeeded in connecting the muzzle flash with the report, nor with the bullet that had crushed the bone just below his knee.

24

Gunvald Larsson still had his eyes on the hands of his watch when he heard the second shot. It was followed immediately by at least four more.

Like most watches in the country, his showed common standard Swedish time, that is, fifteen degrees or one hour East Greenwich, and since it was well-cared-for and neither lost nor gained as much as one second a year, his observations were exact.

The first shot was heard at precisely twelve ten. The next four, possibly five, all came in the course of two seconds, that is, between the fourth and the sixth second from the starting point. Which was twelve ten.

Guided by commendable instinct and a correct assessment of direction and distance, Gunvald Larsson and Kollberg acted together during the next two minutes.

They jumped into the nearest car, which happened to be Gunvald Larsson's red BMW.

Gunvald Larsson hit the ignition, peeled some rubber and raced off – not the way he had come, around the central hospital, but past the old heating plant and along the narrow drive that wound up towards Dalagatan between the maternity ward and the Eastman Institute. Then he turned one hundred and eighty degrees to the left and out on to the flagstone court in front of the Institute, braked hard, skidded, and came to a stop with the car slightly at an angle between the fountain and the broad stone steps to the building.

Even before they had time to open the doors and get out, both Gunvald Larsson and Kollberg saw that a uniformed policeman was lying on his back among the spruce branches in the basin. They also saw that he was wounded but alive, and that there were a number of other people in the area. Of these, three were lying on the ground, wounded, dead or trying to find cover, and the rest were standing still, probably wherever they had found themselves when the shots were fired. A patrol car was just coming to a stop on the road up out of Vasa Park. There was a constable at the wheel and he started to open the left front door even before the car had come to a halt.

They got out simultaneously, Gunvald Larsson on the left and Kollberg on the right.

Gunvald Larsson didn't hear the next shot, but he saw his Chinese fur hat leave his head and land on the steps, and he suddenly felt as if someone had drawn a red-hot poker along the hairline from his right temple to a point just above his ear. He hadn't even had time to straighten up, and now his head was knocked to one side and he heard a shot and a shrill whistling, a dry crack and a whining ricochet, and then in two huge leaps he flung himself up the eight steps and pressed himself against the stone wall to the left of the entrance with its three rectangular pillars. He put his hand to his cheek and it came away covered with blood. The bullet had ploughed a furrow in his scalp. The wound was bleeding copiously and his kid jacket was ruined. Already, and for good.

Kollberg reacted as quickly as Gunvald Larsson. He ducked back into the car and was quick-witted enough to vault over into the back seat. Immediately afterwards, two shots cracked through the roof of the car and burned into the stuffing of the front seat.

He could see Gunvald Larsson in the entrance, flat up against the wall and apparently wounded. He knew he had to get out of the car and up the steps at once, and in an almost reflex action he kicked open the right-hand front door with his foot and at the same time hurled himself out through the left-hand rear. Three shots, all aimed at the right side of the car, but Kollberg was already outside on the left where he grabbed hold of the first of the four iron handrails, swung himself up the eight steps without even touching them, and landed with his head and right shoulder in Gunvald Larsson's gut.

Then he took a deep breath, struggled to his feet and pressed himself against the wall beside Gunvald Larsson, who was grunting oddly, probably from surprise or lack of air.

Nothing happened for several seconds, maybe five or ten. Apparently a brief cease-fire.

The wounded constable still lay in the fountain, and his partner stood by the radio car with his pistol in his right hand and looked around dumbfoundedly. He probably hadn't seen Kollberg and Gunvald Larsson and lacked any sort of general view of the situation. But in any case he did see his wounded buddy, twenty-five feet from where he stood, and he started walking towards him, still with a perplexed expression on his face and his service revolver in his fist.

'What in hell are those two blockheads doing here?' muttered Gunvald Larsson.

And then a second later yelled, 'Kvant! Stop! Cover!'

Where, Kollberg wondered.

Because there wasn't any cover.

Gunvald Larsson appeared to have realized the same thing, because he didn't yell again. And for the moment nothing happened except that the blond policeman straightened up and stared in the direction of the entranceway and then went on walking. Apparently he couldn't distinguish the two men in the shadows.

A red double-decker bus drove past heading south on Dalagatan. Someone screamed hysterically for help.

The constable had reached the fountain, put one knee on the rim and leaned down over the wounded man.

There was a little ledge on the inside of the stone basin, presumably for small children to sit on during the summer and splash their bare feet in the water. His leather jacket gleamed in the sun as the policeman laid his pistol on the ledge to free his hands. He turned his broad back upward towards the sky, and the two rifle bullets struck him less than a second apart, the first in the back of the neck and the other directly between his shoulder blades.

Kurt Kvant fell at right angles on top of his partner. He didn't make a sound. Kristiansson had had time to see the exit wound made by the first bullet as it emerged neatly halfway between Kvant's Adam's apple and his collar. Then he felt the weight of Kvant's body across his own hips, and then he passed out, from pain, and fear, and loss of blood. They lay in a cross on the spruce branches, one of them unconscious and the other one dead.

'God damn,' said Gunvald Larsson. 'God damn it to hell!'

Kollberg was seized by a strong sense of unreality.

He had been waiting for something to happen. Now something was happening, but it was as if it were taking place in another dimension from the one where he himself still lived and moved.

Something else happened. Someone moved, walked into the magic flagstone square. A little boy with a moss-green quilted jacket, blotchy jeans in various shades of blue, and green wellies with reflecting tape. Blond curly hair. He couldn't have been more than five. The boy walked slowly and hesitantly towards the fountain.

Kollberg felt the quivering in his body, the automatic physical preparation for rushing out of the doorway and picking up the child in his arms. Gunvald Larsson noticed it too, and without taking his eyes from the macabre scene before them, he put his large bloody hand on Kollberg's chest.

'Wait,' he said.

The boy stood by the edge of the basin and stared down at the crossed bodies. Then he stuck his left thumb in his mouth, put his right hand to his left ear, and burst into tears.

Stood for a moment with the tears trickling down his plump cheeks, his head on one side. Turned suddenly and ran back the way he'd come. Across the pavement and the street. Out of the flagstone quadrangle. Back to the land of the living.

No one shot at him.

Gunvald Larsson looked at his watch.

Twelve twelve and twenty-seven.

'Two minutes and twenty-seven seconds,' he said to himself.

And Kollberg thought, by association but a little oddly: Two minutes and twenty-seven seconds, not generally thought to be a very long time. But in certain contexts it could mean a lot. A good Swedish sprinter, Björn Malmroos for example, could theoretically run the hundred metres fourteen times. That's a lot.

Two policemen shot, one of them already dead for sure. In all probability the other one too.

Gunvald Larsson a quarter of an inch from death. Two inches himself.

And then the little boy in the moss-green jacket.

That's also a lot.

Lennart Kollberg looked at his own watch.

It already said twenty past.

In certain other respects he was a perfectionist, but in some circumstances he simply didn't make it.

On the other hand, it was an Exakta, a Russian watch, and he'd bought it for sixty-three kronor. It had been running nicely for over three years, and if you set it and wound it at regular intervals it even told the time.

Gunvald Larsson's chronometer had cost 1,500 kronor.

Kollberg lifted his hands, looked at them, and cupped them around his mouth.

'Hello! Hello!' he roared. 'Anyone who can hear me! The area is dangerous! Take cover!'

He took a deep breath and started again.

'Attention! This is the police! The area is dangerous! Take cover!'

Gunvald Larsson turned his head and looked at him. The expression in his china-blue eyes was peculiar.

Then Gunvald Larsson looked at the door leading into the Institute. It would of course be locked on a Saturday. The entire big stone building was undoubtedly empty. He eased closer to the door and kicked it in with superhuman strength.

It should have been impossible, but he did it. Kollberg followed him into the building. The next door was unlocked and made of glass, but he kicked in that one too. Splinters flew.

They came to a telephone.

Gunvald Larsson picked up the receiver, dialled 90000 and asked for emergency.

'This is Gunvald Larsson. There's a madman in the building at Dalagatan 34. He's shooting from the roof or the top floor with an automatic weapon. There are two dead constables lying in the fountain in front of the Eastman Institute. Alert all the central precincts. Block off Dalagatan and Västmannagatan from Norra Bantorget to Karlbergsvägen, and Odengatan from Odenplan to St Eriksplan. And all the cross streets in the area west of Västmannagatan and south of Karlbergsvägen. Have you got that? What? Notify command? Yes, notify everybody. But wait a minute. Don't send any patrol cars to that address. And no one in uniform. We'll assemble at . . .'

He lowered the receiver and frowned.

'Odenplan,' said Kollberg.

'Right,' said Gunvald Larsson. 'Odenplan'll be fine. What? I'm inside the Eastman Institute. In a few minutes I'll go over and try to take him.'

He banged down the receiver and went into the nearest men's room. Wet a towel and wiped the blood off his face. Took another and tied it around his head. Spots of blood appeared immediately on the provisional bandage.

Then he unbuttoned his kid jacket and his coat. And drew his pistol, which he carried clipped to his belt. He examined it grimly, then looked at Kollberg.

'What kind of a weapon you got?'

Kollberg shook his head.

'Oh, that's right,' said Gunvald Larsson. 'You're some sort of a pacifist.'

His pistol, like all his possessions, was not like other people's. A Smith & Wesson .38 Master, which he'd bought because he didn't like the standard Swedish police model, the 7.65 mm Walther.

'You know what?' said Gunvald Larsson. 'I've always thought you were a fucking idiot.'

Kollberg nodded.

'How d'you reckon we'll get across the street?' he said.

25

The house in Segeltorp could hardly be called imposing – a little wooden building which, to judge from the architecture, had been built as a summer house at least fifty years before. The original paint was worn clear through to grey wood in places, but it was still apparent that the house had once been bright yellow with white trim. The fence around the yard, which seemed large in proportion to the house, had been painted Falun red not so very many years ago. As had the handrail on the steps, the outer door and the latticework around a small verandah.

It stood quite some distance above the main road, and since the gate was open Rönn drove up the steep drive all the way to the back of the house.

Martin Beck got out immediately and took several deep breaths while he looked around. He felt a little ill, as he often did when he rode in a car.

The garden was neglected and full of weeds. A partially over-grown path led to an old rusted sundial that looked pathetic and out of place on its cement pedestal surrounded by scrubby bushes.

Rönn slammed the door to the car.

'I'm starting to get a bit peckish,' he said. 'Think we've got time for a quick bite when we're through here?'

Martin Beck looked at his watch. Rönn was used to eating lunch at this time of day, it was already ten minutes after twelve. Martin Beck was careless about meals himself. He didn't really like to eat while he was working and preferred having his dinner in the evening.

'Sure,' he said. 'Come on, let's go in.'

They walked around the corner of the house, up the steps and knocked at the door. It was opened immediately by a man in his seventies.

'Come in,' he said.

He stood silently by and looked at them inquiringly as they hung up their coats in the crowded front hall.

'Come in,' he said again, and stood to one side so they could pass.

There were two doors at the other end of the front hall. One of them led through a short hall to the kitchen. From this second hall, a staircase led up to the second floor or attic. The other door led into the living room. The air inside was damp and stale, and rather dim because of the tall fern-like potted plants that stood in the windowsills and kept out most of the daylight.

'Please sit down,' said the man. 'My wife will be right here. With some coffee.'

The room was dominated by a rustic dining suite – a straight-backed pine sofa and four chairs with striped upholstered seats around a large table topped by a massive slab of beautifully veined fir. Martin Beck and Rönn sat down at opposite ends of the sofa. A door stood ajar at the far end of the room, and through it they could see the cracked end of a mahogany bedstead and a wardrobe with oval mirrors on its doors. The man walked over and closed the door before sitting down in one of the chairs on the other side of the table.

He was thin and bent, and the skin on his face and bald head was grey and covered with light brown liver spots. He was wearing a thick hand-knitted sweater over a grey-and-black chequered flannel shirt.

'I was just saying to my wife when we heard the car that you gentlemen made very good time. I wasn't sure my directions were so good on the phone.'

'It wasn't hard to find,' Rönn said.

'No, that's right, you're policemen, so you know your way around – in town and out. Åke got to know the city awfully well from being a policeman.'

He took out a flattened pack of John Silvers and held it out. Martin Beck and Rönn both shook their heads.

'Well, it was to talk about Åke you gentlemen came,' said the man. 'Like I told you on the phone, I really don't know what time he left. Mother and I thought he might stay the night, but he must have gone home instead. He often stays overnight. It's his birthday today, so we thought he'd stay and have breakfast in bed.'

'Does he have a car?' Rönn asked.

'Oh yes, he's got a Volks. Here's Mother with the coffee.'

He stood up when his wife came in from the kitchen. She was carrying a tray and put it down on the table. Then she dried her hands on her skirt and shook hands with the two guests.

'Mrs Eriksson,' she said when they stood up and said their names.

She served the coffee and put the tray on the floor, then sat down next to her husband and folded her hands in her lap. She looked to be about the same age as he. Her hair was silver grey, severely permed into small stiff curls, but her round face was almost completely wrinkle-free and the red colour in her cheeks didn't look like makeup. She stared down at her hands, and when she suddenly threw a timid glance at Martin Beck he wondered if she were afraid or simply shy with strangers.

'There are a few questions we'd like to ask you about your son, Mrs Eriksson,' he said. 'If I understood your husband correctly, he was here last night. Do you know what time he left?'

She looked at her husband as if hoping he would answer for her, but he stirred his coffee and said nothing.

'No,' she said hesitantly. 'I don't know. I suppose he left after we'd gone to bed.'

'And when was that?'

She looked at her husband again.

'Yes, what time was that, Otto?'

'Ten thirty. Eleven maybe. We usually go to bed earlier, but since Åke was here . . . I reckon it was probably closer to ten thirty.'

'So you didn't hear him go?'

'No,' the man said. 'But why do you want to know? Has anything happened to him?'

'No,' said Martin Beck. 'Not as far as we know. This is just routine. Tell me, what's your son doing these days?'

The woman had gone back to staring at her hands, and her husband answered.

'He's still repairing lifts. It's a year now since he started that.'

'And before that?'

'Oh, he did a little of everything. He was with a plumbing firm for a while, and then he used to drive a taxi, and he's been a night watchman, and just before he went to work for this lift company he drove a lorry. That was while he was training for this new thing, this lift thing.'

'When he was here last night,' said Martin Beck, 'did he seem himself? What did he talk about?'

The man didn't answer right away, and the woman took a biscuit and started breaking it into small pieces on her plate.

'I suppose he was pretty much like always,' said the man finally. 'He didn't say much, but he never does any more. I reckon he was worried about the rent, and then this business with Malin.'

'Malin?' said Rönn.

'Yes, his little girl. They took his little girl away. And now he's going to lose his flat too.'

'Excuse me,' said Martin Beck. 'I don't quite understand. Who took his daughter away from him? I assume it's his daughter you mean?'

'Yes, Malin,' said the man, and patted his wife on the arm. 'She was named after my mother. I thought you knew that. That the Child Welfare Board took Malin away from Åke.'

'Why?' asked Martin Beck.

'Why did the police murder his wife?'

'Please answer the question,' said Martin Beck. 'Why did they take the child away from him?'

'Oh, they've tried before, and now they finally managed to get some sort of paper that says he can't take care of her. We offered to take her here, of course, but we're too old they said. And this house isn't good enough.'

The woman looked at Martin Beck, but when he met her glance she looked quickly down into her coffee cup. And then she spoke up, quietly but indignantly.

'As if it was better for her to live with strangers. And anyway this is better than in the city.'

'You've taken care of your granddaughter before, haven't you?'

'Yes, many times,' the woman said. 'There's a room in the attic where she can stay when she's here. Åke's old room.'

'The kinds of jobs Åke's had, he couldn't always take care of her,' the man said. 'They thought he was unstable, whatever that means. That he couldn't hold down a job, I think that's what they meant. That's not so easy these days. Unemployment just gets worse and worse all the time. But he's always been so good to Malin.'

'When did all this happen?' asked Martin Beck.

'With Malin? They came and got her the day before yesterday.'

'Was he very upset about it last night?' Rönn asked.

'Yes, I suppose he was, though he didn't say much about it. Then there was this thing about the rent too, but there's no way we can help him with our little pension.'

'Couldn't he pay his rent?'

'No. And now they're about to evict him, he said. With rents so high it's a wonder people can afford to live anywhere.'

170

'Where does he live?'

'On Dalagatan. In a brand-new building. He couldn't find anything else when they tore down the place he was living before. And he was making better money then, of course, so he reckoned he could make it. But that doesn't matter so much. The worst part was this thing with his little girl.'

'I'd like to know a little more about this business with the Child Welfare people,' said Martin Beck. 'They don't just take a child away from its father, not just like that.'

'Don't they?'

'They claim, at least, that they make a thorough investigation first.'

'Yes, I suppose so. Some people came out here and talked to the wife and me and looked at the house and asked all sorts of questions about Åke. He wasn't very happy, not after Marja died, but you can understand that. They said his depression – that he was so gloomy all the time – had an injurious effect on the child's mental state. I remember that's what they said, they always have to talk so fine. And that it wasn't good he had so many different jobs and such funny hours. Yes, and then he had money troubles, couldn't pay the rent and so forth, and then, of course, there were some of his neighbours in the building who complained to the Child Welfare that he left Malin alone too much at night and that she didn't eat properly and so on.'

'Do you know who else they talked to?'

'The people he'd worked for. I think they tried to get hold of every boss he'd ever had.'

'The ones in the police department too?'

'Yes, of course. That was the most important one. Apparently.'

'And apparently he didn't give him much of a recommendation,' said Martin Beck.

'No, Åke said he wrote some sort of a letter that absolutely ruined his chances of keeping Malin.'

'Do you know who it was that wrote this letter?' asked Martin Beck.

171

'Yes. It was that Inspector Nyman, the same one who let Åke's wife lie there and die without lifting a finger.'

Martin Beck and Rönn exchanged a quick glance.

Mrs Eriksson looked from her husband to them, anxious about how they would react to this new accusation. This one was directed at one of their colleagues, after all. She held out the cake dish, first to Rönn, who helped himself to a thick slab of sponge cake, then to Martin Beck, who shook his head.

'Did your son talk about Inspector Nyman when he was here last night?'

'He just said it was his fault that they'd taken Malin. Nothing else. He's not very talkative, our Åke, but last night he was quieter than usual. Wasn't he, Karin?'

'Yes,' said his wife, poking at some crumbs on her plate.

'What did he do while he was here? Last night, I mean,' said Martin Beck.

'He had dinner with us. Then we watched TV for a while. Then he went up to his room and we went to bed.'

Martin Beck had noticed the telephone in the front hall as they came in.

'Did he use the phone at any time during the evening?' he asked.

'Why are you asking all these questions?' the woman said. 'Has Åke done anything?'

'I'm afraid I have to ask you to just please answer our questions first,' said Martin Beck. 'Did he make any calls from here last night?'

The couple across from him sat silent for a moment.

'Maybe,' the man said then. 'I don't know. Åke can use the phone any time he wants to after all.'

'So you didn't hear him talking on the phone?'

'No. We were watching TV. I think I remember he went out for a while and closed the door behind him, and he doesn't usually do that if he's just going to the toilet. The phone's in the hall, and if the TV's on you have to close the door so you won't be disturbed.

We don't hear so well either, so we usually have the sound up pretty high.'

'What time would that have been? That he used the phone, I mean?'

'I don't really know. But we were watching a film, and that was right in the middle of it. About nine, maybe. Why do you want to know?'

Martin Beck didn't answer. Rönn had gobbled down the sponge cake and now suddenly spoke up.

'Your son's a very good shot, as I recall. Among the best in the department at that time. Do you know if he still has any guns?'

The woman looked at Rönn with something new in her eyes, and the man straightened up proudly. It would probably be easy to count the number of times in the last ten years these people had heard anyone praise their son.

'Yes,' the man said. 'Åke's won a lot of prizes. We don't have them here, unfortunately. He keeps them in his flat on Dalagatan. And as for guns . . .'

'He ought to sell those things,' the woman said. 'They were so expensive, and he's short of money.'

'Do you know what guns he's got?' Rönn asked.

'Yes,' the man said. 'I do. Did a lot of target shooting myself when I was younger. First of all, Åke's got his weapons from the Home Guard or the Civil Defence or whatever they call it these days. He took night courses and got a commission too, not bad, if I do say so myself.'

'Do you know what kinds of weapons?' said Rönn stubbornly.

'First of all, his Mauser rifle. And then his pistol, he's terrific with a pistol, won his first gold medal years ago.'

'What kind of pistol?'

'Hammerli International. He showed it to me. And then he's got . . .'

The man hesitated.

'Got what?'

'I don't know . . . he's got a licence for those two I mentioned, of course, as you gentlemen realize . . .'

'I assure you we're not thinking of arresting your son for illegal possession of weapons,' said Martin Beck. 'What else does he have?'

'An American automatic rifle. Johnson. But he must have a licence for that one too, because I know he's entered competitions with it.'

'Not a bad arsenal,' Martin Beck muttered.

'What else?' said Rönn.

'His old carbine from the Home Guard. But that's not worth much. For that matter it's upstairs in the closet. But the bore is worn, and then those carbines never were much good. But I think that's the only one he keeps up here. He certainly doesn't have all his other things here.'

'No, he keeps them at home, of course,' Rönn said.

'Yes, I suppose he does,' the man said. 'Of course he's still got his room upstairs here, but naturally he's got all his important stuff at home on Dalagatan. Well, if they won't let him stay in that nice flat he can always move back in here until he can find something else. It isn't very big, the attic, I mean.'

'Would you mind if we took a look at his room?' said Martin Beck.

The man looked at them uncertainly.

'No, I suppose that's all right. But there's not much to see.'

The woman stood up and brushed cake crumbs from her skirt.

'Oh my,' she said. 'I haven't even been up there today. It may be in a mess.'

'It's not so bad,' her husband said. 'I looked in this morning to see if Åke had slept there last night, and it didn't look so bad at all. Åke's very neat.'

The man looked away and went on talking in a lower voice.

'Åke's a good boy. It's not his fault he's had a hard time. We've worked all our lives and tried to raise him as good as we could. But everything went wrong, for him and for us. When I was a

174

young worker I had something to believe in, I thought everything would be fine. Now we're old and no one bothers about us and everything's all wrong. If we'd known what society was coming to, we wouldn't have had any children at all. But they've just been leading us on all these years.'

'Who?' said Rönn.

'The politicians. The party leaders. The ones we thought were on our side. Just gangsters, all of them.'

'Please show us the room,' said Martin Beck.

'Yes,' the man said.

He walked ahead of them out into the hall and up a steep, creaking wooden staircase. Right at the top of the stairs was a door, which he opened.

'This is Åke's room. Of course it was nicer looking when he was a boy and lived at home, but he took most of the furniture when he got married and moved away. He's here so seldom now.'

He stopped and held open the door, and Martin Beck and Rönn walked into the little attic room. There was a window in the sloping roof, and the walls were covered with faded flowered wallpaper. In one wall was a door covered with the same paper, probably to a closet or a storage room. A narrow folding bed with a grey army blanket for a spread stood against the wall. From the ceiling hung a pale yellow lampshade with a long dirty fringe.

On the wall above the bed there was a small picture in a frame with a broken piece of glass. It depicted a little golden-haired girl sitting in a green meadow and holding a lamb in her arms. Under the foot of the bed was a pink plastic pot.

There was an open weekly magazine and a ballpoint pen on the table, and someone had thrown down an ordinary white kitchen towel with a red border on to one of the wooden chairs.

There was nothing else in the room.

Martin Beck picked up the towel. It was worn thin from many washings and was somewhat stained. He held it up against the light. The stains were yellow and reminded him of the fat that comes on genuine pâté de foie gras. The shape of the stains suggested that someone had wiped off a knife on the towel. The yellow fat made the linen almost transparent, and Martin Beck rubbed the material thoughtfully between his fingers before bringing it to his nose to smell. At the very moment that he realized what the stains consisted of and how they had come about, Rönn interrupted him.

'Look here, Martin,' he said.

He was standing by the table, pointing at the magazine. Martin Beck leaned down and saw that something had been written with a ballpoint pen in the upper margin above the crossword puzzle on the right-hand page. Nine names, arranged in three groups.

The names were unevenly printed, and had been gone over several times. His gaze locked on the first column.

STIG OSCAR NYMAN †
PALMON HARALD HULT †
MARTIN BECK †

He managed to notice that among the other names were those of Melander, the Superintendent, the National Chief of Police. And Kollberg.

Then he turned to the man by the door. He stood with his hand on the doorknob and looked at them questioningly.

'Where on Dalagatan does your son live?' said Martin Beck.

'Thirty-four,' said the man. 'But –'

'Go down to your wife,' Martin Beck interrupted him. 'We'll be right there.'

The man went slowly down the stairs. On the bottom step he turned around and looked in bewilderment at Martin Beck, who waved at him to go on into the living room. Then he turned to Rönn.

'Call Strömgren or whoever the hell's there. Give them the number here and tell him to get in touch right away with Kollberg

176

at Mount Sabbath and tell him to call here immediately. Have you got anything in the car so we can take some prints up here?'

'Yes, sure,' Rönn said.

'Good. But make that call first.'

Rönn went down to the telephone in the hall.

Martin Beck looked around the cramped little attic room. Then he looked at his watch. Ten minutes to one. He heard Rönn come up the stairs in three great leaps. Martin Beck looked at Rönn's pale cheeks and unnaturally wide-open eyes and knew that the catastrophe he'd waited for all day had taken place.

26

Kollberg and Gunvald Larsson were still inside the Eastman Institute when the sirens began their chorus. First they heard the sound of a single vehicle that seemed to come from Kungsholm and drive across St Erik's Bridge. Then other cars in other parts of the city joined the song; their howling seemed to come from every direction, it filled the air but never came really close.

They found themselves in the centre of a silent circle. Something like walking out into a meadow on a summer night and the crickets stop chirping all around you but only right where you're standing, Kollberg thought.

He had just taken a look out towards Dalagatan and noted that nothing had changed for the worse, while a few things had gotten better. The two policemen still lay in the round basin, but there were no other dead or wounded on the street. The people who'd been there before had disappeared, even the ones who'd been lying on the ground. So apparently they'd not been wounded.

Gunvald Larsson still hadn't answered the question about how they were going to get across the street. Instead, he was chewing thoughtfully on his lower lip and staring past Kollberg at a row of white dentist's gowns hanging on hooks along one wall.

The alternatives were obvious.

Go straight across the flagstone square and across the street, or sneak out through one of the windows on to Vasa Park and take a detour.

Neither one seemed very appealing. The first was a little too much like suicide, and the second took too much time.

Kollberg looked out again, carefully and without moving the curtains.

He nodded towards the fountain with its somewhat surreal ornamentation – a globe with a child kneeling on Scandinavia and two crossed policemen.

'Did you know those two?' he asked.

'Yes,' said Gunvald Larsson. 'Radio patrol from Solna. Kristiansson and Kvant.'

Silence for a moment.

'What were they doing here?'

And then Kollberg asked a more interesting question.

'And why should anyone want to shoot them?'

'Why does anyone want to shoot us?'

That was a good question too.

Someone obviously took a great interest in the matter. Someone equipped with an automatic rifle with which he'd dropped two uniformed officers and done his very best to shoot down Kollberg and Gunvald Larsson. But someone who didn't seem to care to shoot at anyone else, despite the fact that to start with there'd been plenty of live targets.

Why?

One answer presented itself immediately. Whoever did the shooting had recognized Kollberg and Gunvald Larsson. He knew who they were and really wanted to kill them.

Had whoever it was also recognized Kristiansson and Kvant? Not necessarily, but the uniforms made them easy to identify. As what?

'It seems to be someone who doesn't like policemen,' muttered Kollberg.

'Mmm,' said Gunvald Larsson.

He weighed the pistol in his hand.

'Did you see if the bastard was up on the roof or in one of the flats?' he asked.

'No,' said Kollberg. 'I really didn't have time to look.'

Something happened out on the street. Rather prosaic, but remarkable all the same.

An ambulance rolled up from the south. It stopped, backed up towards the fountain and stopped again. Two men in white coats got out, opened the back doors and pulled out two stretchers. They moved calmly and didn't seem to be the least bit nervous. One of them glanced up towards the nine-storey building on the other side of the street. Nothing happened.

Kollberg grimaced.

'Yes,' said Gunvald Larsson immediately. 'There's our chance.'

'Dandy chance,' said Kollberg.

He didn't feel particularly enthusiastic, but Gunvald Larsson had already taken off his kid jacket and suit coat and was searching energetically through the white surgical gowns.

'I'm going to try it anyway,' he said. 'This one looks pretty big.'

'They only make three sizes,' said Kollberg.

Gunvald Larsson nodded, clipped his pistol to his belt and wriggled into the white gown. It was very tight across the shoulders.

Kollberg shook his head and reached out his arm for the largest gown in sight. It was too tight. Across the stomach.

He had a strong feeling that they looked like a pair of comics out of a silent film.

'I think maybe it'll work,' said Gunvald Larsson.

'Maybe is the word,' said Kollberg.

'Okay?'

'Okay.'

They walked down the steps, across the stone pavement and past the ambulance crew, who had just lifted Kvant on to the first stretcher.

Kollberg glanced down at the dead man's face. He recognized him. A constable he'd seen a few times at long intervals, and who had once done something notable. What? Captured a dangerous sex criminal? Something like that.

Gunvald Larsson was already halfway across the street. He looked very odd in his ill-fitting doctor's gown and a white rag around his head. The two ambulance attendants stared after him in astonishment.

A shot rang out.

Kollberg ran across the street.

But this time it wasn't aimed at him.

A black-and-white police car was moving east along Odengatan with its siren on. The first shot came just as it passed Sigtunagatan, and it was followed at once by a whole series. Gunvald Larsson took a couple of steps out on to the pavement to get a better look. At first the car sped up, then it started to wobble and skid. The firing had stopped by the time it passed the intersection of Odengatan and Dalagatan and disappeared. Immediately afterwards came an ominous crash of metal against metal.

'Idiots,' said Gunvald Larsson.

He joined Kollberg in the foyer, ripped open his white gown and drew his pistol.

'He's on the roof, that's for sure. Now we'll see.'

'Yes, he's on the roof now,' Kollberg said.

'What do you mean?'

'I don't think he was on the roof before.'

'We'll see,' repeated Gunvald Larsson.

The building had two entrances on the street side. This was the one on the north, and they took it first. The lift wasn't working and there were several nervous tenants on the stairs.

The sight of Gunvald Larsson in a torn coat, bloody bandage, pistol in hand didn't ease their fears. Kollberg had his identification in the pocket of his coat, and his coat was back in the building

181

across the street. If Gunvald Larsson was carrying any papers, he conscientiously avoided showing them.

'Out of the way,' he said gruffly.

'Stick together down on the ground floor here,' Kollberg suggested.

It wasn't so easy to calm them down, these people – three women, a child and an old man. They'd probably seen what had happened from their windows.

'Just keep calm,' said Kollberg. 'There's no danger.'

He thought about this statement and laughed hollowly.

'No, now the police are here,' said Gunvald Larsson over his shoulder.

The lift was stopped about six floors up. The door was open on the floor above and they could look down the shaft. The elevator looked to be highly unusable. Someone had intentionally put it out of action. This someone was in all probability the man on the roof. So now they knew something else about him. He was a good shot, he recognized them, and he knew something about lifts.

Always something, Kollberg thought.

Another flight up they were stopped by an iron door.

It was locked and closed and probably barred and blocked from the other side, just how was hard to say.

On the other hand they could immediately determine that it couldn't be opened by ordinary means.

Gunvald Larsson wrinkled his bushy blond eyebrows.

'No point trying to beat it down,' said Kollberg. 'It won't help.'

'We can kick in the door to one of the flats down here,' said Gunvald Larsson. 'Then we can climb out of a window and try to get up that way.'

'Without ropes or ladders?'

'Right,' said Gunvald Larsson. 'It won't work.'

He thought for a few seconds and went on.

'And what would you do on the roof? Without a gun?'

Kollberg didn't answer.

'Of course it'll be the same story in the other entry,' said Gunvald Larsson sourly.

It was the same story in the other entry, with the exception of an officious older man who claimed to be a retired army captain and who was holding the few people there under strict supervision.

'I was thinking of letting all the civilians take shelter in the basement,' he said.

'Splendid,' said Gunvald Larsson. 'That's just what we'll do, Captain.'

Otherwise it was a dismal repetition. Closed iron door, open lift door and ruined lift machinery. Chances of getting anywhere: zero.

Gunvald Larsson scratched himself thoughtfully on the chin with the barrel of his pistol.

Kollberg looked at the weapon nervously. A fine pistol, polished and well cared for, with a fluted walnut grip. The safety was on. He had never noticed a penchant for unnecessary gunfire among Gunvald Larsson's many reprehensible qualities.

'Have you ever shot anyone?' he asked suddenly.

'No. Why do you ask?'

'I don't know.'

'What do we do now?'

'I have a feeling we ought to get over to Odenplan,' said Kollberg.

'Maybe so.'

'We're the only ones with any real knowledge of the situation. At least we know what's happened.'

It was evident that this suggestion didn't appeal to Gunvald Larsson. He jerked a hair from his left nostril and examined it absentmindedly.

'I'd like to get this character down off the roof,' he said.

'But we can't get up there.'

'No, we can't.'

They went back down to the ground floor. Just as they were about to leave the building they heard four shots.

'What's he shooting at now?' said Kollberg.

'The patrol car,' said Gunvald Larsson. 'He's practising.'

Kollberg looked at the empty patrol car and saw that both blue blinkers and the searchlight on the roof had been shot to pieces.

They left the building, keeping tightly to the wall, and turned immediately to the left on Observatoriegatan. There wasn't a person in sight.

As soon as they'd rounded the corner they dropped their white coats on the pavement.

They heard a helicopter overhead, but they couldn't see it.

The wind had risen a bit and it was biting cold, despite the deceptive sunshine.

'Did you get the names of whoever lived up there?' asked Gunvald Larsson.

Kollberg nodded.

'Apparently there are two penthouse apartments, but one of them seems to be vacant.'

'And the other one?'

'Somebody named Eriksson. A man and his daughter, as I understood it.'

'Check.'

In summary: someone who was a good shot, had access to an automatic weapon, recognized Kollberg and Gunvald Larsson, didn't like policemen, knew something about lifts, and might be named Eriksson.

They walked swiftly.

Sirens were wailing in the distance and nearby.

'We'll probably have to take him from outside,' Kollberg said.

Gunvald Larsson didn't seem convinced.

'Maybe,' he said.

If there were no people to be seen on Dalagatan or in its immediate vicinity, there were all the more in Odenplan. The triangular square was literally swarming with black-and-white cars and uniformed policemen and, not surprisingly, this massive deployment had drawn a large audience. The roadblocks so hastily thrown up had caused chaos in the traffic. The effects were in fact visible all through central Stockholm, but right here they were most spectacular. Odengatan was jammed with stationary vehicles all the way to Valhallavägen, a score of buses were stuck fast in the muddle on the square itself, and all the empty taxis already in the square when the confusion began didn't make matters any better. To a man, the drivers had abandoned their taxis and were mingling with the police and the crowd.

Everyone wondering what it was all about.

More and more people arrived steadily from every direction, but especially up out of the metro. A mass of motorcycle policemen, two fire engines and a traffic surveillance helicopter completed the picture. Here and there were groups of uniformed police, trying to obtain elbow room under baffling circumstances.

It couldn't have looked worse if the late Nyman had been directing it all himself, thought Kollberg, as he and Gunvald Larsson pushed their way towards the metro entrance, which seemed to mark the focus of activity.

And where they also found a man it might be useful to talk to, namely, Hansson of the Fifth Precinct. Or rather Lieutenant Norman Hansson, an Adolf Fredrik veteran who really knew his precinct inside out.

'Are you running this show?' Kollberg asked him.

'Good God, no.'

Hansson looked around in alarm.

'Who is then?'

'There seem to be quite a few candidates, but Superintendent Malm just got here. He's in the van over there.'

They pushed their way over to the van.

Malm was a trim, elegant man in his fifties, with a pleasant smile and curly hair. Rumour had it he stayed in condition by horseback riding on Djurgården. His political reliability was above all suspicion and on paper his credentials were superb. But his qualifications as a policeman were more open to question – indeed there were those who questioned their very existence.

'Good heavens, Larsson, you look terrible,' he said.

'Where's Beck?' Kollberg asked.

'I haven't been in touch with him. And anyway, this is a case for specialists.'

'What specialists?'

'From the regular police, of course,' said Malm irritably. 'Now it turns out the Commissioner is out of town and the Chief of the Metropolitan Police is on leave. But I've been in touch with the National Chief. He's out in Stocksund, and . . .'

'Splendid,' said Gunvald Larsson.

'What do you mean by that?' said Malm suspiciously.

'That he's out of range,' said Gunvald Larsson innocently.

'What? Well, in any case I've been given this command. I understand you've just come from the scene. How do you assess the situation?'

'There's some crazy son of a bitch sitting on a roof with an automatic rifle shooting policemen,' said Gunvald Larsson.

Malm looked at him expectantly, but nothing else was forthcoming.

Gunvald Larsson beat his arms against his sides to keep warm.

'He's well entrenched from the inside,' Kollberg said. 'And the surrounding roofs are lower. Part of the time he's in a flat up there, what's more. So far we haven't had a glimpse of him. In other words, it may be hard to get at him.'

'Oh yes, there are lots of ways,' said Malm loftily. 'We're the ones with the resources.'

Kollberg turned to Hansson.

'What happened to that car that got shot up on Odengatan?'

'Too much,' said Hansson sullenly. 'Two men wounded, one in the arm and one in the leg. May I make a suggestion?'

'What?' said Gunvald Larsson.

186

'That we move away from here. To somewhere inside the cordon, for example the gasworks car park on Torsgatan.'

'Where the old gasometer was,' said Kollberg.

'Right. They tore it down. They're going to build a cloverleaf.'

Kollberg sighed. The old brick gas-holder had been a unique piece of architecture, and a few people with foresight had mounted a campaign to save it. Unsuccessfully, of course. Could anything be more important than a cloverleaf?

Kollberg shook himself. Why was he always thinking things that were irrelevant? He was definitely getting a little dotty.

'Can the helicopters land there?' Malm asked.

'Yes.'

Malm threw a look at Gunvald Larsson.

'Is it . . . out of range?'

'Yes. Unless the bastard's got a mortar.'

Malm paused for quite a while. Then he looked at his colleagues and made his announcement in a loud, clear voice.

'Gentlemen. I have an idea. We will move individually to the gasworks area on Torsgatan. Regrouping there . . .'

He looked at his watch.

'In ten minutes.'

27

By the time Martin Beck and Rönn got to Torsgatan it was one thirty p.m. and everything seemed to be pretty well organized.

Malm had established himself in the old gatehouse at the west entrance to the hospital, and he was surrounded not only by considerable material resources but also by most of the policemen who had so far played significant roles in the drama. Even Hult was there, and Martin Beck walked straight over to him.

'I've been looking for you.'

'Oh? What for?'

'It doesn't matter any more. It was just that Åke Eriksson used your name when he called the Nymans' last night.'

'Åke Eriksson?'

'Yes.'

'Åke Reinhold Eriksson?'

'Yes.'

'Is he the one who murdered Stig Nyman?'

'So it seems.'

'And who's sitting up there right now?'

'Yes. Probably.'

Hult said nothing more and his face was expressionless, but he clenched his meaty red fists so the knuckles stood out like bone-white spots beneath the skin.

As far as anyone knew, the man on the roof hadn't made a move since taking target practice on the abandoned patrol car an hour before.

Despite the fact that they were now studying the building through field glasses, no one actually knew if he was even still alive. And so far the police hadn't fired a single shot.

'But the net is closing,' said Malm, looking pleased.

This cliché was so moth-eaten that no one even had the strength to smile inwardly. What's more, for once it gave a fairly accurate picture of the situation.

Police had infiltrated the entire block the apartment building stood in. Most of them were equipped with walkie-talkies and could maintain contact with each other and with the mobile radio control parked outside the old hospital gate. There were tear-gas experts in the attics of the nearest buildings, and sharpshooters lay ready at what were considered important strategic points.

'There are only two such points,' said Gunvald Larsson. 'The roof of the Bonnier Building and the cupola of Gustav Vasa Church. Do you think the minister will let us send a sniper up his steeple?'

No one was really listening to him.

The immediate plan had been determined. First, the man on the roof would be given a chance to surrender. Failing that, he would be taken by force, or shot. No more policemen's lives were to be risked. The decisive action would be taken from outside the building.

Hook-and-ladder trucks stood waiting on Observatoriegatan and Odengatan, ready to go into action if the situation seemed to demand it. They were manned by firemen, since someone had to operate the machinery, but also by policemen in firemen's uniforms.

Martin Beck and Rönn were able to contribute some important information. Namely that Eriksson – if it was Eriksson, that qualification still had to be made – was armed with an American-made Johnson automatic rifle and an ordinary army model semi-automatic rifle, both of them probably equipped with telescopic sights. Also with a target pistol, type Hammerli.

'Johnson automatic,' said Gunvald Larsson. 'Jesus Christ. It weighs less than fifteen pounds and it's exceptionally easy to handle and it's as good as a machine gun. Has a short recoil and raps out a hundred and sixty rounds a minute.'

The only one listening was Rönn, who grunted thoughtful assent.

Then he yawned. No one got the better of nature.

'And with the Mauser he can hit a louse on a visiting card at six hundred metres. With good visibility and a little luck he could hit a man at over a thousand.'

Kollberg, who was leaning over a map of the city, nodded.

'Imagine what he can do just to amuse himself,' said Gunvald Larsson.

Gunvald Larsson had been amusing himself by working out ranges. From the roof where he'd entrenched himself, Eriksson lay 150 metres from the intersection of Odengatan and Hälsingegatan, 250 from the central hospital at Mount Sabbath, 300 from Gustav Vasa Church, 500 metres from the Bonnier Building, 1,000 from the first skyscraper at Hötorget, and 1,100 from the City Hall.

Malm waved away these observations patronizingly and irritably.

'Yes, yes,' he said. 'Don't worry about that now.'

The only one who wasn't thinking much about tear-gas bombs and helicopters, water cannon and walkie-talkies was Martin Beck.

He was standing quietly in a corner, and not just because of his usual claustrophobia and aversion to crowds. He was thinking about Åke Eriksson and the circumstances that had driven the man into the absurd and desperate situation in which he now obviously found himself. It was possible that Eriksson's mind was completely in eclipse, that he was beyond communication and human contact, but it wasn't certain. Someone was responsible for all of this. Not Nyman, because he had never understood what responsibility for human beings actually meant, or even that such an idea existed. Not Malm of course, for whom Eriksson was quite simply a dangerous madman on a roof, with no other connection to the police than that it was their job, one way or another, to put him out of action.

And Martin Beck felt something growing stronger and stronger in his mind. A sense of guilt, a guilt he might actively have to come to terms with.

Ten minutes later, the man on the roof shot a policeman standing on the corner of Odengatan and Torsgatan, five hundred metres from the window from which the shot had clearly been fired. The surprising thing was not so much the distance as the fact that he'd been able to get a clear shot through all the leafless branches in the park.

However it happened, the shot went home, striking the officer in the shoulder. Since he was wearing a bulletproof vest, the wound was not too serious, at least not critical.

Eriksson fired just that one shot – maybe it was some kind of a show of strength, or a purely reflex action. A demonstration of the fact that he shot at policemen wherever he could find them.

'Is it possible he's got the little girl up there with him?' Kollberg asked suddenly. 'As a hostage?'

Rönn shook his head.

The child was in good hands, out of danger.

Out of danger from her father? Had she ever been in danger in his presence?

A little while later everything was ready for the crucial assault.

Malm inspected the specially trained policemen who were to carry out the capture itself. Or liquidation, if that proved to be necessary. In all probability it would prove to be necessary. No one seriously believed that the man on the roof would simply surrender. But of course the possibility existed. Many similar situations in criminal history had ended with the desperado – the universally accepted term for persons of Eriksson's type – suddenly growing tired of the whole affair and giving himself up to superior force.

The specialists who were to put an end to the terror – the same old well-worn expressions cropped up again and again, there didn't seem to be any others – were two young policemen with comprehensive training in hand-to-hand combat and surprise attack.

Martin Beck also went out and talked to them.

One of them was a redhead named Lenn Axelsson. His smile had a sort of hard-won self-assurance that was very likeable. The other was blonder and more serious but inspired equal confidence. Both were volunteers, though the special branch of the force they represented took it for granted that even difficult assignments would be executed promptly and voluntarily.

They both seemed clever and pleasant, and their faith in their own ability was infectious. Good, dependable men, with first-rate training. The department had no great abundance of such men – capable, brave, and far more intelligent than average. Thanks to both theoretical and practical instruction, they were well acquainted with what was expected of them. It seemed somehow that the whole exercise would go off smoothly and easily. These boys knew their special mission and were very sure of themselves. Axelsson joked and even told and laughed at a story of how, as a cadet, he had approached Martin Beck with a show of camaraderie, and less than the most fortunate results. Martin Beck couldn't remember the incident at all, but to be on the safe side he laughed anyway, if somewhat weakly.

The two men were well equipped, with bulletproof vests as well as bulletproof breeches. Steel helmets with plexiglass visors, gas masks and, as their primary armament, light, effective automatic weapons of the kind called machine-pistols in Sweden. They also carried tear-gas grenades for all eventualities, and their physical training guaranteed that, in the event of hand-to-hand combat, either one of them could easily overpower a person like Åke Eriksson.

The plan of attack was seductively simple and direct. The man on the roof was first to be put out of action by a concentrated rain of tear-gas cartridges and grenades, then the helicopters would fly in low and set down the two police commandos on either side of the criminal. He would be taken from two directions and, already incapacitated by gas, his chances should be minimal.

Only Gunvald Larsson seemed opposed to the plan, but he couldn't manage or wouldn't take the trouble to state any objection other than that, in spite of everything, he still preferred the idea of trying to get at Eriksson from inside the building.

'We're going to do this the way I say,' said Malm. 'I don't want any more risky schemes and personal heroics. These boys have been trained for situations like this. We know they've got a ninety per cent chance of succeeding. And the prospects of at least one of them making it completely uninjured are just about one hundred per cent. So no more amateurish objections. Understood?'

'Understood,' said Gunvald Larsson. 'Heil Hitler!'

Malm jumped as if someone had run him through with a red-hot poker.

'I won't forget that,' he said. 'You can count on it.'

Everyone in hearing looked at Gunvald Larsson reproachfully. Even Rönn, who was standing beside him.

'That was a hell of a dumb thing to say, Gunvald,' he said under his breath.

'Says you,' said Gunvald Larsson dryly.

So the final phase began, calmly and systematically. A loudspeaker van was driven up through the hospital grounds to almost in sight of the roof. But only almost. The speaker horn was aimed, and Malm's voice thundered up towards the besieged building. He said exactly what everyone had a right to expect him to say.

'Attention, please! This is Superintendent Malm. I don't know you, Mr Eriksson, and you don't know me. But I can give you my word as a professional that it's all over. You're surrounded, and our resources are unlimited. But we don't want to use more force

193

than the situation demands, especially considering all the innocent women and children and other civilians who are still in the danger area. You've already caused enough, more than enough suffering, Eriksson. You now have ten minutes in which to surrender of your own free will. Like a man of honour. I beg you, for your own sake, show some compassion, and accept the compassion we offer you now.'

It sounded fine.

But there was no answer. Not even a shot.

'I wonder if he's acted in anticipation of events,' Malm said to Martin Beck.

Yes, the language really was impoverished.

Exactly ten minutes later the helicopters took off.

They whirled out in wide arcs, at first quite high, and then moved in towards the roof with its small balconies and two penthouse apartments. From two directions.

At the same time, tear-gas projectiles began to rain down on the building from every side. A few of them broke windows and exploded inside, but most of them landed on the roof and the balconies.

Gunvald Larsson was in perhaps the best position to follow the events of the final phase. He had gone up to the roof of the Bonnier Building and was lying behind the parapet. When the tear-gas bombs started popping and the sickly clouds of gas began spreading out across the roof, he stood up and put his field glasses to his eyes.

The helicopters carried out their pincer movement impeccably. The one from the south arrived a little before the other, but that was according to plan.

Now it was already hovering over the south part of the roof. The plexiglass bubble opened and the crew started lowering the commando on a line. It was the redhead, Axelsson, and he looked formidable in his bulletproof clothing, his machine gun grasped firmly in both hands. Gas grenades hooked to his belt.

Two feet from the ground he lifted his face guard and started putting on his gas mask. He came closer and closer to the roof, the machine gun at the ready in the crook of his right arm.

And now Eriksson, if that's who it was, should come stumbling out of the cloud of gas and throw down his weapons.

When likeable, red-haired Axelsson was six inches from the roof, a single shot was fired. Bulletproof clothing may be all very well, but it can never protect the entire face.

In spite of the distance, Gunvald Larsson could see all the details. The body, which gave a start and went limp, even the bullet hole between the eyes.

The helicopter leapt upwards, paused for several seconds, then swept across the tops of the buildings and in over the hospital complex, with the dead policeman dangling on a line from the body of the ship. The machine gun was still hanging on its sling, and the dead man's arms and legs swayed limply in the wind.

He had never got the gas mask more than halfway on.

For the first time, Gunvald Larsson now caught a glimpse of the man on the roof. A tall figure in some kind of an overall shifted position quickly not far from the chimney. He couldn't spot any weapon, but he saw clearly that the man was wearing a gas mask.

The second helicopter had broken off its part of the pincer movement from the north and now hovered motionless several yards above the roof, the door in its plexiglass bubble already open, stormtrooper number two ready to descend.

And then came the fusillade. The man on the roof had gone back to his Johnson automatic and in less than a minute fired off at least a hundred rounds. The shots could not be seen, but the range was so short that almost all of them must have struck.

The helicopter swept away towards Vasa Park, wobbled, and lost altitude. Missed the top of the Eastman Institute by inches, tried with a roar to right itself, slipped sideways and crashed thunderously in the middle of the park, where it lay on its side like a shotgunned crow.

The first helicopter was already back at the take-off point with a dead policeman swinging between its landing gear. It came down on the gasworks car park. Axelsson's body bounced on the ground and was dragged for several yards.

The rotors stopped.

Then came the impotent substitute for revenge. Hundreds of different weapons belched out bullets towards the building on Dalagatan. Few of them with any definite target, and none of them with any effect.

The police opened fire, futilely, but presumably to regain their courage. Shots were fired from hopeless angles and impossible ranges.

No shots were fired from the Bonnier Building or from Gustav Vasa Church.

It took several minutes for the gunfire to die down and stop.

That anyone might have hit Åke Eriksson (if in fact that's who it was) seemed utterly out of the question.

28

The temporary headquarters was an exceptionally cute little yellow wooden house with a black metal roof, an enclosed porch, and a tall hood on the chimney.

Twenty minutes after the unsuccessful airborne landing, most of the assembly were still in shock.

'He shot down the helicopter,' said Malm in disbelief and probably for the tenth time.

'Oh, so you've come to that conclusion too,' said Gunvald Larsson, who had just returned from his observation post.

'I'll have to ask for military assistance,' said Malm.

'Oh I don't think . . .' said Kollberg.

'Yes,' said Malm. 'That's our only chance.'

The only chance to dump the responsibility on someone else without too great a loss of prestige, thought Kollberg. What could the army do?

'What can the army do?' said Martin Beck.

'Bomb the building,' said Gunvald Larsson. 'Barrage this part of town with artillery. Or . . .'

Martin Beck looked at him.

'Or what?'

'Call in the paratroops. Might not even have to use people. We could drop a dozen police dogs.'

'Sarcasm is extremely out of place at this particular moment,' said Martin Beck.

Gunvald Larsson didn't reply. Rönn suddenly spoke up instead. For some reason he had chosen this moment to study his notes.

'Well, I see this happens to be Eriksson's thirty-sixth birthday.'

'Hell of a funny way to celebrate,' said Gunvald Larsson. 'But wait a minute. If we set up the police orchestra on the street and play "Happy Birthday to You", that might put him in a jolly mood. And then we could drop him a poison birthday cake with thirty-six candles.'

'Shut up, Gunvald,' said Martin Beck.

'We haven't used the fire service,' said Malm.

'No,' said Kollberg. 'But after all it wasn't the fire service that killed his wife. He's got damned good vision, and as soon as it dawns on him that there are disguised policemen among the firemen...'

He stopped.

'What does Eriksson's wife have to do with this?' Malm asked.

'A good deal,' said Kollberg.

'Oh, that old story,' said Malm. 'But there is something to what you say. Maybe some relative could talk him into giving up. His girl friend, for example.'

'He doesn't have one,' Rönn said.

'Okay, but anyway. Maybe his daughter or his parents.'

Kollberg shivered. It seemed more and more evident that the Superintendent had picked up his knowledge of police work at the movies.

Malm got up and walked out to the cars.

Kollberg looked long and searchingly at Martin Beck. But Martin Beck didn't meet his gaze. He was standing by the wall in the old gate-keeper's room and looked somehow sad and inaccessible.

Nor did the situation warrant any particular optimism.

There were now three people dead – Nyman, Kvant and Axelsson – and with the crash of the helicopter, the number of injured had risen to seven. Those were sinister statistics. Kollberg hadn't had time to feel anything in particular while he was trying to save his own life outside the Eastman Institute, but now he was afraid. Afraid, partly, that further recklessness would cost the lives of still more policemen, but mostly that Eriksson would suddenly abandon the principle of shooting only at the police. Because at that instant the scope of the disaster would expand enormously. There were all too many people within his range, most of them in the hospital complex or in the flats along Odengatan. And what could anyone do about it? If time really counted, there was only one way out. To somehow storm the roof. And what would that cost?

Kollberg wondered what Martin Beck was thinking. He wasn't used to being left in the dark on that point, and it irritated him to be so now. But it didn't last long, because just then the Superintendent appeared in the doorway, and Martin Beck looked up at him.

'This is a one-man job,' he said.

'For who?'

'For me.'

'I can't permit that,' said Malm at once.

'If you'll excuse me, it's my decision to make.'

'Just a minute,' said Kollberg. 'What are you basing that conclusion on? Technical considerations? Or moral ones?'

Martin Beck looked at him but said nothing.

For Kollberg that was answer enough. Both.

And if Martin Beck had made the decision, Kollberg wasn't the man to oppose it. They knew each other too well for that, and too long.

'How are you planning to do it?' said Gunvald Larsson.

'Get into one of the flats below him and go out through a window facing the courtyard. The window under the balcony on the north. And go up with a grappling ladder.'

'Yes, that might work,' said Gunvald Larsson.

'Where do you want Eriksson?' Kollberg asked.

'Towards the street, and preferably on the upper roof, on top of the north penthouse.'

Kollberg wrinkled his forehead and put his left thumb against his upper lip.

'He probably won't go there willingly,' said Gunvald Larsson. 'Because he'd be vulnerable there. For a good shot.'

'Wait a minute,' Kollberg said. 'If I've got the construction of that roof straight, the penthouses sit on the actual roof of the building like boxes. They're a couple of yards in from the street, and between the penthouse roofs and the outer edge there's a slanting glass roof that slopes in. So there's a hollow there.'

Martin Beck looked at him.

'Yes, that's right,' Kollberg went on, 'and I have the feeling he was lying right there when he shot at the car on Odengatan.'

'But at that point he wasn't running the risk of getting shot at himself,' Gunvald Larsson objected. 'But by this time a sharpshooter on top of the Bonnier Building or up in the church tower . . . no, wait, I guess not from the Bonnier Building.'

'And he hasn't thought of the church tower,' Kollberg said. 'For that matter, there isn't anyone up there anyway.'

'No,' said Gunvald Larsson. 'Stupidly enough.'

'Okay. Now to get him over there, or at least to get him up on the penthouse roof, we'll have to do something to draw his attention.'

Kollberg furrowed his brow again and everyone else was quiet.

'That building is a little further from the street than the ones on either side,' he said. 'Roughly six feet. I reckon if we do something right down in the corner, in the angle where the two buildings come together, and as close to them as possible, he'll have to get up on the upper roof in order to see. He'd hardly dare just lean out over the rail on the lower level. We could have one of the fire engines . . .'

'I don't want any firemen involved,' said Martin Beck.

'We can use the police that are already in firemen's uniforms. And if they stick close to the walls he can hardly get at them.'

'Unless he's got some hand grenades,' said Gunvald Larsson pessimistically.

'And what will they do?' asked Martin Beck.

'Make noise,' Kollberg said. 'That's enough. I'll take care of that detail. But you, on the other hand, you've got to be quiet as hell.'

Martin Beck nodded.

'Yes,' said Kollberg. 'I expect you know that.'

Malm looked narrowly at Martin Beck.

'Am I to regard you as a volunteer?' he asked finally.

'Yes.'

'I have to say I admire you,' said Malm. 'But frankly I don't understand you.'

Martin Beck didn't answer.

He entered the building on Dalagatan fifteen minutes later. He'd stuck close to the walls, with the interlinking light metal ladders under his arm.

At the same time, one of the fire engines, siren wailing, swung around the corner from Observatoriegatan.

He was carrying the little shortwave radio in his coat pocket and his 7.65 mm Walther in its shoulder holster. He waved away one of the plainclothes officers who'd sneaked in by way of the furnace room and started slowly up the stairs.

When he reached the top he opened the apartment door with a master key that Kollberg had somehow produced, went in, hung his overcoat and jacket in the hall.

He automatically glanced around at the apartment, which was tastefully and pleasantly furnished, and wondered for a moment who lived there.

The deafening bellow of the fire engine went on through it all.

Martin Beck felt calm and relaxed. He opened the window at the back of the building and took his bearings. He was directly under the north balcony. He assembled the ladder, threaded it out through the window and hooked it fast to the rail of the balcony ten feet further up.

Then he stepped down from the window, walked back into the apartment and switched on his radio. He made contact with Rönn at once.

From his viewpoint on top of the Bonnier Building, five hundred yards to the southwest and over twenty storeys above the ground, Einar Rönn stared across the hospital complex towards the building on Dalagatan. There were tears in his eyes from the fresh wind, but he could quite distinctly see the spot he was supposed to observe. The roof of the penthouse on the north.

'Nothing,' he said into the radio. 'Still nothing.'

He heard the fire engine howling, and then he saw a shadow slither across the little sunlit piece of roof and he put his mouth to the radio.

'Yes. Now,' he said, rather excitedly. 'Now he's up there. On this side. He's lying down.'

Twenty-five seconds later the siren stopped. For Rönn, half a kilometre away, the difference was slight. But only an instant later he again saw the patch of shadow on the roof over there far away, and he saw a figure rise to its feet and he said, 'Martin! Come in!'

This time his voice was really excited. No one answered.

If Rönn had been a good shot, which he wasn't, and if he'd had a rifle with a telescopic sight, which he didn't, he would have had a chance of hitting the figure on the roof. If he'd had the nerve to shoot, which he doubted. By this time, the person he saw might actually be Martin Beck.

For Einar Rönn, it didn't mean much that a fuse blew in the fire engine and the scream of the siren stopped.

For Martin Beck, it meant everything.

As soon as he got Rönn's signal he put down the radio, twisted out through the window and climbed quickly up to the balcony. Directly in front of him he had the windowless rear of the penthouse and a narrow, rusty iron ladder.

When the protecting siren was cut off, he found himself on the way up this ladder with his pistol in his right hand.

In the wake of the massive, vibrating howl came what seemed like total silence.

The barrel of his pistol hit the right side of the iron ladder with a light echoing clang.

Martin Beck heaved himself up to the roof, had his head and shoulders already over the edge.

Six feet in front of him stood Åke Eriksson, his feet set wide on the roof, his target pistol aimed straight at Martin Beck's chest.

He himself was still holding his Walther pointed up and to one side, caught in the middle of a movement.

What did he have time to think?

That it was too late.

That he recognized Eriksson more readily than he'd expected to – the blond moustache, the combed-back hair. The gas mask pushed around to the back of his neck.

That's what he had time to see. Plus the oddly shaped Hammerli with its huge grip and the steel-blue material of the square barrel. The pistol staring at him with death's small black eye.

He'd read that somewhere.

Most of all, that it was too late.

Eriksson shot. He saw the blue eyes just in that hundredth of a second.

And the flash from the muzzle.

The bullet struck him in the middle of the chest. Like a sledgehammer.

29

The little balcony was roughly six feet deep and ten feet long. A narrow iron ladder was firmly bolted to the inside wall, and led up to the black sheet-iron roof. On the two short walls there were closed doors into the building, while on the side facing the court-yard was a high railing of thick opaque glass plates, and above it an iron beam that ran between the outside corners of the two side walls. On the glazed brick tiles of the balcony floor stood a collapsible rack for beating carpets.

Martin Beck lay on his back on this sparse network of galvanized iron pipes. His head was bent back and his neck rested against the heavy pipe that constituted the frame of the carpet rack.

He slowly regained consciousness, opened his eyes and looked up into the clear blue sky. His vision began to swim and he closed his eyes again.

He remembered, or rather perhaps still felt, the terrible impact against his chest and how he had fallen. But he had no memory of landing. Had he plunged down into the yard, the whole height of the building? Could a man survive a fall like that?

Martin Beck tried to lift his head to look around, but when he tensed his muscles the pain was so piercing that for a moment he passed out again. He didn't repeat the attempt, but looked around from under half-closed lids as well as he could without moving his head. He could see the ladder and the black edge of the roof, and realized that his fall hadn't been more than a couple of yards.

He closed his eyes. Then he tried to move his arms and legs one at a time, but the pain stabbed at him as soon as he moved a muscle anywhere. He realized he'd been hit by at least one shot in the chest, and he was mildly surprised to be alive. He was not, however, gripped by the dizzying joy that the people in novels seemed to feel in these situations. Nor, oddly enough, was he afraid.

He wondered how much time had passed since he'd been hit, and whether he'd been hit again after losing consciousness. Was the man still up there on the roof? He didn't hear any shots.

Martin Beck had seen his face, at once the face of a child and of an old man. How was that possible? And his eyes – insane with fear or hate or desperation, or maybe just utterly vacant.

Martin Beck had somehow imagined that he understood this man, that a part of the fault was his own, that he must help, but the man on the roof was beyond all help. At some point during the last twenty-four hours he had taken the decisive step across the border into insanity, into a world where nothing existed except revenge, violence and hate.

Now I'm lying here and maybe dying, thought Martin Beck, and what kind of guilt do I atone for by dying?

None at all.

He was frightened by his own thoughts and it suddenly seemed to him he'd been lying there motionless for an eternity. Had the man on the roof been killed or captured, was it all over and he had been forgotten, left to die, alone, on a little balcony?

Martin Beck tried to shout, but all that came out was a gurgling sound and he tasted blood in his mouth.

He lay completely still and wondered where the powerful roaring noise came from. It was all around him and sounded like strong wind in the tops of trees or like breakers on an ocean beach, or was it perhaps coming from some air-conditioning machinery somewhere nearby?

Martin Beck felt himself sinking in a soft, silent darkness where the roar died away, and he didn't bother to fight it. He came back to the roar and shimmering phosphorescent flashes in the blood-red light behind his eyelids, and before he sank again he realized that the rushing sound was somewhere inside himself.

His consciousness left him and came back and left him and came back, as if he were being rocked on a heavy, listless swell, and through his brain passed visions and fragments of thought he no longer had the strength to grasp. He heard mumbling and distant sounds and voices from inside the growing roar, but nothing concerned him any more.

He was plunging down into a thundering shaft of darkness.

30

Kollberg rapped his shortwave radio nervously with his knuckles.

'What happened?'

The radio gave a short burst of static, but for the moment that was all.

'What happened?' he repeated.

Gunvald Larsson walked up to him with long strides.

'To the fire engine? They had a short circuit.'

'I don't mean the fire engine,' said Kollberg. 'What happened to Martin? Yes, hello? Hello? Come in.'

It crackled again, a little louder this time, and then Rönn's voice came through, vague and uncertain.

'What happened?' it said.

'I don't know,' Kollberg shouted. 'What can you see?'

'Nothing right now.'

'What did you see before?'

'Hard to say. I think I saw Eriksson. He came out to the edge of the roof, and I gave Martin the signal. Then . . .'

'Yes?' Kollberg said impatiently. 'Hurry up.'

'Well, then the siren stopped and right afterwards Eriksson stood up. I think so anyway. He stood straight up, with his back towards me.'

'Did you see Martin?'

'No, not once.'

'And now?'

'Nothing at all,' Rönn said. 'There's no one there.'

'Fuck!' said Kollberg and dropped the hand with the walkie-talkie.

Gunvald Larsson grunted unhappily.

They were standing on Observatoriegatan, quite close to the corner of Dalagatan and less than a hundred yards from the building. Malm was there too, and a lot of other people with him.

A fire service official walked up to them.

'You want the hook-and-ladder to stay out there?'

Malm looked at Kollberg and Gunvald Larsson. He no longer seemed quite so eager to give orders.

'No,' said Kollberg. 'Have them drive it back. There's no point in their exposing themselves any longer than necessary.'

'Well,' said Gunvald Larsson. 'It doesn't look like Beck made it, does it?'

'No,' said Kollberg quietly. 'It doesn't.'

'Wait a minute,' someone said. 'Listen to this.'

It was Norman Hansson. He said something into his radio, then he turned to Kollberg.

'I've got a man up in the church tower now. He thinks maybe he sees Beck.'

'Yes? Where?'

'He's lying on the north balcony overlooking the yard.'

Hansson looked at Kollberg gravely.

'He seems to be injured.'

'Injured? Is he moving?'

'Not now. But my man thinks he saw him move a couple of minutes ago.'

This observation might be accurate. Rönn couldn't see the back of the building from Bonnier's. But the church was to the north, and what's more, two hundred yards closer.

'We have to get him down from there,' Kollberg muttered.

'We have to put an end to this whole spectacle,' said Gunvald Larsson gloomily.

'For that matter,' he went on, a few seconds later, 'it was a mistake to go up there alone. One hell of a mistake.'

'Keep your peace in front of men and slander them behind their backs,' Kollberg said. 'Do you know what that is, Larsson?'

Gunvald Larsson looked at him for a long time.

'This isn't Moscow or Peking,' he said then, with unusual severity. 'The cabbies don't read Gorky here, and the cops don't quote Lenin. This is an insane city in a country that's mentally deranged. And up there on the roof there's some poor damned lunatic and now it's time to bring him down.'

'Quite right,' said Kollberg. 'For that matter, it wasn't Lenin.'

'I know.'

'What the hell are you talking about?' said Malm nervously.

Neither of them even looked at him.

'Okay,' said Gunvald Larsson. 'You go get your pal Beck, and I'll take care of the other one.'

Kollberg nodded.

He turned to walk over to the firemen but then stopped himself.

'Do you know what I reckon your chances are of getting off that roof alive? By your method?'

'Roughly,' said Gunvald Larsson.

Then he looked at the people standing around him.

'I'm going to blow the door and storm the roof from the inside,' he said in a loud voice. 'I'll need one man to help me. Two at the most.'

Four or five young policemen and a fireman raised their hands, and right behind him a voice said, 'Take me.'

'Don't misunderstand me now,' said Gunvald Larsson. 'I don't want anyone who thinks it's his duty, and no one who thinks he's great stuff and wants to impress everybody. The chances of getting killed are better than any of you dream.'

'What do you mean?' said Malm bewilderedly. 'Who do you want then?'

'The only ones I'm interested in are the ones who really want to take a chance at getting shot. Who think it's fun.'

'Take me.'

Gunvald Larsson turned around and looked at the man who'd spoken.

'Yes, you,' he said. 'Hult. Yes, that's fine. I suppose you'd like to go all right.'

'Hey, here,' said one of the men on the pavement. 'I'd like to go.'

A slim blond man in his thirties, wearing jeans and a leather jacket.

'Who are you?'

'Name's Bohlin.'

'Are you even a policeman?'

'No, I'm a construction worker.'

'How did you get here?'

'I live here.'

Gunvald Larsson examined him thoughtfully.

'Okay,' he said. 'Give him a pistol.'

Norman Hansson immediately took out his service automatic, which he was carrying quite simply in the breast pocket of his coat, but Bohlin didn't want it.

'Can I use my own?' he said. 'It'll only take a minute to get it.'

Gunvald Larsson nodded. The man left.

'That's actually illegal,' said Malm. 'It's . . . wrong.'

'Yes,' said Gunvald Larsson. 'It's wrong as all hell. Most of all that there's anyone with a gun to volunteer.'

Bohlin was back in less than a minute with the gun in his hand. A .22 Colt Huntsman, with a long barrel and ten rounds in the magazine.

'Well, let's get going then,' said Gunvald Larsson.

He paused and looked at Kollberg, who was already on his way around the corner with two long coils of rope on his arm.

'We'll let Kollberg go up first and bring down Beck,' he went on. 'Hansson, get some men to drill and set the charges in the doors.'

Hansson nodded and walked away.

A little while later they were ready.

'Okay,' said Gunvald Larsson.

He walked around the corner, followed by the other two.

'You take the south entrance,' he said when they got to the building. 'I'll take the north. When you've lit the fuse, run down at least one flight. Preferably two. Can you make it, Hult?'

'Yes.'

'Good. And one more thing. If either of you kills him up there, then whoever does it will have to answer for it later.'

'Even if it's in self-defence?' Hult asked.

'Right. Even if it's in self-defence. Now let's synchronize our watches.'

Lennart Kollberg turned the handle to the apartment. The door was locked, but he already had a passkey in his hand and quickly opened it. He noticed Martin Beck's coat on a hanger and the shortwave radio on a table as he entered the front hall, and as soon as he went on into the apartment he saw the open window and the lower part of the metal ladder outside. It looked frail and fragile, and he'd gained a good many pounds since the last time he'd climbed such a ladder, but he knew it was built to support heavier bodies than his and he climbed up into the window without hesitating.

He made sure the two coils of rope, which were over his shoulders and crossed on his chest, wouldn't get in his way or catch on the ladder, and then he climbed slowly and carefully up to the balcony.

Ever since Rönn reported what he'd seen through his field glasses, Kollberg had been telling himself that the worst could have happened, and he thought he was prepared. But when he heaved himself up to climb over the railing and saw Martin Beck lying bloody and lifeless only three feet away, he gasped for breath.

He launched himself over the railing and leaned down over Martin Beck's pale yellow upturned face.

'Martin,' he whispered hoarsely. 'Martin, for God's sake . . .'

And as he said it he saw an artery working in Martin Beck's taut throat. Kollberg put his fingers carefully on the pulse. It was beating, but very sluggishly.

He checked over his friend's body. As far as he could tell, Martin Beck had been hit by only one shot, in the middle of his chest.

The bullet had made an amazingly small hole between the buttons. Kollberg ripped open the shirt, which was drenched with blood. To judge by the oval shape of the wound, the bullet had struck slightly from one side and continued on into the right half of the thorax. He couldn't determine if it had come out the other side or was still inside the chest.

He looked at the floor underneath the rack. A pool of blood had gathered, not particularly large, and the flow of blood from the wound had almost stopped.

Kollberg slipped the coils of rope over his head, hung one of them on the carpet rack's upper crossbar, then paused with the other in his hand and listened. There wasn't a sound from the roof. He unrolled the line and slipped one end carefully under Martin Beck's back. He handled the rope quickly and silently, and when he was done he checked to see that it lay around Martin Beck the way it should, and that the knots were properly tied. Finally he felt in Martin Beck's pockets, found a clean handkerchief, and took his own somewhat less clean one from his trouser pocket.

He took off his cashmere scarf, tied it around Martin Beck's chest and put the two folded handkerchiefs between the knot and the wound.

He still didn't hear a sound.

Now came the hard part.

Kollberg leaned over the balcony railing and looked down, then moved the ladder so it hung right beside the open window. Then he carefully slid the rack up to the railing, took the loose end of the rope he'd tied around Beck, wound it a couple of turns around the railing where the ladder had been, and knotted it around his own waist.

He lifted Martin Beck carefully over the edge while exerting a counter force with his own body so that the rope stayed taut. When Martin Beck was hanging free on the other side of the glass balustrade, Kollberg started loosening the knot at his waist with his right hand while he held the entire weight of the other man's body with his left. When he'd undone the knot he slowly started lowering Martin Beck. He held tightly with both hands and without looking over the rail tried to estimate how much line he needed to play out.

When, according to his calculations, Martin Beck ought to be hanging outside the open window, Kollberg leaned over to look. He let out a few more inches and tied the line firmly around the iron railing above the glass.

Then he picked up the other coil of rope from the carpet rack, put it over his shoulder, climbed quickly down the ladder and in through the window.

Apparently lifeless, Martin Beck hung a foot and a half below the window ledge. His head had fallen forward and his body was suspended slightly at an angle.

Kollberg made sure his footing was secure and leaned out over the windowsill. He grasped the line with both hands and started to haul. He shifted his grip to one hand, caught hold of the rope under Martin Beck's arms, lifted him up, grabbed him under the shoulders and dragged him through the window.

When he'd removed the rope and laid him on the floor, he climbed the ladder again, untied the rope from the railing and let it fall. When he was back in the window, he unhooked the ladder and brought it down.

Then he lifted Martin Beck on to his back and started down the stairs.

Gunvald Larsson had six seconds left when he discovered he'd committed what was probably the worst oversight of his career. He was standing in front of the iron door, looking at the fuse he was supposed to light, and he had no matches. Since he didn't smoke, a lighter wasn't part of his equipment. When, very rarely, he went out to the Riche or the Park he generally stuffed a couple books of their monogrammed matches in his pocket. But he'd changed coats countless times since the last time he'd been out to eat.

His jaw dropped, as the saying goes, and with his mouth still open in perplexity, he drew his pistol, took off the safety, held the muzzle against the end of the fuse – with the barrel aimed at an angle against the door so he wouldn't get a ricochet in some inconvenient place, his stomach for example – and pulled the trigger. The bullet whined around in the stone stairwell like a hornet, but in any case the fuse was lit, fizzing away with a merry blue flame, and he ran down the stairs. One and a half flights down, the house vibrated from the detonation in B-entry and then his own charge went off, four seconds late.

But he was faster than Hult, and probably faster than Bohlin too, and he made up one or two of those seconds in his rush up the stairs. The iron door had disappeared, or, that is, it was lying flat on the landing where it belonged, and half a flight further up was a steel-reinforced glass door.

He kicked it down and found himself on the roof. To be exact, right next to the chimney between the two penthouse apartments.

He saw Eriksson at once, standing legs astraddle on the penthouse

214

roof with the much discussed Johnson automatic in his hands. But Eriksson didn't see Gunvald Larsson. His interest was apparently completely occupied by the first explosion and his attention was directed to the south half of the building.

Gunvald Larsson put one foot on the guard rail facing the street, gathered his weight and landed on the penthouse roof. Eriksson turned his head and looked at him.

The distance between them was only twelve feet and the outcome was clear. Gunvald Larsson had the man in his sights and his finger on the trigger.

But Eriksson didn't seem to care. He went on turning, swinging the automatic around towards his antagonist. And Gunvald Larsson didn't shoot.

He stood motionlessly with his pistol aimed at Eriksson's chest, and the barrel of the rifle continued to swing.

Just then Bohlin fired. It was a masterful shot. His view was largely blocked by Gunvald Larsson, but with unerring precision he nevertheless put a bullet in Eriksson's left shoulder, from a range of more than sixty feet.

The automatic rifle rattled down on to the metal roof, and Eriksson twisted halfway around and sank down on all fours.

Then Hult was there, slamming the flat side of his pistol into the back of Eriksson's head. The blow made a cruel-sounding smack.

The man on the roof lay unconscious, with blood streaming from his head.

Hult was breathing hard. He lifted his weapon again.

'Hold it,' said Gunvald Larsson. 'That's plenty.'

He put his own pistol back on its clip, straightened the bandage on his head and flicked a fat, oily grain of soot from his shirt with his right index finger.

Bohlin too climbed up on the roof and looked around.

'For Christ's sake, why didn't you shoot?' he said. 'I don't get it –'

'No one expects you to,' Gunvald Larsson interrupted him. 'By the way, have you got a licence for that pistol?'

Bohlin shook his head.

'In that case you're probably in trouble,' said Gunvald Larsson. 'Now come on, let's carry him down.'

P.S.

Ideas,
interviews
& features . . .

A Policeman's Lot is Not a Happy One

IN 1879, BRITISH composers Gilbert & Sullivan produced their comic opera, *Pirates of Penzance.* Its rhyming couplet, 'When constabulary duty's to be done, to be done, A policeman's lot is not a happy one, happy one' has a lot to answer for, since this seems to have originated the notion of solemn sleuths, glum gumshoes and discontented, dispirited detectives, a theme taken up only eight years later by Arthur Conan Doyle when his creation Sherlock Holmes made his entrance in *A Study in Scarlet.* Aided by his chum, the dependable, resolutely cheerful but rather less than rapier-witted Dr Watson, Holmes is the most celebrated fictional detective, a brilliantly rational sleuth, but prone to boredom, depression and the use of cocaine to alleviate his frequent longueurs.

Since then, it seems that the majority of fictional detectives, private or public, have had the blues, and Martin Beck is no exception, admitting as much in the majority of the novels, ranging from his acknowledgement of the 'policeman's occupational disease' to the gloomy fact that 'no other professional group suffered from such role fixation or dramatized its daily life as did the police'. Towards the conclusion of the Beck series, there are several rumours, as well as an official decision, that he will be made commissioner. Yet due to a combination of chance and another error of judgement from his superiors, he's not promoted. Ironically, he seems much better off as he is and promotion to a safer, desk-bound job would only add to his malaise, reaffirming his awareness that he wasn't, as he puts it, a 'Cheerful Charlie'.

An enthusiastic fan of Raymond Chandler's classic 'Philip Marlowe' novels, the poet W.H. Auden noted that they were 'powerful but extremely depressing', largely because Marlowe is a lone wolf, professionally, legally and romantically, and much given to sitting on his own in his dingy office or flat with only a bottle of booze for company and bemoaning the meagre rewards accorded to his life and life in general. Though Beck is married with a family and has a secure job that's reinforced by the support of capable colleagues and the judicial might of the authorities, he too is disillusioned by the emptiness of his life. While they're not in the same league of lowness as the Marlowe novels, the Beck books do share a similar sense of gloom and futility. This is partly due to the nature of the police officer's job but also perhaps because of the actual *work* itself – taking notes at a crime scene, shoving the grisly images to the back of one's mind while focusing on an interminable spiral of myriad details, before wading through a paper mire, the stultifying welter of facts and figures that make up a person's life. Long, weary hours spent immersing oneself in the grind of canvassing, phoning, burrowing through the detritus of the victim's past, straining bloodshot eyes and struggling to uncover a name, a number, some indistinct piece of information that ▶

❝ The majority of fictional detectives, private or public, have had the blues, and Martin Beck is no exception. ❞

A Policeman's Lot is Not a Happy One *(continued)*

◄ might, if examined more closely, actually have some significance.

These streets down which the detectives go may be mean, as Chandler put it, but they are also dreary and endless, and behind their doors are sullen types, stubbornly unhelpful, their grim faces radiating mistrust and a desire to be left alone. This is not exciting, rewarding work, and there is no thrill of the chase. Bored by the long periods of inaction and inertia, frustrated by the apparent lack of success, stymied by the rigidity and dogmatic loopholes of the law, much of their life is unadulterated tedium, very occasionally punctuated by moments of peril or even triumph, and its cumulative effect is such that, in all likelihood, happiness may not actually be important to these men any more. But that may well actually be the point; that perhaps the most miserable investigators are also the best.

But if the work is difficult and not entirely rewarding, can the disconsolate detective, assuming he's not a lone wolf but part of a unit, take refuge in team spirit and the companionship of his peers? Well, not really. Although Beck and Kollberg are good friends and have known each other for decades, they remain very different individuals, with the latter being much more of the sensualist than his diffident and rather dyspeptic ally. Apart from this, while there is a certain amount of respect, there's little or no camaraderie among the men. Indeed, Sjöwall and Wahlöö delight in dishing up a double whammy by not just making the policemen a miserable bunch but also pretty unpopular. Totally dissimilar, Rönn and Larsson nevertheless have something approaching a mutual affection, but the latter is disliked by almost everybody else. Beck finds Rönn annoying and petty, and doesn't greatly care for Larsson, who is, in turn, intensely disliked by Kollberg, although a begrudging respect between them creeps in slowly during the later books.

Larsson's unpopularity, which doesn't remotely bother him, may stem from the fact that, unlike most of his colleagues, he is a man of action, not given to ruminating over endless paperwork and more inclined to pound a confession out of a suspect than pounding the pavement trying to prise information from members of the public, especially since these usually prove to be indifferent, reluctant to be involved or just plain hostile. At times he seems to have wandered in from another crime novel, one of a more dramatic, if commonplace, variety. His strength, dynamism, spontaneity and willingness to break the law to apprehend a lawbreaker are so radically different from the methodical cud-chewing and line-toeing favoured by the majority of his peers that they make him unique and also help to explain why he remains so heartily disliked. Ironically, this bold and fearless approach to his job doesn't appreciably elevate Larsson's mood, since he grumbles incessantly about the hours he has to work, his colleagues, the criminals he's pursuing, and reserves his ▶

‘ The Beck novels are characterized by a sense of gloom and futility. This is partly due to the nature of the police officer's job but also perhaps because of the actual *work* itself. ’

A Policeman's Lot is Not a Happy One *(continued)*

◄ most stinging and insolent complaints for his superiors. Unlike the majority of his peers, he's a bachelor and is perhaps in agreement with another careworn cop, Inspector Kurt Wallander, the creation of Swedish crime novelist Henning Mankell, whose attitude towards matrimony was decidedly gloomy: 'Policemen were divorced. That's all there was to it.' ■

Society is to Blame

SJÖWALL AND WAHLÖÖ wanted to construct a series of crime novels that mirrored the society shaped by the Swedish welfare state, an aim in which they succeed admirably. So, it's not just the police, the politicians or the criminals that are under scrutiny in the ten Martin Beck books, but the whole of Swedish society, including the bureaucrats, urban planners, legal practitioners, the wealthy, the poor, the dissolute and the disenfranchised. The one genus conspicuous by their absence in the authors' world is the one that might be considered 'normal', leaving the reader to draw the somewhat uncomfortable conclusion that perhaps such people don't actually exist any more.

Despite the apparently popular perception of the welfare experiment as being so successful that it earned itself the sobriquet 'the Third Way' (between Communism and Capitalism) and the more enticing-sounding, 'the Swedish Method', Sjöwall and Wahlöö clearly looked on it as a kind of social poison, infecting the country from top to (mainly) bottom. In all of the ten books, the downside of the welfare venture is markedly apparent – with the majority, though not all, of the victims being the young. As the series unfolds, the energetically promoted notion of Sweden as a kind of paradise, home of the sauna and the smorgasbord, basking in its international reputation for sexiness and pleasure, is revealed to be nothing more than a desperately enforced myth. In Beck's eyes, ▶

> ❛ Beck's world is crowded with hordes of teenage runaways, single mothers and drug users; adolescent nihilists drifting into a sordid, seemingly inescapable spiral of addiction, prostitution, petty crime and, at the furthest extreme, murder. ❜

Society is to Blame *(continued)*

◄ it's a kind of *demi-monde*, an inferno riven by poverty, rampant drug abuse, corruption at all levels, steeped in murder and crimes of violence.

There is also the damning statistic, which is difficult to ignore, that Stockholm has one of the highest suicide rates in the world, a fascinating subject for Beck and one 'that had begun to interest him more and more'. As the omniscient narrator notes in *The Locked Room*, 'the so-called Welfare State abounds with sick, poor and lonely people, living at best on dog food, who are left uncared for until they waste away and die in their rat-hole flats', whilst in the penultimate novel, *Cop Killer*, Beck himself informs us, concerning the popularity of suicide, that 'Sweden led the world by a margin that seemed to grow larger from one report to the next'. Certainly, his world is crowded with hordes of teenage runaways, single mothers and drug users; adolescent nihilists drifting into a sordid, seemingly inescapable spiral of addiction, prostitution, petty crime and, at the furthest extreme, murder. From his perspective, Sweden's cities are full of them; abandoned, repressed or misunderstood by parents with different values and neglected by a society caught at a crossroads, from which it's unable to embark. ■

Police and Policies

THE STORY OF A CRIME is the subtitle for the entire sequence of Beck novels and the crime in question would appear to be a political one – the nationalization of Sweden's police force in 1965, a development that led to it becoming a more paramilitary organization, with greater use of firearms and military equipment, bigger and more centrally orchestrated operations and a greater prominence of the National Police Commissioner, whose fictional counterpart in the books is a generally vilified figure. As if to confirm this, in the eighth novel, *The Locked Room*, there is the telling remark that what various high-ranking members of the police force 'actually wanted, was power'. Despite the fact that their central character, Beck, has no interest in politics, and virtually none of the other characters, unlike their creators, are particularly politically informed, the novels all possess a political undertone, set as they are against the ever-shifting backdrop of the sixties and seventies, a period of tumultuous social change when young people began to involve themselves in world affairs.

As the story of Beck and his world gradually picks up pace, political references, initially veiled, begin to take centre stage, especially since, being public servants, Beck and his colleagues have to deal with the invariably calamitous results of political misjudgements and chicanery. Alongside this, and the frequent mentions of anti-Vietnam demonstrations usually dealt with in an amusing, if cynical, manner, more ▶

> ❝ The novels all possess a political undertone, set as they are against the ever-shifting backdrop of the sixties and seventies, a period of tumultuous social change. ❞

Police and Policies *(continued)*

◄ and more political commentary begins to emerge.

As a young man Per Wahlöö was engaged in various radical causes (at least one of which saw him deported from Franco's Spain in 1957), wrote several political novels detailing different aspects of dictatorship, and along with his wife was a committed Marxist and member of the Leftist Communist Party, called VPK in Sweden. But in the early Beck novels, Sjöwall and Wahlöö proceeded cautiously, restricting themselves to tangential observations of the chaotic political machinations taking place in Sweden and it's not until around the fourth or fifth book, towards the middle of the series, that they start to grow rather more energetic in their banner-waving.

From there on, more pointed criticism of the Swedish government begins to appear though always contributed by the omniscient third-person narrator, a discreet if voluble presence who hovers over each book. Used by the authors to affirm their message, he is nonetheless, as they admitted in an interview, 'a little afraid of making our characters too politically aware. They might start to seem unreal.' From the second half of the series, politics start to shade almost every aspect of the story, including plot, background, and most of the characters, even the criminals. For while they too are rendered early on as fairly tenebrous, indistinct characters, clearly villains but little more than that, in the later books, as the socio-political waters are muddied and grow more opaque, the bad guys become more rounded individuals – and perhaps are not so bad after all. Some of them even start to seem sympathetic. In *The Locked Room*, for instance, Monita, setting a fine example of multi-tasking, is a single mother, waitress and bank robber, who (literally) gets away with murder but she is also responsible for the arrest of her former lover, an incorrigible professional criminal who might otherwise have gone free.

It's not just the reader who feels sympathy towards the felons, either. In the sixth novel, *Murder at the Savoy*, Beck is moved to feel more sorry for the killer than he is for the victim, a wealthy, corrupt businessman who, we are gently coaxed into thinking, pretty much deserved to die. Unlike the majority of crime novelists writing at this time, certainly Swedish ones, Sjöwall and Wahlöö deliberately present the characters, their settings and their histories in such a way as to ensure that one's sympathies drift irresistibly towards those who might be regarded as bad. The only one of their contemporaries employing similar subtleties was Patricia Highsmith and there is more than a touch of her *legerdemain* in the way the two slyly subvert our precious preconceptions about good and evil. As with many of Highsmith's novels, and especially the brilliant Mr Ripley series, Sjöwall and Wahlöö tear down the black-and-white, papier-mâché gimcrack of conventional morality and reveal in its place a much more complex and substantial structure, multi-layered, many-hued and infinitely more intriguing. ■

6 Sjöwall and Wahlöö tear down the black-and-white, papier-mâché gimcrack of conventional morality and reveal in its place a much more complex and substantial structure. 9

Life at a Glance

MAJ SJÖWALL (1935–) was born in Stockholm, Sweden. She studied journalism and graphics and worked as a translator, as well as an art director and journalist for some of the most eminent magazines and newspapers in Sweden. She met her husband Per Wahlöö in 1961 through her work, and the two almost instantly became a couple. They had two sons together and, after the death of Per Wahlöö, Sjöwall continued to translate. She also wrote several short stories and the acclaimed crime novel *The Woman Who Resembled Greta Garbo*, with the Dutch crime writer Tomas Ross. She is arguably Sweden's finest translator and is still at work today.

PER WAHLÖÖ (1926–1975) was born in Lund, Sweden. After graduating from the University of Lund, he worked as a journalist, covering criminal and social issues for a number of newspapers and magazines. In the 1950s Wahlöö was engaged in radical political causes and his activities resulted in his deportation from Franco's Spain in 1957. After returning to Sweden, he wrote a number of television and radio plays, and was the managing editor of several magazines, before becoming a full-time writer. Per Wahlöö died of cancer in 1975, only weeks after *The Terrorists*, the final instalment of the Martin Beck series, was published.

From 1965 to 1975, Sjöwall and Wahlöö together wrote ten novels, all featuring

Martin Beck. Perhaps chief among the many factors that make the series so special and so unique, was the authors' decision to do ten books and no more and to have each one act as a separate chapter in the whole work. Within this Decalogue, which was subtitled *The Story of a Crime*, they successfully constructed an incisive and realistic portrait of 1960s Sweden. ■

True Crime – Just the Facts?

EVEN AS SJÖWALL AND WAHLÖÖ were skilfully depicting Swedish society through its crimes, they were also spreading their net further afield and seemingly adapting some of the most controversial crimes of the sixties and seventies for inclusion in the Beck books. While *The Man on the Balcony*, with its grisly slaying of children, may have something of the infamous Moors Murders case in the north of England in the early 1960s, many of the other books have elements from other major crimes, such as one of the bank robberies in *The Locked Room*, carefully planned and flawlessly carried out, which is reminiscent of the Great Train Robbery in England in 1963, and the shoot-out near the end of *The Abominable Man*, with the rifleman picking off his targets from the roof of a tall building, which recalls the slayings from the University of Texas Tower in 1966. Also notable are the assassinations and the lengthy description of the motorcade in the final novel, *The Terrorists*, which recall the activities of the Baader Meinhof gang (or Red Army Faction, as they were later known), and the Palestinian Liberation Organization, alongside the Kennedy assassination of 1963. The crimes perpetrated in this novel seem to reflect most aspects of the latter in that they feature both a conspiracy of trained killers and a lone gunman, or woman, in this instance. In the novel, set in 1974, the day of both the attempted and the actual assassination,

November 21, is just one day short of the eleventh anniversary of Kennedy's death – November 22, 1963.

The climactic shoot-out in *The Abominable Man* is powerfully redolent of the tragic saga of Charles Whitman. A former marine, Whitman killed his wife and mother, and then went to the top of the University of Texas in Austin and began firing at passers-by, killing fifteen and wounding thirty-one until he was finally shot by the police. Reported around the world, this carnage took place in 1966, just as Sjöwall and Wahlöö had begun writing their books. While it almost certainly caught the attention of the pair, Whitman's killing spree has also inspired a plethora of references throughout popular culture, ranging from novels like Stephen King's *The Dead Zone* and James Patterson's *Cat & Mouse*; numerous movies, including one, *The Deadly Tower*, which featured Kurt Russell as Whitman; several songs by artists as diverse as Steely Dan, Kinky Friedman, Harry Chapin, Tom Waits and the band Macabre and countless name checks in television shows, including cartoons *The Simpsons*, *King of the Hill* and *South Park*, snipers in towers apparently proving to be a rich vein for animators.

Possibly the most horrific crime of this period, but one that Sjöwall and Wahlöö never seemed to consider borrowing for their fiction, was the Manson killings of 1969, where Charles Manson and his band ▶

6 Sjöwall and Wahlöö spread their net further afield and adapted some of the most controversial crimes of the sixties and seventies for inclusion in the Beck books. 9

True Crime – Just the Facts?
(continued)

◄ of disciples, known as his 'family', slaughtered Sharon Tate and her friends and then, a couple of days later, did the same to a wealthy married couple, the LaBiancas, in Los Angeles. Possibly this was just too horrendous for the pair to write about, or to transpose to Sweden, or perhaps the nature of the crimes, with their twin emphasis on Satanic cults and Hollywood-esque pursuit of fame (Manson's followers were both delighted and proud when his picture graced the cover of *Life* magazine) were just too far out and too apolitical for Sjöwall and Wahlöö even to contemplate. ■

Have You Read?

The next three books in the Martin Beck series

Read on

The Locked Room

In this double-edged mystery, a retired longshoreman with a bullet through his skull is discovered in a room locked on the inside with no weapon present, and a young woman robs a bank, shooting the hapless citizen who tries to stop her. Martin Beck is certain that there is a common denominator, but when he finds one, the pieces refuse to fall neatly into place.

'Admirers of the series – and who is not an admirer? – will find the usual deftness, the fine shades of characters'
New York Times Book Review

'Probably the best book in the series' *Time*

'*The Locked Room* is flat out one of my favourites in the series. I am blown away by the authors' wonderful and original take on a standard mystery contraption – a locked room murder. I am in awe of the novel as a showcase of Martin Beck at his brooding best' MICHAEL CONNELLY

Cop Killer

In a Swedish country town, a woman is brutally murdered and left buried in a swamp. On a quiet suburban street a midnight shootout takes place between three cops and two teenage boys. Martin Beck, Chief of Sweden's National Homicide ▶

17

Have You Read? *(continued)*

◄ Squad, and his partner, Lennart Kollberg, are called in on both cases. And in an unfamiliar small-town setting they encounter figures from their earlier cases.

'Martin Beck is as always very believable: this, we feel, is what it must mean to be an honest and intelligent policeman in modern Sweden; or anywhere else'
Times Literary Supplement

'An intensely interesting and disturbing picture of what lurks just below the surface'
Publishers' Weekly

....

The Terrorists
First Detective Inspector Martin Beck of the Stockholm National Police Force is in charge of security for a visiting US senator whom a group of international terrorists is determined to assassinate. At the same time he becomes involved with the murder of a millionaire porno filmmaker and the misadventures of a young Swedish girl caught up in bureaucratic red tape. As the terrorists move closer to their goal, there is a totally unexpected climax, and Beck himself is faced with what appears to be imminent death.

'Of all the [Sjöwall/Wahlöö] books, this one may be the tightest in organization and the most suspenseful'   *New York Times*

'The crime novel at its best'   *Irish Times*